Collector's Encyclopedia of

COMPACTS

CARRYALLS &
FACE POWDER BOXES

LAURA M. MUELLER

COLLECTOR BOOKS
A Division of Schroeder Publishing Co., Inc.

On the cover:
Top left: Lady Arlene, face powder box — 3"sq x 1⅝". $45.00 – 60.00.
Center left: Unmarked, silvertone, pressed powder compact — 2"dia x ¾". Rare.
Center right: Mavco, plexiglas, loose powder compact — 5"dia x ½". $65.00 – 80.00.
Bottom left: Unmarked, goldtone, loose powder vanity case — 3" x 2⅜" x ⅜". $75.00 – 100.00.
Bottom right: Unmarked, white metal, rigid handle triple vanity case — 3½" x 2⅛" x ⅜". $225.00 – 250.00.

SEARCHING FOR A PUBLISHER?

We are always looking for knowledgeable people considered to be experts within their fields. If you feel that there is a real need for a book on your collectible subject and have a large comprehensive collection, contact us.

COLLECTOR BOOKS
P.O. Box 3009
Paducah, Kentucky 42002-3009

Cover design by Beth Summers
Book design by Gina Lage

Additional copies of this book may be ordered from:

Collector Books
P.O. Box 3009
Paducah, Kentucky 42002-3009

@ $24.95. Add $2.00 for postage and handling.

Printed by IMAGE GRAPHICS, INC., Paducah, Kentucky

Dedication

---◆---

To My Mother
Mae Ott Mueller
A Haunting Memory

◆◆◆◆◆◆◆◆

Harry Addison Mowery
Collaborator, Counsel
Critic & Chauffeur

◆◆◆◆◆◆◆◆

<u>Photography</u>
Brent Turner
BLT Productions, Inc.
7575 Deer Park Way
Reynoldsburg, Ohio 43068

◆◆◆◆◆◆◆◆

Acknowledgments

This serendipitous adventure took a serious turn in 1989 when Roselyn Gerson's book on ladies' compacts was published. Collecting information was finally available on or about the most neglected of women's accessories. Always a historian first and collector second, I began assembling a collection that would represent the rise and fall of compacts; trying to gather the best examples of each quirk and turn of design. This took some fancy footwork and a sense of balance.

To maintain this balance, I was graciously granted loans from several important collections which had items I lacked. My thanks to: Ann Mueller Zdeb, Ruth A. Forsythe, Ellen Foster and Barbara Bauman Mueller. The powder box chapter owes its life to Susan Rutter and Robin Doty.

And thanks to those who looked over my shoulder, and undangled my participles: Kathleen Geyer Malone, Harry Addison Mowery, Stephen Vincent Mueller, and Beth Wilxman Schodorf.

Contents

Preface

Reflections on the Fair Vanity —
An Overview on Collecting

Mello-Glo Art Deco Gift Set. Goldtone, loose powder compact, (see page 15, #8); face powder box — 4"sq x 1"; glass perfume — 2¼" x 1⅝"; box — 10⅜" x 1½". Set: $350.00 – $400.00.

On Friday, April 3rd, 1987, in Geneva, Switzerland, a six piece 18kt gold vanity purse set belonging to the Duchess of Windsor was auctioned by Sotheby's for $660,000. The set, made by Van Cleef & Arpels, consisted of: powder compact, pill box, scent bottle, lipstick tube, cased comb, and notebook holder. Various gemstone charms and stickpin fronts were affixed to the items. One wonders what the Duchess' first powder carrier looked like when she was Bessie Wallis Warfield of Baltimore, Maryland. Of genteel poverty, did she have a powder rag in a cardboard box, or maybe only a rabbit's foot and some rice powder, and what was the cost? Always adventurous, surely she tried a cosmetic or two to heighten her unique look and had to shop discreetly to avoid being socially exiled. Did she ever think that one of her jewel encrusted compacts would be in London's Victoria & Albert Museum Jewel Room or a Cartier gold and diamond nécessaire du soir of hers would be valued at almost $300,000? Her style and lifespan of ninety years puts bookends on the history of women's compacts and vanity cases.

Buffeted by wars, economic disasters, and the ultimate break of both written and unwritten social rules, women's cosmetics have had more ups and downs than a trampoline. As the public eye applied makeup and the powder box became portable, the vanity case arrived "with bells on" — literally. Cases were not only made to impress, compress and outdress; many had features that were not so obvious. Certain manufacturers had nail-friendly cases that opened without a struggle and a metal nail file; there were right and left-handed interior powder door latches. Mirrors sometimes came in three different magnifications, and teasing tricks were played on powder loading.

Evalyn Walsh McLean of Hope Diamond notoriety had Cartier attach a two part vanity case to a man's pigskin watch band. In 1938 Black, Starr & Frost Gorham featured: "The New Compact-Bracelet...Gold with Rubies and Diamonds...Detachable," and a lipstick lapel clip: "gold cylinder in which a lipstick is cunningly concealed." A mirror was not included.

With all this inventiveness a major design puzzle exists: why did so many cases have a monogram cartouche? This quirk became a design obsession so forced that the best motifs suffered, sparing only those items that had a strong logo identity. Persisting up into the fifties, the monogram box was moved to the interior powder door lid or a space on the case back. All this energy for what — how many cases on view today have monograms?

Another question also puzzles collectors — when it was obvious that the Evans lipstick would not open or close properly, why did the company persist in using it until almost the end? Did Mrs. Evans invent it? And finally, why was the Coty envelope case so popular? It really didn't hold much powder, the puff skittered out, and pressure from the lid closure snap eventually cracked the mirror. Did Hitchcock's mistaken use of this case in his film, *Marnie*, start the fad?

He had his character popping out the mirror frame to gain access to a hidden compartment. Don't try this unless you plan on buying another case.

Collecting cosmetic cases and boxes is a recent interest still settling down to some broad guidelines. The range is so wide that any book must be slanted towards a particular taste. Several other collections were included here for better balance, but the major assemblage is based on commercial items that were available to any woman with modest or better means. Intrinsic precious metals and materials are not covered, nor are elaborate mesh or beaded bags — these deserve a book of their own.

A major attempt has been made to seek out the historical background of the compact — one of woman's most maligned accessories. Spoofed and ridiculed, compacts were depicted as frivolous and superficial. Fair game in cartoons and the performing arts, the point was lost on the artistic aspects of a now esteemed object whose industry was totally supported by women. The last laugh is being heard today in the world's finest auction houses.

This historical overview also includes a time when women were able to participate in a male world — World War II. The patriotic, plastic and non-metal cases featured here are as important to a respected collection as the Dali Bird or a Volupté Hand. Their very fragility demands that they be gathered now as a safeguard against future careless handling and continued lack of respect in the collectible marketplace.

Another new collectible featured here is the face powder box — again an important part of feminine history and deserving of an honored place in any collection. Values fluctuate widely as the boxes are sought for different reasons. Artwork is very important; matching advertising has already secured a market niche with collectors. The major threat to powder boxes is paper price stickers. After surviving almost a century these lovely works of art are now being defaced by stickers at a rapid rate. They have no value with such graffiti damage. Using tagged clear baggies, string tags, or faintly penciling prices on the inner lid would help conserve an endangered historical object for future appreciation.

The values listed in this book are at best an educated guess as no attempt has been made to set a market price. Too many factors are present: geography, fragility, personal preference, and the minds of collectors and dealers. The only hard and true fact is condition. As the accompanying notes explain, some cases have different scales of condition. Use these notes as tools and with discretion; do not become enticed into accepting poor condition by the word *unique*. Unless it is obvious that an item is handmade or personally assembled, it is questionable whether a manufactured object is one-of-a kind.

Every collector has a bad day, but as your knowledge expands you will have more answers than questions and more good deals than bad ones. Acquire a sense of what truly belongs in your collection, be tenacious in your goals, and remember that a quality collection reflects back on your good taste and judgment.

Chapter One

COMPACTS & FLAPJACKS

Unmarked — Goldtone, Loose Powder Compact. Tambourine case with yellow and red chenille ball fringe, metallic red borders, framed mirror, case has scenic transfers of Flamenco dancers and bull fight; 4"dia x ¾". Very rare.

"...'KEEP YOUR POWDER DRY' WOULD BE OLD STUFF TO THE MODERN COMPACT, WHICH MANAGES TO ACCOMPLISH MUCH MORE THAN THIS WITH THE GREATEST OF EASE. IT MUST NOT ONLY BE SUPREMELY GOOD-LOOKING; BUT ALSO MECHANICALLY PERFECT. EASY TO OPEN. CONVENIENT TO USE. JAM-PROOF. SPILL PROOF. AND DUST PROOF."
WOMAN'S HOME COMPANION, 1936

American engineers were late in their exploration of outer space for one very simple reason: they were too busy inventing ways to keep women's face powder in compacts. For forty years — more or less — the challenge of designing women's compacts which would not allow powder to infiltrate purses, pockets, etc., may have been a special course in engineering schools. Pressed, compressed, or cake, powder made an early appearance in sample tins, which were given or for a few cents mailed to patrons of the soap and lotion companies.

A 1909 ad for PLEXO face powder bragged about "the perfect powder in a perfect box...just right for carrying in your purse or bag." It was a forced marriage of a box lid (1¾" in diameter) and a puff, using the lid as a handle — no mirror. Until World War I, most compacts were really just containers for powder bags or "rags." Both appear in ads showing the bags and rags as needed but unsanitary. Jergens' Woodbury line, however, had the rags for sale at 25¢ a box and they were merely washable chamois. The unsavory aspects might have been infrequent washing.

When "nose" mirrors were added to the boxes and cans for a quick dab, compacts began to assume a tiny amount of design, and by 1913 a Detroit druggist was offering a handsome little accessory, gold finished with (powder) pad, bag and reducing mirror with a 50¢ powder box purchase. In 1917 *Vanity Fair* had "...the refillable case...heavily gold plated... $1.00." Until after WWI almost all women's cosmetic items and cases were sold by druggists; some were better than others.

The advent of New York beauty salons in the twenties, as the best place to socialize by the cosmetic houses of Rubinstein, Arden, and Hudnut's Du Barry, put cosmetics and compacts on every woman's status list. A composite of the Fifth Avenue salons was deftly skewered by author Clare Boothe in her play and later movie *The Women;* (try counting the number of compacts depicted). Other French houses, eager to promote their products, saw the benefit of a classy compact as a gift item that needed refilling. This gift incentive, appealing to men who wouldn't cross the carpet into a lingerie department or risk a squirt or two from a high powered commissioned perfume sales woman, were only too happy to do their shopping with their friendly druggist or local jewelry store. Literally, thousands of compacts and vanity cases suitably inscribed were sold on Valentine's Day. Ads were slanted more towards this gift trade.

Once the divorce was granted between the cosmetic houses using compacts as another container for their products and the case manufacturers who were seeking wider markets, the golden age of compacts surfaced. Each new decade following had its own image.

The twenties waffled back and forth between the pressed and loose powder choice which affected compact design. Norida pushed their patented "Can Not Spill" case for loose powder, digressing from the "product first/case second" policy. The 1925 Paris Exposition Des Arts Decoratifs did not impact the American houses until late in the decade, but the French houses of Houbigant and Richard Hudnut moved fast to feature the new look — except Coty. Coty's long artistic union with René Lalique and the Art Nouveau motif hindered them and forestalled their unique case designs to another decade.

American case manufacturers, regardless of the Depression and hard times, absorbed the Art Deco and Moderne lines with passion and frugality. Price was paramount for a product that was an impulse purchase at the best of times. Cases were pulled down in workmanship and trimmed of features. The chic new deco mode helped sales, but the required enameling suffered as did interior case fittings. A monthly druggist trade magazine, with ads by Coty, Tre-Jur, and Yardley, warned of neglect in stocking the "10¢" table with name brand cosmetics. Tre-Jur was offering a 'glove' enameled compact for 50¢. Coty held their own, asking $1.00 for a metal lipstick tube.

The late thirties, which blended into that almost forgotten pre-war period of 1940 – 1941 when times were improving, was the apogee of the compact case. Design and quality were unparalleled, and most of the truly classic cases came from this period. As early as 1937 craftsmen were fleeing Europe and uncertain future, bringing their skills and tools to an awaiting industry. Also the major French houses shifted emphasis to New York and introduced line after line to the American woman, who now had a bit of pocket money.

When the war hit, there was no hesitation in accepting major unknown challenges. As each new corner was turned, people and industry turned with no qualms. Some corners became permanent, however. The cosmetic industry was not allowed to look back; the American woman, war-weary with the impossible tasks of coping with home, job, and restrictions, wanted a different look. The battle was on. Pancake make-up, creme powder, and foam rubber sponge pads instead of cotton puffs slid the compact case into unknown regions — and it lost its way.

Postwar exhilaration was reflected in the compact. Mink covered cases and pavé rhinestone lids looked more like wretched excess than inventive design, as jewelry houses crossed over to compacts, trading on their name, and case houses dabbled in jewelry. Although plastic as a dress compact for loose powder diminished and metallics returned, bigger continued to be better. The huge carryalls were hauled out with the compact playing only a minor role. Sterling, which had an unrestricted ride during the war returned to the jewelry stores from whence it came, leaving behind a strange legacy of hybrid matings.

The compact of today is a ghost of its former self. The industry (going past the many who think a compact is an automobile or a musical disk, and trying to reach those discerning few who recognize a compact as a cosmetic adjunct) has a hard act to follow. No longer a necessity or a gift choice, the compact now has a new image — a curiosity.

"Such Stuff as Dreams are Made on"...

Those immortal words from Shakespeare's *Tempest* express the intangible and indescribable character
of Beauty—that which makes a woman's face stand out, remembered, beloved, across the miles, across the years.
And Beauty, literally the stuff of dreams, can be so wonderfully enhanced by Elizabeth Arden's new Pink Powders.
Renoir Pink for daytime, Paradise Pink for evening, each used over Mat Foncé to give incredible
results, banishing the look of strain and fatigue that comes with modern living, adding new lustre to loveliness.

Renoir Pink Powder *for Daytime*, 1.75 and 3.00 . . . Paradise Pink Powder *for Evening*, 1.75 and 3.00
Mat Foncé *to use under them*, 1.75 and 3.00 . . . All Day Foundation Cream, Light Rosetta Bronze, 1.00
Radiant Peony Lipstick, 1.50 . . . Eye Shado, Opal Blue and Soft Brown, 1.25 each . . . Eye Cosmetique, Brown, 1.50
(prices plus taxes)

Elizabeth Arden

Harper's Bazaar, 1944

10

```
1   3   6
2   4   7
    5
```

1. Norida — Goldtone, Loose Powder Can Compact. Engine-turned lid design, twist-off bottom for exterior powder refill, case signed, framed mirror, 2½"dia x ⅝". Ref: 1925 ad. $65.00 – $85.00.

2. Pompeian — Goldtone, Pressed Powder Can Compact. Lid indentation motif, case signed, framed mirror, 2½"dia x ⅝". $75.00 – $90.00.

3. La Bara — Goldtone, Pressed Powder Can Compact. Bas-relief head of Cleopatra on lid with circled legend, framed mirror, 2½"dia x ⅝". $125.00 – $150.00.

Lid design is silent film actress, Theda Bara, in her famous 1917 role; probably endorsed by American Products Co. to compete with Rigaud/Mary Garden line.

4. Mary Garden — Goldtone, Pressed Powder Can Compact. High-relief profile with circled legend on lid: Rigaud — Paris, framed mirror, 2½"dia x ⅞". Ref: 1920 ad. $75.00 – $90.00.

Mary Garden made her Paris debut in 1906 and was the leading operatic diva at Chicago Lyric Opera from 1910 to 1934. Her public endorsement of lipstick and powder as early as 1918 with the prominent Parfumerie Rigaud, hastened the social acceptance in America for women's cosmetics without the "mail only, plain brown wrapper" directions.

5. Cheramy — Goldtone, Pressed Powder Can Compact. Embossed multi-floral lid motif, Cappi name on lid, case signed, framed mirror, 2¼"dia x ⅝". $65.00 – $80.00.

6. Babbitt — Goldtone, Pressed Powder Can Compact. Moon/Stars and floral spray lid indentation, case signed, framed mirror, 2"dia x ¼". $50.00 – $65.00.

7. Djer-Kiss — Goldtone, Pressed Powder Can Compact. Embossed bellflower rim motif with green highlights, case signed, framed mirror, 2½"dia x ⅝". Ref: Pat. 1917. $50.00 – $65.00.

1	4	7
2	5	8
3	6	9

McCall's Magazine, **1920**

1. Richard Hudnut — Goldtone, Loose Powder Compact. Engine-turned cross-line lid motif with floral square, case signed and Three Flowers logo, framed mirror, 2⅛"dia x ⅜". Ref: Pat. 1927. $45.00 – $60.00.

2. Lazell — White Metal, Pressed Powder Compact. Engine-turned linear lid motif with circle monogram cartouche, case signed, and de Meridor logo, framed mirror, 2¼"dia x ½". Ref: 1915 ad. $45.00 – $60.00.

3. Lanchère — White Metal, Pressed Powder Compact. Rose indentation lid motif, case signed and Blue Rose logo, framed mirror, 2"dia x ⅜". $35.00 – $50.00.

4. Colgate — Goldtone, Pressed Powder Can Compact. Laurel wreath rim motif with faint blue highlights, case signed, framed mirror, 1½"dia x ⅝". Ref: Pat. 1917. $35.00 – $50.00.

5. Elizabeth Arden — Goldtone, Loose Powder Compact. Engine-turned fine linear lid motif, case signed and Ardenette logo, framed mirror, 2"octagon x ⅜". Ref: 1931 ad. $50.00 – $65.00.

6. Armand — White Metal, Pressed Powder Compact. Minimal stamped lid motif with name, framed mirror, 1¾" x 1½" x ¼". $35.00 – $50.00.

7. Unmarked — Goldtone, Loose Powder Compact. Engine-turned linear band lid motif with oval monogram cartouche, no identification, framed mirror, 2"dia x ⅜". $35.00 – $50.00.

8. Yardley — Goldtone, Loose Powder Compact. Faceted lid and case, embossed raised center circle with floral spray and blue highlights, case signed, framed mirror, 2¼"dia x ⅜". $45.00 – $60.00.

9. Mello-Glo — Goldtone, Loose Powder Compact. Engine-turned linear band lid motif with scrolled rim, case signed, framed mirror, 2"octagon x ⅜". Ref: Pat. 1925. $60.00 – $75.00.

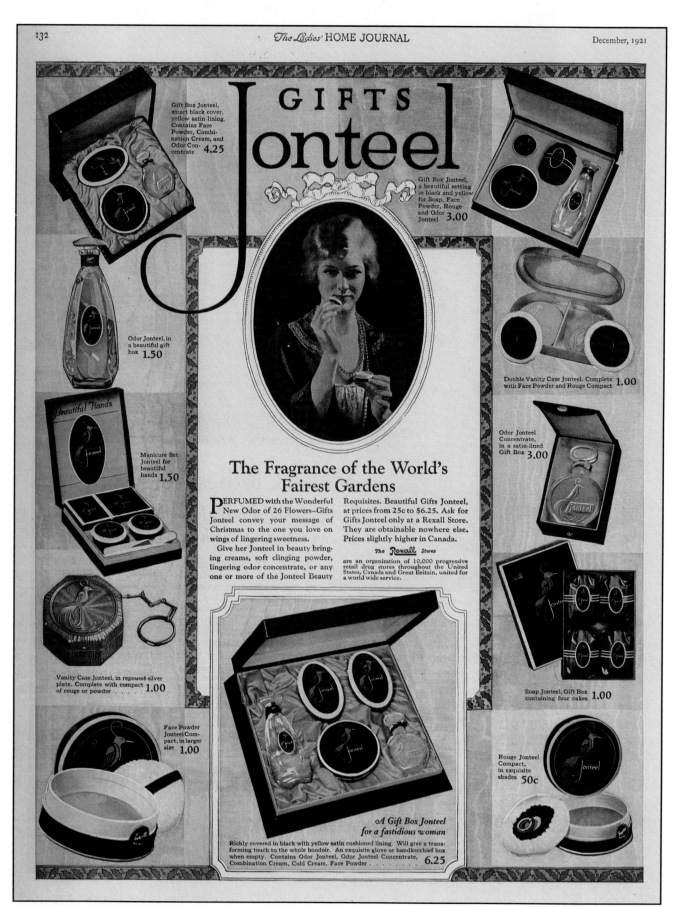

The Ladies' Home Journal, 1921

```
        1        7
    2       5    8
    3            9
    4       6
```

1. Tre-Jur — White Metal, Pressed Powder Compact. Engine-turned banded lid with "The Little One" logo center motif, case signed, framed mirror, 2"dia x ¼". Ref: 1926 ad. $35.00 – $50.00.

2. Lazell — White Metal, Pressed Powder Compact. Engine-turned banded lid with scrolled frame and center monogram cartouche, case signed and de Meridor logo, framed mirror, 1½"octagon x ⅜". Ref: 1915 ad. $45.00 – $60.00.

3. Doray — White Metal, Loose Powder Compact. Engine-turned banded lid with applied silver foil oval seal with logo, (only case identification) framed mirror, 1½"octagon x ⅜". $75.00 – $90.00.

4. Armand — White Metal, Pressed Powder Compact. Engine-turned circular banded lid, center with femme silhouette logo, case signed, framed mirror, 2¼"dia x ½". Ref: Pat. 1924. $45.00 – $60.00.

5. Vivienne — Goldtone, Pressed Powder Compact. Brushed finish with stenciled smoky blue votary silhouette and banding, paper insert: Supreme (only case identification), framed mirror, 1½"dia x ½". $90.00 – $100.00.

6. Jonteel — White Metal, Pressed Powder Pendant Compact. Bark-like "Sheffield Plate" case finish with high relief Bird-of-Paradise logo, 4" broad bar finger-ring chain, no case identification, framed mirror, 1½"octagon x ¾". Ref: 1921 ad. $75.00 – $90.00.

7. Norida — White Metal, Pressed Powder Compact. Hammered finish with bas-relief eighteenth century couple, paper insert: Fleur Sauvage, case signed and Aderon logo, framed mirror, 2"dia x ⅜". $75.00 – $90.00.

This compact does not have the patented Norida "no-spill" interior, and the lid design is a major logo departure. It may have been a later attempt around 1925 to introduce a new line with different market identification.

8. Mello-Glo — Goldtone, Loose Powder Compact. Engine-turned Art Moderne 'Lightning Flash' lid design with outline stylized femme silhouette and signed logo, framed mirror, 1⅞" x 1½" x ⅜". Ref: Pat. 1925. $65.00 – $80.00.

Although this is a loose powder compact, there is no screen or powder wheel for containment — a 'one-holer' with only case pressure against the puff as a stopper.

9. Norida — White Metal, Loose Powder Compact. Hammered finish with bas-relief eighteenth century femme figure logo, revolving powder sifter with interior release for refill, case signed, framed mirror, 2⅛"dia x ½". Ref: 1925 ad. $45.00 – $60.00.

```
        1       4
    2       3   5
                6
```

1. Unmarked — Sterling, Loose Powder Compact.
Open, black enameled case, engraved floral lid motif,
vermeil interior, framed mirror, see page 126, 2" x 1⅞"
x ⅜". $150.00 – $175.00.

2. Coty — "Platinum Tone," Pressed Powder Compact.
#1162, Black "Coffret" with snap closure, box signed:
L'Origan, lid crest, case signed, metallic mirror, 1⅞"sq
x ⅜". Ref: 1930 ad. $125.00 – $150.00.

3. Luxor — White Metal, Pressed Powder Compact.
Black enamel, raised sun rays with boxed monogram
logo, case signed, framed mirror, 2"dia x ¼". Ref: Pat.
1926. $65.00 – $80.00.

**4. Colgate — Black Enamel, Pressed Powder Can
Compact.** "#100 Black Box," engraved lid initials and
acanthus border, instruction papers, case signed, framed
mirror, 2½"dia x ⅝". Ref: 1924 ad. $90.00 – $105.00.

*The three sets of papers in the box (shown): instruct
the engraver on proper monogramming techniques
and recommended styles, advise the new owner (Flo
Chandler) to use the enclosed maroon flannel pouch
to protect the enamel, and includes a paper tissue
with refill information.*

**5. Colgate — Black Enamel, Pressed Powder Can
Compact.** Mini #100, engraved acanthus lid border,
case signed, framed mirror, 1½"dia x ⅝". Ref: 1924 ad.
$65.00 – $80.00.

**6. Harriet Hubbard Ayers — White Metal, Loose
Powder Glove Compact.** Black enameled, embossed
diamond monogram logo: "HHA," case signed,
framed mirror, 2" x 1½" x ¼". $35.00 – $50.00.

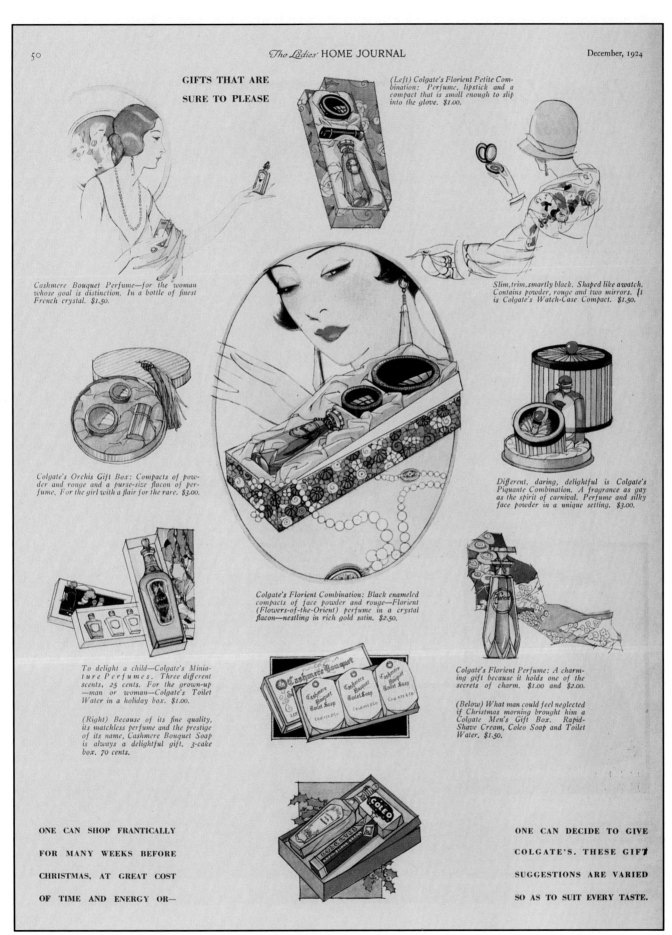

The Ladies' HOME JOURNAL   December, 1924

GIFTS THAT ARE
SURE TO PLEASE

(Left) Colgate's Florient Petite Combination: Perfume, lipstick and a compact that is small enough to slip into the glove. $1.00.

Cashmere Bouquet Perfume—for the woman whose goal is distinction. In a bottle of finest French crystal. $1.50.

Slim, trim, smartly black. Shaped like a watch. Contains powder, rouge and two mirrors. It is Colgate's Watch-Case Compact. $1.50.

Colgate's Orchis Gift Box: Compacts of powder and rouge and a purse-size flacon of perfume. For the girl with a flair for the rare. $3.00.

Different, daring, delightful is Colgate's Piquante Combination. A fragrance as gay as the spirit of carnival. Perfume and silky face powder in a unique setting. $3.00.

Colgate's Florient Combination: Black enameled compacts of face powder and rouge—Florient (Flowers-of-the-Orient) perfume in a crystal flacon—nestling in rich gold satin. $2.50.

To delight a child—Colgate's Miniature Perfumes. Three different scents, 25 cents. For the grown-up —man or woman—Colgate's Toilet Water in a holiday box. $1.00.

(Right) Because of its fine quality, its matchless perfume and the prestige of its name, Cashmere Bouquet Soap is always a delightful gift. 3-cake box. 70 cents.

Colgate's Florient Perfume: A charming gift because it holds one of the secrets of charm. $1.00 and $2.00.

(Below) What man could feel neglected if Christmas morning brought him a Colgate Men's Gift Box. Rapid-Shave Cream, Coleo Soap and Toilet Water. $1.50.

ONE CAN SHOP FRANTICALLY FOR MANY WEEKS BEFORE CHRISTMAS, AT GREAT COST OF TIME AND ENERGY OR—

ONE CAN DECIDE TO GIVE COLGATE'S. THESE GIFT SUGGESTIONS ARE VARIED SO AS TO SUIT EVERY TASTE.

The Ladies' Home Journal, 1924

```
                3
        1       4       6
        2       5       7
```

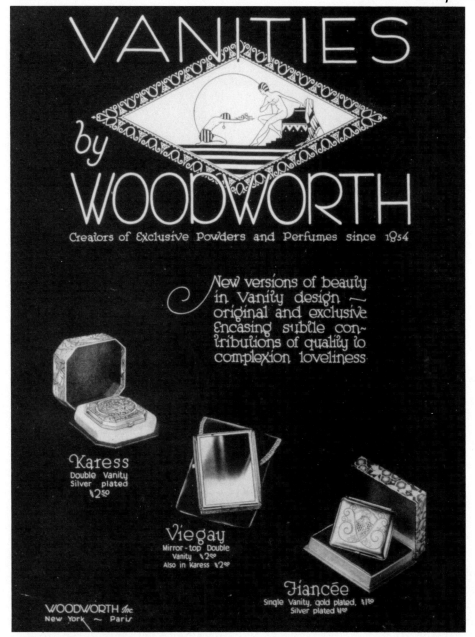

Theatre Magazine, 1928

1. Plough's — White Metal, Pressed Powder Compact. Engine-turned banded lid motif with oval monogram cartouche, case signed with Black & White logo, framed mirror, 2"dia x ⅜". $35.00 – $50.00.

2. Richard Hudnut — White Metal, Pressed Powder Compact. Embossed multi-floral lid motif with ribbons, lambswool Art Moderne patterned puff, case signed and Three Flowers logo, framed mirror, 2¼"dia x ½". $45.00 – $60.00.

3. Djer-Kiss — White Metal, Pressed Powder Compact. Fancy presentation box with purple silk lining, hammered case finish with center lid monogram cartouche, no case logo, box has sticker: "Chair Compact" and logo, framed mirror, 2¼"dia x ⅜". $125.00 – $150.00.

The tassel is detachable and fits through the looped push piece. There is a separate indentation in box for loose tassel.

4. Woodworth — Silver Plated, Pressed Powder Compact. Art Nouveau case with niello accented floral lid motif, Karess logo, case signed, framed mirror, 2" x 1⅝" x ⅜". Ref: 1928 ad. $90.00 – $105.00.

5. Woodworth — White Metal, Pressed Powder Compact. Incised lid motif: blue bells with tendrils, faint blue coloring, case signed and Karess logo, Fiancée on puff (refill?), framed mirror, 2" x 1¾" x ⅜". Ref: 1928 ad. $45.00 – $60.00.

6. Evans (Unmarked) — White Metal, Loose Powder Compact. Cloisonné center lid motif with enamel accented floral sprays, framed mirror, 2¼"dia x ⅜". $35.00 – $50.00.

7. Woodworth — Silver Plated, Pressed Powder Compact. Engine-turned snowflake lid motif, case signed and Viegay logo, framed mirror, 2"dia x ½". Ref: Pat. 1916. $45.00 – $60.00.

```
1       3       6
2       4       7
        5
```

1. Dovell — Goldtone, Loose Powder Compact. Blue enamel on diagonal ribbed case with squared center monogram cartouche, no case identification, puff with logo shown, framed mirror, 2¼" x 1⅞" x ½". $35.00 – $50.00.

2. Langlois — White Metal, Pressed Powder Compact. Heavy ribbed case lid with bas-relief flower basket, Cara Nome logo in cartouche, case signed, framed mirror, 2⅛"dia x ½". Ref: Pat. 1924. $45.00 – $60.00.

3. Langlois — White Metal, Pressed Powder Compact. Incised flower basket motif, black plastic shoulders, Cara Nome logo, case signed, metallic mirror, 2¼" x 2" x ⅜". $35.00 – $50.00.

The hinged flange closure of this model was only in use during the middle Depression years. Coty and Marie Earle used the same cases to the late thirties, while Houbigant stayed with it until the early forties. The idea might have begun as a cost saving device. However, usually the flanges did not stay closed, and puff and powder escaped regularly. Another wrong idea was to substitute plated metal

for a glass mirror; distortion and corrosion met equally aggravating flaws.

4. Girey — Goldtone, Loose Powder Compact. High gloss finish with trough rim, attached rhinestone and crown bijou, no case identification, puff with logo, framed mirror, 2¾" x 2¼" x ⅜". $45.00 – $60.00.

5. Nymfaun — Goldtone, Pressed Powder Compact. Engine-turned banded case design, rectangular monogram cartouche, case signed, framed mirror, 2½" x 2" x ½". $75.00 – $90.00.

6. Woodworth — Goldtone, Pressed Powder Compact. Engine-turned sun ray lid motif with stylized Greek key rim, faint blue accents, Karess logo, case signed, handmade blue silk puff shown, framed mirror, 2¼"shield x ½". $65.00 – $80.00.

7. Pompeian — Goldtone, Pressed Powder Compact. Brushed finish with Art Nouveau votary figure, purple shaded incised tendrils and scrolled rim, paper and sticker logos, case signed, framed mirror, 2½"dia x ½". $125.00 – $150.00.

1	3	6
2	4	7
	5	

1. Coty — Goldtone, Pressed Powder Disk Compact. Coral/gold spangled plastic lid inset, paper label on reverse: L'Aimant, case signed, framed mirror, 2¾"dia x ½". $25.00 – $40.00.

Pressed powder made a come-back in the early/middle fifties with publicity emphasis on creme additives such as Lanolin. The compact was suddenly thrown into the minor role of merely the powder carrier, and plastic throw-away compacts began dominating the marketplace. Metallic compacts were reprieved for a time by the use of a small hole or plug in the case bottom, allowing the replacement of the used pressed powder disk. Some cases also had alternative fittings for loose powder.

2. Charles of the Ritz — Goldtone, Loose Powder Compact. Silver color overlay in ribbed chevron lid design, alternating with glossy goldtone, case signed, case glued mirror, 2½"dia x ½". $30.00 – $40.00.

3. Coty — Goldtone, Pressed Powder Disk Compact. Plastic classic Coty logo lid inset, case signed and L'Origan logo, framed mirror, 2½"dia x ½". $25.00 – $30.00.

4. Lucor — Goldtone, Pressed Powder Disk Compact. Silvertone on glossy goldtone, circled lid design with center figure logo, reverse paper label: Antoine De Paris, disk replacement hole, label signed, case glued mirror, 2¾"dia x ½". Ref: 1958 ad. $25.00 – $30.00.

5. #4711 — Goldtone, Pressed Powder Disk Compact. Plastic coated green/black snowflake lid inset, reverse legend: "Tosca, Made in England," disk replacement button, case signed, framed mirror, 2"dia x ⅜". $25.00 – $30.00.

6. Fuller — Goldtone, Pressed Powder Disk Compact. Engine-turned circled lid motif with stylized monogram lid cartouche, paper label: The Fuller Brush Co., puff: The House of Fuller, case signed, case glued mirror, 2¾"dia x ½". $35.00 – $50.00.

7. Coty — Goldtone, Loose Powder Compact. Paris blue and maroon enameled lid, enhanced by goldtone raised dots and center domed motif, case signed, framed mirror, 2¾"dia x ½". Ref: 1942 ad. $45.00 – $60.00.

```
                    2    5
              1     3    6
                    4    7
```

.1. Revlon — Goldtone, Pressed Powder Disk Compact. Futurama white champlevé enamel lid with glossy goldtone raised laurel wreath and crowned crest with "R" monogram, disk replacement holes, case signed, case glued mirror, 2⅝"dia x ½". Ref: 1958 ad. $15.00 – $20.00.

As formal metallic compacts retreated in the late fifties, a surprising regression occurred; the case shapes began to revert to the earlier powder can format both in a lack of imaginative design and mechanical features.

2. Revlon — Goldtone, Conversion Powder Compact. Moiré case pattern, presentation box legend: "Case designed by Van Cleef & Arpels," case has interior framing only and paper label instructions for pressed or loose powder choice, case signed, framed mirror, 3¼" x 2¼" x ½". $50.00 – $65.00.

3. Elizabeth Arden — Goldtone, Pressed Powder Disk Compact. Fine incised linear case motif with circled rhinestones, "Made in Switzerland," case signed, puff has Ardena logo, framed mirror, 2¾"dia x ⅜". $45.00 – $60.00.

4. Coty — Goldtone, Pressed Powder Disk Compact. Ribbed lid design with Coty crest, reverse gold foil label: "French Flair," disk replacement holes, no case identification, case glued mirror, 2⅝"dia x ½". Ref: 1959 ad. $15.00 – $25.00.

5. Elizabeth Arden — Goldtone, Pressed Powder Disk Compact. Pearlized champlevé enamel lid with glossy goldtone raised laurel wreath and Napoleonic monogram and crest, disk replacement hole, foil case label and case signed, puff with Ardena logo, case glued mirror, 2¾"dia x ½". Ref: 1953 ad. $25.00 – $35.00.

6. Richard Hudnut — Goldtone, Pressed Powder Disk Compact. Engine-turned concentric circle lid design with attached rhinestone enhanced Du Barry crest, disk replacement hole, foil case label, puff with Du Barry logo, no case identification, case glued mirror, 2¾"dia x ½". $35.00 – $50.00.

7. Elgin American — Goldtone, Conversion Powder Compact. Engine-turned sun rays and quatrefoil flower lid motif, center circle monogram cartouche, disk replacement slot, case signed, case glued mirror, 2⅝"dia x ⅜". $45.00 – $60.00.

Unlike the Revlon Conversion Compact with no interior fittings, this model has both powder door and powder disk.

Totally new compact make-up with the <u>loose-powder-look</u> (in golden metal case incredibly, only 1.50)

COMPOUNDED AND COPYRIGHTED IN U.S.A. BY COTY, INC. HAT BY LILLY DACHÉ

No greasy foundation to mask... blotch...streak...or change shade!

At last! That delicate glow . . . that light and lovely "loose-powder look" . . . the look all those compact powders with heavy foundations try to capture—but can't! FRENCH FLAIR is *pure* beauty! Nothing to cake up your make-up, nothing to pile up your powder—*nothing* to suppress its excitement! Like a silken mist, Coty's FRENCH FLAIR covers small flaws, shadows, lines— those aging signs—softly and subtly, with a clinging caress of color. So new . . . so beautiful . . . that only Coty, the most famous name in face powder, could create it! In 12 heavenly hues!

It's unspillable...refillable...and it looks like fine jewelry!

Coty French Flair 1.50

COTY...THE ESSENCE OF BEAUTY THAT IS FRANCE

Refill 1.10

1	3	6
2	4	7
	5	

1. Pilcher — Bimetal, Loose Powder Compact. Copper case with attached high relief goldtone rose spray, no case identification, puff with logo, framed mirror, 3¼"sq x ⅝". $65.00 – $80.00.

Another failed attempt at loose powder control. The powder screen is a pocket with a non-porous backing. The idea was to fill the screen pocket and tap for powder release.

2. Dorset Fifth Avenue — Goldtone, Loose Powder Compact. Tri-color transfer: black, rose and green broad band stylized flora lid design, no case identification, puff with logo, case glued mirror, 3⅛"sq x ¾". $45.00 – $60.00.

3. Studio Girl — Goldtone, Pressed Powder disk Compact. Brushed finish, attached crown and rose bijou, foil label, no case identification, puff with logo, disk replacement hole, case glued mirror, 3" x 2" x ½". $25.00 – $35.00.

4. Dorset Fifth Avenue — Goldtone, Loose Powder Compact. Silver overlay on glossy goldtone lid, with engine-turned floral panel and diagonal lines, no case identification, puff with logo, case glued mirror, 3⅛"dia x ¾". $35.00 – $45.00.

5. Gallery Originals — Aluminum, Pressed Powder Compact. Brushed finish, with square cut faux sapphires lid insets and dual ribbing, paper instructions, no case identification, puff with logo shown, case glued metallic mirrors, 2¾"sq x ½". $25.00 – $35.00.

6. Sternmill — White Metal, Loose Power Compact. Chromed finish, minimal lined lid design with rectangular monogram cartouche, no case identification, puff with logo: "Made In England" shown, framed mirror, 2⅝"sq x ¼". $60.00 – $75.00.

7. Dorset Fifth Avenue — Bimetal, Loose Powder Compact. Glossy Goldtone with high repoussé copper floral lid inset, no case identification, puff with logo, case glued mirror, 3⅛"sq x ⅝". $45.00 – $60.00.

28

1 4
2 5
3 6

1. Volupté — Goldtone, Loose Powder Compact. Modified chevron lid detail with tiny center monogram cartouche, case signed, framed mirror, 2⅞"sq x ⅜". $65.00 – $80.00.

2. Metalfield — Goldtone, Loose Powder Compact. Alternate fine/broad lid ribbons, rectangular monogram lid cartouche, case signed, framed mirror, 2½"sq x ½". $45.00 – $60.00.

3. Unmarked — Goldtone, Loose Powder Compact. Engraved sun rays, only case information: "Made In Switzerland," framed mirror, 3⅛"dia x ¼". $50.00 – $65.00.

4. Primrose House — Goldtone, Loose Powder Compact. Rising sun with rays, reverse monogram cartouche, case signed, framed mirror, 2¼"sq x ⅜". $45.00 – $60.00.

All these compacts have fine workmanship. They are also very heavy, indicating a quality use of brass.

5. Unmarked — Goldtone, Loose Powder Compact. Circle monogram cartouche, with ribbed ascending circles, no case identification, case glued mirror, 3¼"dia x ⅜". $35.00 – $50.00.

6. Easterling of Boston — Goldtone, Loose Powder Compact. Strong diagonal bands of glossy and brushed goldtones, box monogram cartouche, case signed, framed mirror, 3¼"sq x ¼". Ref: 1947 ad. $65.00 – $80.00.

1   4
2   5
3   6

1. Dorset — Goldtone, Loose Powder Compact. Pink enamel with glossy goldtone stylized eye and scrolls in bas-relief, no case identification, puff with logo, case glued mirror, 3½"sq x ½". $65.00 – $80.00.

2. Evans — Goldtone, Loose Powder Compact. Glossy goldtone embossed scattered petals on granulated background, no case identification, puff with logo, framed mirror, 2⅜"rounded sq x ⅜". $35.00 – $50.00.

3. Dorothy Gray — Goldtone, Loose Powder Compact. New Moon and Star lid motif in glossy and brushed tones, case signed, framed mirror, 3¼"dia x ¼". Ref: 1947 ad. $65.00 – $80.00.

The Dorothy Gray cases are always a delight in design, imagination and control of the compact size limitation. This skill brings the wish of a name or signature to identify these artisans. Although possessing talent of the highest caliber, the compact designers — with few exceptions — remain a mystery.

4. Elgin American — Goldtone, Loose Powder Compact. Bubbles and Ribbons motif in glossy and brushed tones, American Beauty paper ad, case signed, glued mirror, 2¾"sq x ¼". $35.00 – $50.00.

5. Dorothy Gray — Goldtone, Loose Powder Compact. Savoir Faire raised mask with incised ribbons on a rhinestone studded brushed tone background, case signed, framed mirror, 3¾"oval x 3" x ½". Ref: 1947 ad. $75.00 – 90.00.

6. Elgin American — Goldtone, Loose Powder Compact. Mardi Gras masks in glossy relief on an incised background, case signed, framed mirror, 2¾"sq x ¼". $25.00 – $40.00.

1	4
2	5
3	6

1. Elgin American — Goldtone, Loose Powder Compact. Chameleon effect with alternating gold and silver tone braiding, slight incising, paper ad with federal tax and puff replacement information, case signed, case glued mirror, 3¾" x 3¼" x ⅜". Ref: 1945 ad. $65.00 – $80.00.

The Chameleon effect on these compacts is the result of light reflections created by lacquer, interacting glossy and brushed finished, or gold with silver-tones. The design depends on highlights in surface texture to bring the design to life. The motif is almost always without case relief. The nature of this delicate casework prohibits rough handling and harsh cleaners. Any use of stickers for pricing or identification may rapidly discolor the design. The prices reflect fine to mint lacquer condition.

2. Wadsworth — Goldtone, Loose Powder Compact. Chameleon effect with cross hatching of brushed gold and silver bands, ribbed shoulders, case signed, framed mirror, 3⅛"sq x ⅜". $75.00 – $90.00.

3. Newport — Goldtone, Loose Powder Compact. Chameleon effect, glossy and brushed goldtones with faint incising, stylized honor playing card of femme figure, no case identification, puff with logo, case glued mirror, 3½" x 2⅜" x ⅜. $65.00 – $80.00.

4. Pilcher — Goldtone, Loose Powder Compact. Chameleon effect, glossy and brushed goldtone with linear squarings, no case identification, papers, puff with logo, case glued mirror, 3½" x 2¼" x ¼". $50.00 – $65.00.

5. Pilcher — Bimetal, Loose Powder Compact. Chameleon effect, "Gold Plate on Silver Finish" with foil label on mirror, slight pinwheel incising, case signed, framed mirror, 3¼"dia x ⅜". Ref: 1948 ad. $75.00 – $90.00.

6. American Beauty — Goldtone, Loose Powder Compact. Chameleon effect, floral spray created by glossy and brushed tones, case signed, framed mirror, 3¼"squared oval x 2½" x ¼". $35.00 – $50.00.

1   4
2   5
3   6

1. Volupté — Goldtone, Loose Powder Compact. Broad band lattice in high relief, no case identification, puff with logo, case glued mirror, 2⅜"sq x ⅜". $25.00 – $35.00.

2. Volupté — Goldtone, Loose Powder Compact. Gift Box, glossy case with brushed rectangle gift card and bow-tied cord in raised relief, case signed, framed mirror, 3"sq x ½". Ref: 1947 ad. $75.00 – $90.00.

3. Columbia Fifth Avenue — Goldtone, Loose Powder Compact. Brushed finish with glossy door knocker motif in high relief, no case identification, puff with logo, case glued mirror, 3¼"dia x ½". Ref: 1946 ad. $25.00 – $35.00.

4. Majestic — Goldtone, Loose Powder Compact. Envelope purse with faux button closure, in engine-turned bas-relief moiré pattern, lid button acts as monogram cartouche, no case identification, case glued mirror, 2¾"sq x ¼". $45.00 – $60.00.

5. Dorothy Gray — Goldtone, Loose Powder Compact. Brushed tone buckle in relief on faux shagreen, case signed, framed mirror, 2¾"sq x ⅜". Ref: 1942 ad. $50.00 – $65.00.

6. Elizabeth Arden — Goldtone, Loose Powder Compact. Square coiled embossed rope lid motif in glossy relief, case signed, framed mirror, 2¾"sq x ⅜". $35.00 – $50.00.

```
1        5
2        6
3        7
4
```

1. DeVilbiss — Goldtone, Loose Powder Compact.
Glossy case, affixed white enameled dogwood florets with rhinestone centers in ultra high relief, attached dual leaf sprays, case signed, framed mirror, 2½" x 2¼" x ⅜". $150.00 – $175.00.

2. Richard Hudnut — Goldtone, Loose Powder Compact. High embossed spiraling sun and ribbed rays, case signed, framed mirror, 2⅜"dia x ½". $45.00 – $60.00.

3. Zell — Goldtone, Loose Powder Compact. Attached embossed glossy flower bud in high relief on brushed finish, no case identification, puff with logo, case glued mirrors, 3⅛" x 2¼" x ⅜". $35.00 – $45.00.

4. Evans — Goldtone, Loose Powder Compact. Antiqued finish, Orchid raised lid attachment in high embossed relief, paper advertising for the Clocker fitted clutch, no case identification, puff with logo, framed mirror, 2½"dia x ¾". $35.00 – $45.00.

5. Tre-Jur — Goldtone, Loose Powder Compact. Art Deco high embossed flora lid motif, monogram car-touche on reverse, "Little One" case logo, case glued mirror, 3"dia x ⅜". $45.00 – $60.00.

Hampden has this case in spun aluminum. Both puff and case have logos.

6. Richard Hudnut — Goldtone, Pressed Powder Compact. Black enameled lid with engine-turned reverse, chased glossy goldtone Art Deco Lotus center motif, case signed, framed mirror, 2½"dia x ⅜". $65.00 – $75.00.

7. Zell — Goldtone, Loose Powder Compact. Bicolor brushed silver and goldtone finish, high relief glossy attached lid ornament of stylized leaves and block 'O,' no case identification, box logo, framed mirror, 3⅜"octagon x ¾". $50.00 – $65.00.

Zell Compacts are rarely identified by case signing, relying on original puff logoes. If the original puff is missing, the compact has two other identifying characteristics — the powder well liners are usually of heavy ivory pearlized paper, and the powder door has a stamped acanthus motif.

1   4   6
2   5   7
3   8

1. Volupté — Goldtone, Loose Powder Compact. Model #74-351, brushed silvertone case with engraved Delta Tau Delta fraternity Greek initials, twisted rope edging, "Prettiest Faces" paper ad, case signed, framed mirror, 3⅛"dia x ⅜". $45.00 – $60.00.

2. Unmarked — Silvertone, Loose Powder Compact. "Made In Austria," case signed, gray faux snakeskin enamel finish with silvertone banding, chromed interior, chamois puff, framed mirror, 3"sq x ⅜". $65.00 – $75.00.

3. Unmarked — White Metal, Loose Powder Compact. Engine-turned case with faux turquoise prong set stones, superimposed on embossed affixed leaves, elaborate bow tie opener, "Made In USA" logo, framed mirror, 2¼"sq x ⅜". $50.00 – $65.00.

4. Wadsworth — Goldtone, Loose Powder Compact. Spun Silvertone case finish with attached goldtone insignia: "Flying Wheel/Indianapolis Speedway" sou-

venir, case signed, framed mirror, 3⅛"dia x ¼". $75.00 – $90.00.

5. Volupté — White Metal, Loose Powder Compact. Engine-turned linear cushion case with box monogram cartouche, chromed interior, case signed, framed mirror, 2½"sq x ½". $45.00 – $60.00.

6. Crown — White Metal, Loose Powder Compact. Damascene case finish, oriental scene, case signed, framed mirror, 3"dia x ½". $45.00 – $60.00.

7. Stratton — White Metal, Loose Powder Compact. Foil sticker: "Real Diamond Cut Front," circle monogram cartouche, case signed: (Hand logo), framed mirror, 2¾"sq x ¼". $50.00 – $65.00.

8. Unmarked — Sterling, Loose Powder Compact. Heavy chased lid design of village, reverse inscribed: "India, 1944," no identification, framed mirror, 2¾"dia x ½". $125.00 – $140.00.

1	4
2	5
3	6

1. Dorset Fifth Avenue — Goldtone, Loose Powder Compact. Clear plastic lid dome covering pink silk flowers on lavender velour ground, no case identification, puff with logo, case glued mirror, 3⅛"dia x 1". $35.00 – $45.00.

2. Unmarked — White Metal, Loose Powder Compact. Two-tone walnut veneer lid and reverse, scotty dogs in relief, bead rim, paper insert with instructions for filling envelope puff to prevent leakage, no case identification, framed mirror, 2⅞"sq x ½". $50.00 – $65.00.

3. Dorset Fifth Avenue — Goldtone, Loose Powder Compact. Clear lucite encased silver spangles as highly raised lid inset, chased border, no case identification, puff with logo, case glued mirror, 2⅞" x 2½" x ¾". $50.00 – $65.00.

4. Monette — Goldtone/Plastic, Loose Powder Compact. Mottled lavender plastic case with goldtone/enameled plastic lid, multi-colored dragon motif over silver foil ground, case signed: "S.G.D.G., Brevette," framed mirror, 2¾"sq x ⅜". $75.00 – $90.00.

5. "S" — Goldtone, Loose Powder Compact. Clear plastic domed lid with floral nosegay on lace with ivory pearlized ground, pale green ground on reverse, inked lettering: "Paris," powder well signed: "Made in France," framed mirror, 2¾"dia x ¾". $50.00 – $65.00.

6. Majestic — Goldtone, Loose Powder Compact. Milk lucite cutout exposing leaping gazelle lid scene with multicolor accents, lucite in high relief border, case signed, framed mirror, 2¾"sq x ½". $90.00 – $110.00.

The 'cutout' Lucite carving gives the paper design an intagio effect. Individual carved segments are hand set to continue the total outline concept — very heavy case.

```
1      3      6
2      4      7
       5
```

1. Unmarked — Goldtone, Loose Powder Compact. Petit point lid cover, dual figure pastoral scene, case identification, "Made in U.S.A.," framed mirror, 3¼" x 2¼" x ⅜". Ref: Pat. 1931. $75.00 – $90.00.

2. Dorette — Goldtone, Loose Powder Compact. Foil sticker: "Handmade (sic) Genuine Snake Skin," padded red snake skin cover, no case identification, puff with logo, case glued mirror, 3" x 2¼" x ½". $65.00 – $90.00.

3. Schildkraut — Goldtone, Loose Powder Compact. Foil sticker: "Genuine Hand Made Petit Point…1650 Stitches to the Square Inch." 16 page booklet enclosed: "The Romance of Petit Point," no case identification, puff with logo, case glued mirror, 2¾" x 2⅜" x ⅞". $90.00 – $125.00.

4. Zell Fifth Avenue — Goldtone, Loose Powder Compact. Passementerie needlework on black velvet, puff with logo, no case identification, pearlized powder liner and acanthus door embossing, framed mirror, 2¾"sq x ½". $50.00 – $65.00.

Zell has several signatures: "Styled by Zell," "Zell Fifth Avenue," and "Zell."

5. Gwenda — White Metal, Loose Powder Compact. Red plaid taffeta lid with pale green enamel reverse, Tap-Flap powder dispenser with paper instructions, original plaid paper box, case signed, framed mirror, 2¼"dia x ¼". $65.00 – $75.00.

6. D.R.P. — White Metal, Loose Powder Compact. Embossed red leather case with Comma motif, case signed, framed mirror, 2¾"sq x ½". $45.00 – $60.00.

7. Rowenta — White Metal, Loose Powder Compact. Gold and silver needlework on ivory silk, lid inset, black enameled case, elaborate tricolor floral embroidery on ivory silk puff, case signed: "Foreign," framed mirror, 2½" x 2⅛" x ⅜". $90.00 – $105.00.

1	4
2	5
3	6
	7

1. Unmarked — Goldtone, Loose Powder Compact. Pink and white enamel on copper, artist signed femme head with hat design, no case identification, framed mirror, 2¾"sq x ½". $45.00 – $60.00.

2. Weisner of Miami — Goldtone, Loose Powder Compact. White cloisonné with multicolor pansies, foil sticker: "Hand painted genuine cloisonné by Weisner of Miami," no case identification, case glued mirror, 2¾" x 2⅜" x ½". $35.00 – $50.00.

3. Stratton — Goldtone, Conversion Powder Compact. Green and white Wedgwood-like lid inset of mythological figure, scalloped rim, boxed signature, framed mirror, 3¼"dia x ½". $50.00 – $65.00.

4. Unmarked — Goldtone, Loose Powder Compact. White porcelain domed lid with transfer pastoral fig-ures, pink enamel reverse, no case identification, case glued mirror, 2½"dia x ½". $25.00 – $40.00.

5. Evans — Goldtone, Loose Powder Compact. Royal blue lid enamel with domed oval porcelain affixed ornament, stepped shoulders, hammered reverse, with engraving: "Queen — 1940," case signed, framed mirror, 2½"sq x ½". $50.00 – $65.00.

6. Unmarked — Goldtone, Loose Powder Compact. White porcelain with transfer multicolor floral border, no case identification, case glued mirror, 2¾" x 2⅜" x ½". $25.00 – $40.00.

7. Evans — Goldtone, Loose Powder Compact. Pink cloisonné lid inset with wreath of pink roses, ribbed reverse, hammered interior, case signed, framed mir-ror, 2⅝"sq x ⅜". $50.00 – $65.00.

1   3   6
2   4   7
      5

1. Stratnoid — White Metal, Loose Powder Compact. Plastic reverse transfer lid inset with Art Deco dancing couple on patterned blue foil ground, case signed, "Made in England," case mounted metallic mirror, 2"sq x ⅜". $75.00 – $90.00.

2. Rion — White Metal, Pressed Powder Compact. Black plastic tropical view silhouette over iridescent butterfly wings background, lid signed: "Rio" and "Bill" paper: Brasil, case signed, framed mirror, 2"dia x ⅜". $65.00 – $80.00.

3. Wiesner of Miami — Goldtone, Combination Set. M.O.P., box foil sticker: "Genuine Mother of Pearl," reverse protective paper backing, paper insert: "Trickettes by Wiesner of Miami," puff with logo, no case identification, case glued mirror, see #6 — lipstick, 2¾"dia x ⅝". Ref: 1954 ad. $50.00 – $65.00 set.

4. Volupté — Goldtone, Loose Powder Compact. M.O.P., twisted goldtone rope wrapping, case signed, framed mirror, 2⅞"sq x ½". $65.00 – $75.00.

5. Zell — Goldtone, Loose Powder Compact. M.O.P., snowflake lid design, pearlized tag, box, powder well liner and information papers, puff logo and powder door Acanthus motif, no case identification, framed mirror, 3"dia x ⅜". $50.00 – $65.00.

6. Wiesner of Miami — Lipstick. See #3.

7. Gwenda — White Metal, Loose Powder Compact. Black enameled case, plastic lid reverse transfer with multicolor kingfisher bird on patterned blue foil ground, case signed: "Made in England — Tap-Flap," powder dispenser, case mounted metallic mirror, 2¼"octagon x ¼". $75.00 – $90.00.

1
2
3

4
5
6

1. Kramer — Goldtone, Loose Powder Compact.
Mesh link rhinestones with floral petit point lid inset, rope border, pouch with logo, no case identification, case glued mirror, 2¾" x 2⅜" x ½". Ref: 1951 ad. $75.00 – $90.00.

2. Kramer — Goldtone, Loose Powder Compact.
Mesh link rhinestone encrusted lid, rope border, no case identification, reverse engraved: "Mother 8-30-52," case glued mirror, 2¾" x 2⅜" x ½". $65.00 – $80.00.

3. Unmarked — Goldtone, Loose Powder Compact.
Mink fur lid cover with prong mounted rhinestone border, "Made in U.S.A.," powder door monogram cartouche, no case identification, case glued mirror, 2¾" x 2⅜" x ½". $65.00 – $75.00.

4. Unmarked — Goldtone, Loose Powder Compact.
Black bead case with embroidered pink bead floral sprays, no case identification, "Made in France," framed scalloped bevel mirror, 3⅛"dia x ½". $75.00 – $90.00.

5. Wand Art — Goldtone, Loose Powder Compact.
Black enameled case with glued spangles and painted gilt ribbon borders, paper information: "Original Art Design," puff with logo, no case identification, case glued mirror, 2¾" x 2½" x ⅜". $45.00 – $50.00.

The paper insert continues: "This jewel painted article is not subject to Federal Excise Tax." The glued spangles shed at the lightest touch negating any benefit the original owner might have gained by the 'no tax' ploy. To qualify in the current market, the compacts should have <u>most</u> of the original design intact.

6. Wand Art — Goldtone, Loose Powder Compact.
Brushed goldtone case with hand painted nosegay centered with multicolor glued spangles, puff with logo, no case identification, case glued mirror, 2¾" x 2½" x ⅜". $45.00 – 50.00.

```
1    4
2    5
3    6
```

1. Evans — Silvertone, Loose Powder Compact.
#463-503/3, goldtone case with silvertone overlay,
prong mounted handset faceted rhinestone encrusted
lid, exterior and goldtone interior "sun ray" ribbed
motif, case and box signed, "taxable," case glued mirror, 3¼"sq x ⅞". $150.00 – $175.00.

2. Evans — Goldtone, Loose Powder Compact. Prong
mounted handset multicolor faux gemstones in sun
ray lid center, case signed, case glued mirror, 3"dia x
⅝". $90.00 – $115.00.

3. Unmarked — Goldtone, Loose Powder Compact.
Saddle bag, red enameled lid borders, with engine-
turned tiny trefoil case motif, center red enameled "0"
with marcasite banding, case numbered, framed mirror, 2¾" x 2½" x ⅜". $75.00 – $90.00.

*Purchased in London, this compact has exceptional
quality. Case has jeweler's number, fitted piano
hinge, and suede pouch.*

**4. Zell Fifth Avenue — Goldtone, Loose Powder
Compact.** Incised crosshatch lid design with affixed
openwork ripple ornament surmounted by green
rhinestone and pearl bijou in high relief, lid monogram cartouche, puff with logo, no case identification,
framed mirror, 3½"dia x ½". $65.00 – $75.00.

5. K & K — Goldtone, Loose Powder Compact.
Cabochon handset prong mounted faux gemstones
surmounted on rimmed lid, puff with logo, no case
identification, case glued mirror, 2¾"oval x 1¼" x ¾".
$50.00 – $65.00.

6. Volupté — Goldtone, Loose Powder Compact.
Engine-turned wavy lid motif, with affixed floral
bijou accented by rhinestone and faux gemstones in
high relief, case signed, case glued mirror, 2½"sq x ⅜".
$45.00 – $55.00.

1
2
3

4
5
6

1. Volupté — Goldtone, Loose Powder Compact.
Five collet mounted faceted rhinestones ending lid incised diagonal lines, scalloped sided case, case signed, framed mirror, 3⅛" x 2⅜" x ½". Ref: 1945 ad. $65.00 – $75.00.

2. Stratton — Goldtone, Loose Powder Compact.
Incised silvertone lid inlay, surmounted by rhinestone circle and bar, further accented by bicolor blue and clear glass bead dangles, scalloped case, paper sticker with automatic lid mechanism instructions, case "Hand" signed, framed mirror, 3"dia x ¾". Rare.

The bead dangles vary in length and number of beads. The pale blue and clear beads are faceted, while the darker blue are true beads. The large rhinestone bar becomes flexible as it overlaps the case by two stones ending in a larger prong mount. The center of the bar has a large rhinestone. The dangle wires are brass. Unique???

3. Eisenberg — Goldtone, Loose Powder Compact.
Case signed: Original, affixed "Eisenberg Ice...of

Imported Stones Handset in Sterling Silver," framed mirror, 3"sq x ½". Ref: 1947 ad. $175.00 – $200.00.

4. Volupté — Goldtone, Loose Powder Compact.
#74-3171 model, sun ray incised lid design with affixed domed rhinestone cluster, signed case and box, framed mirror, 3"sq x ¾". $65.00 – $75.00.

5. Volupté — Goldtone, Loose Powder Compact.
Black enameled lid, with affixed floral bijou, accented by rhinestones and faux sapphires, paper ad, case signed, framed mirror, 3⅛"sq x ½". $50.00 – $65.00.

6. Elgin American — Goldtone, Loose Powder Compact. Envelope style, Letter Perfect model, brushed finish, with table cut faux topaz buckle ornament, case signed, framed mirror, 3½" x 2⅞" x ½". Ref: 1949 ad. $50.00 – $65.00.

The popularity of the Coty envelope styled compact encouraged other designers to develop variations such as Majestic and Volupté.

1	4
2	5
3	6

1. Elgin American — Goldtone, Loose Powder Compact. #396-10 Model, 1950 commemorative, script date inset with faux pearls attached to lid, other incised dates on alternating glossy and brushed swirls, black satin rigid carrying case with snap flap, case signed, framed mirror, 3⅜"dia x ¾". $50.00 – $65.00.

No hint as to the significance of the dates which start with 1900. A guess at WWI — 1914, 1918; WWII — 1941, 1945, but that leaves six other dates.

2. Unmarked — Goldtone, Loose Powder Compact. Eighteenth century snuff box copy with rhinestone circled faux medallion of French Cardinal Richelieu attached to lid, no case identification, "Made in U.S.A.," purple faille envelope pouch, case glued mirror, 3"oval x 2⅛" x ½". $45.00 – $60.00.

3. Wadsworth — Goldtone, Loose Powder Compact. Eighteenth century snuff box copy with lid encrusted faux pearls and rhinestones accented by engraved Rococo scrolls, metallic powder screen, case signed,

lambswool puff with logo, case glued mirror, 3" x 2¼" x ¾". Ref: 1950 ad. $50.00 – 65.00.

4. K & K — Goldtone, Cigarette Box. Companion to #5.

5. K & K — Goldtone, Loose Powder Box. Bolster snuff box copy with attached rope lattice framed rhinestone lid ornament, paper insert: Kotler & Kopit, no case identification, puff and paper with logo, case glued mirror, 2⅛" x 1¾" x 1¼". $75.00 – $90.00 set.

The revival of the snuff box design for compacts seemed logical. These oval, bolster, and rectangular boxes were priceless gifts of Royalty in previous centuries. The twentieth century copies may have become cherished gifts again.

6. Dorset-Rex Fifth Avenue — Goldtone, Loose Powder Compact. Pavé faux pearl lid adornment with rhinestone square and larger pearls, incised border, case signed: Dorset Fifth Avenue, puff has Rex addition, framed mirror, 3⅛"sq x ½". $45.00 – $55.00.

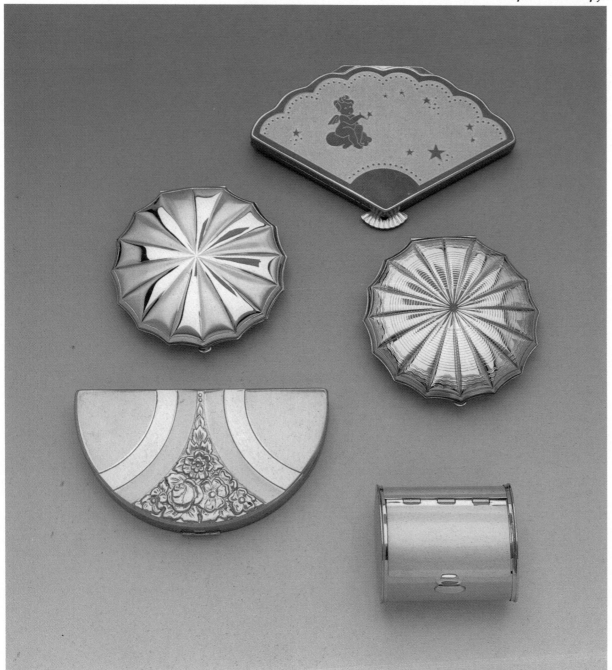

```
1       3
2       4
        5
```

1. Elgin American — Goldtone, Loose Powder Compact. Scalloped knife edged case with alternating ribbed bands of glossy and brushed goldtones, case signed, framed mirror, 3"dia x ½". Ref: 1937 ad. $45.00 – $55.00.

2. Coro — Goldtone, Loose Powder Compact. Lunette case with triangular high embossed center lid motif, alternating bands of glossy and brushed goldtones, case signed, framed mirror, 4" x 2½" x ½". $75.00 – $90.00.

3. Henriette — Goldtone, Loose Powder Compact. Fan, case with brushed silvertone lid overlay, case scallops are followed by lace motif, glossy goldtone cupid on a cloud, scattered stars, ribbed flanged case opener, puff with logo, no case identification, framed mirror, 4¾" x 3" x ⅜". $75.00 – $90.00.

The use of lacquers and metallic overlays rather than case metal work for design will make it difficult to find these compacts in fine to mint condition. The values reflect the quality rather than quantity of these cases.

4. Elgin American. Same case as #1, but with heavily incised circular lid work. $50.00 – $60.00.

5. K & K. See page 44, #5 for information. $35.00 – $40.00.

49

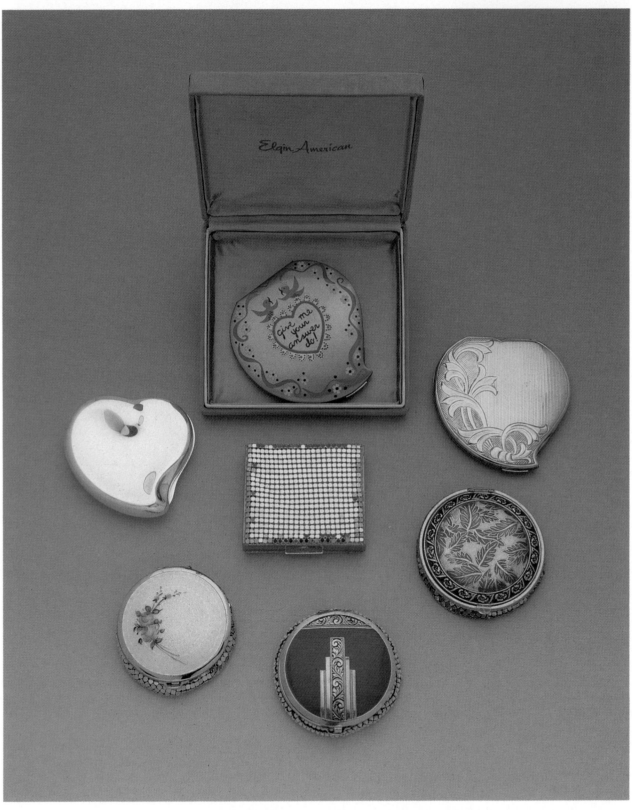

1
2
3
4
5
6
7

Postcard, 1908

1. Halston — Silver Plated, Pressed Powder Compact. Heart, Elsa Peretti case design, paper enclosed provenance, 1988 Christmas limited edition, boxed; puff, liner and box with logo, powder well incised #13697, no case identification, case glued mirror, 3¼" x 3" x ¾". $225.00 – $250.00.

2. Evans — White Metal, Loose Powder Compact. Glossy silvertone mesh pouch case, with "Genuine Dresden Hand-painted Cloisonné," pale yellow lid inset with pink rose spray, tan suede liner, puff with logo, no case identification, framed mirror, 2½"dia x ½". Ref: 1938 ad. $75.00 – $90.00.

3. Elgin American — Goldtone, Loose Powder Compact. Heart, brushed finish with painted lid legend, blue ribbons circle a lace enhanced heart with black lettering: *Give Me Your Answer Do!*, border of bluebirds and yellow daisies, blue enameled reverse, aqua velour presentation case with taffeta lining, case signed, framed mirror, 3½" x 3¼" x ⅜". Ref: 1948 ad. $65.00 – $75.00.

Valentine's Day was the day for compact gift giving, hence the predominance of sentimental designs and motifs. Ads hyped the ideas of gifts for bridesmaids, Mother's Day, anniversaries, graduation, and birthdays. Christmas gifts, however, were skewed to perfumes, jewelry, and furs.

4. Riviera — Goldtone, Loose Powder Compact. Glossy tone all-over link mesh case, not padded, case signed, case glued mirror, 2¾" x 2¼" x ⅝". $45.00 – $50.00.

5. Evans — White Metal, Loose Powder Compact. Red enameled lid inset with Niello Art Moderne embossed lid motif, Armour Mesh pouched case, kid leather liner, case signed, framed mirror, 2½"dia x ½". Ref: 1933 ad. $75.00 – $90.00.

6. Elgin American — Goldtone, Conversion Powder Compact. Heart, deeply chased with lateral lid banding and rococo bordering, has both powder door and pressed powder disk, case signed, framed mirror, 3½" x 3¼" x ⅜". Ref: 1948 ad. $75.00 – $90.00.

The deep chasing requires a very thick base, and this is a very heavy compact. It also shows how long some designs remained popular; this model has been adapted for the later use of the pressed powder disks in the mid-'50s.

7. Rex — Goldtone, Loose Powder Compact. Blue champlevé enamel lid scattered leaf design and embossed floral border, glossy goldtone mesh link pouch case, coated ivory fabric liner, no case identification, puff with logo, framed mirror, 2¾"dia x ½". $50.00 – $65.00.

1
2   3
           4

1. Christian Dior — Goldtone, Loose Powder Compact. All-over ribbed case with lid inset, name plate on powder door, "AGME — Made in Switzerland," framed mirror, 3⅜" x 2⅞" x ½". $125.00 – $150.00.

2. Tussy — Silver Plate, Loose Powder Compact. All-over Persian hunting scene in high relief, case signed, framed mirror, 3¼"dia x ⅜". $65.00 – $90.00.

3. K & K — Sterling, Loose Powder Compact. Deeply chased lid background with tinted flowers, puff with logo, no case identification, framed mirror, 3"dia x ½". $75.00 – $100.00.

4. Unmarked Jonteel — Silvertone, Loose Powder Compact. Domed case with Bird-of-Paradise logo in high relief, framed mirror, 3⅝"dia x ⅜". $65.00 – $90.00.

1   2
           3

1. Coty — Goldtone, Loose Powder Compact. Envelope, shown open.

2. Coty — Goldtone, Loose Powder Compact. Envelope, damask patterned case with faux ruby and filigree affixed bijou, same interior as open model, damask pattern repeated on presentation box and has half round centered faux pearl, box signed: "Envelope — Model #825," puff with logo, case signed, framed mirror, 3½" x 2⅝" x ½". Rare.

3. Coty — Goldtone, Loose Powder Compact. "Envelope, Model #405," puff with logo, envelope box with logo, and enclosed powder packet sample, (shown) signed case, framed mirror, 3½" x 2⅝" x ½". Ref: 1950 ad. $50.00 – $65.00.

Coty hit the design jackpot with this compact, and it is always visible at any collectibles show. However, it is not original to Coty. The French jeweler Van Cleef & Arpels introduced the envelope concept in 1923 in various forms of enameled decoration. Reviving this idea after WWII, Coty went one step further and added presentation cases, and boxes which attracted several levels of buyers.

1   3   5

2   4

1. Unmarked — Enameled, Pressed Powder Glove Compact. Black case, embossed lid floral spray with painted multicolors, framed mirror, 1⅛"dia x ½". $75.00 – $90.00.

This tiny gem is similar to the Divine compacts but does not have a mechanical opener. The Divines in this book all have lunette push piece openers.

2. Divine — Goldtone, Pressed Powder Glove Compact. Mocha enameled case, hand-painted lid scene with eighteenth century couple in yellows and blue, puff with logo, no case identification, paper label, framed mirror, 1⅛"dia x ½". $125.000 – $140.00.

3. Rex Fifth Avenue — Silver Plated, Loose Powder Compact. Lunette case with "Diamond Cut" lateral ribbon lid motif, foil label, puff with logo, no case identification, framed mirror, 5¼" x 2¾" x ½". Ref: 1947 ad. $150.00 – $175.00.

4. Rex Fifth Avenue — Silver Plated, Loose Powder Compact. Flapjack, case incised with floral lid display and center crosshatch band, puff with logo, foil label, no case identification, case glued mirror, 5"dia x ½". $175.00 – $200.00.

The 5" diameter 'Flapjack' or 'Pancake' compact reached the outer limits of usable size. A 1945 Rex ad says it all: "Case of conversational proportions…shows off your face from chin to hair-do." As the upsweep hairdos swept to "conversational proportions," larger and larger mirrors were needed not only to check appearance, they also made great rearview mirrors to check the scene.

5. Divine — Goldtone, Pressed Powder Glove Compact. Glossy finish, hand-painted lid scene with eighteenth century couple superimposed on pink ground, paper insert: "French Process — Hand Made," case signed, no box identification, metallic unframed mirror, puff with logo, (shown). 1⅛"sq x ⅜". $125.00 – $140.00.

54

1
2

3
4

1. Rex Fifth Avenue — Goldtone, Loose Powder Compact. Flapjack, faux veneer vinyl clad case, pink vinyl pierce powder screen with paper instructions, puff with logo, no case identification, case glued mirror, 4½"dia x ½". Ref: 1945 ad. $45.00 – $50.00.

The Rex compacts were the most popular of the generic Fifth Avenues, which included Dorset, Zell, Columbia, and Dale. These were moderately priced and usually promised more than they gave in quality. Rex advertised heavily and was able to meet the WWII metal restrictions by using this patented case and non-silk powder screen. They joined with Dorset in 1951 (Dorset (crown logo) Rex).

2. Rex Fifth Avenue — Goldtone, Loose Powder Compact. Flapjack, "Reverie," ivory vinyl clad case with multicolor pansy floral spray lid display, puff with logo, no case identification, case glued mirror, 4½"dia x ½". Ref: 1945 ad. $40.00 – $45.00.

3. Rex Fifth Avenue — Goldtone, Loose Powder Compact. Baby flapjack, ivory vinyl clad case with pink roses and blue ribbons lid display, puff with logo, no case identification, case glued mirror, 3½"dia x ½". $45.00 – $50.00.

4. Rex Fifth Avenue — Goldtone, Loose Powder Compact. Baby flapjack, faux veneer vinyl clad case, puff with logo, no case identification, case glued mirror, 3½"dia x ½". $35.00 – $50.00.

This is a smaller version of #1.

```
          1     3
            2     4
```

1. Rex Fifth Avenue — White Metal, Loose Powder Compact. Flapjack, silvertone waffle and incised paneled case with goldtone overlays, no case identification, puff with logo, case glued mirror, 3⅞"dia x ⅜". $45.00 – $60.00.

2. Rex Fifth Avenue — Bimetal, Loose Powder Compact. Flapjack, silvertone case with heavy chased "Egg & Arch" lid motif cut through to the background goldtone, sun ray center, case signed, case glued mirror, 3½"dia x ⅜". $65.00 – $80.00.

This model may have been top of the line for Rex. The glossy goldtone interior has a powder well with an engine-turned door with logo (unusual to find a signed Rex case) and also has a button push piece.

3. Rex Fifth Avenue — Sterling, Loose Powder Compact. Flapjack, with incised latticed lid design, case signed: "Sterling," no other case signing, silk puff with logo, case glued mirror, 4"dia x ⅜". $125.00 – $150.00.

4. Rex Fifth Avenue — Bimetal, Loose Powder Compact. Flapjack, silvertone case with heavy chased floral lid border cut through to background goldtone, circle center, no case identification, puff with logo, case glued mirror, 4"dia x ⅜". Ref: 1946 ad. $65.00 – $75.00.

The slight irregularity in workmanship on these compact lids indicates hand tooling. This artistic anomaly by Rex didn't add quality to the case, but did add a touch of unexpected class.

1   2
        3

1. Hingeco/Trueart — Bimetal, Loose Powder Compact. Flapjack, all-over brushed silvertone case with embossed glossy goldtone umbrellas and raindrops, puff and box with logo, no case identification, framed mirror, 3⅞"dia x ⅜". Ref: 1946 ad. $75.00 – $85.00.

2. Dorset Fifth Avenue — Bimetal, Loose Powder Compact. Flapjack, Southern Belle, goldtone case with brushed silvertone overlay with femme figure and nosegays on lid in flat outline decor, puff with logo, no case identification, framed mirror, 3⅞"dia x ⅜". $40.00 – $50.00.

The 'Southern Belle' also appears on an unmarked goldtone of higher quality than #2; this case is similar to the #3 Ritz with smooth reverse but has different interior powder door. Value should follow #3.

3. Ritz — Goldtone, Loose Powder Compact. Flapjack, brushed goldtone case with embossed umbrellas and raindrops, puff with logo, no case identification, framed mirror, 3⅞"dia x ⅜". $65.00 – $75.00.

The two 'Rainy Day' flapjacks have identical interiors and lid design. The Trueart compact, however, has a bark-like embossed reverse, while the Ritz is smooth.

2

1   3

1. Lin-Bren — Goldtone, Loose Powder Compact.
Brushed finish with incised radial lined lid, center
monogram cartouche, case signed, case glued mirror,
3½"dia x ⅜". $40.00 – $50.00.

*The powder well door of this model is another
attempt at loose powder control. The door is dome to
enclose the puff inside the powder well. This solved
the powder-dusted mirror problem somewhat, but
made for a very powdery puff. The Lin-Bren compacts go in a different direction on other features,
such as case closures and powder well doors.*

2. Pygmalion — Goldtone, Loose Powder Compact.
Flapjack, domed center cartouche with enameled City
of London crest, various London scenes are raised on

a granulated ground, "Made in England," puff and
pouch with logo: "Pygmalion 1948," no case identification, case glued mirror, 4"dia x ⅜". $75.00 – $90.00.

3. Zell — Silver Plated, Loose Powder Compact.
Flapjack, embossed fruit lid motif with faint goldtone and colored wash under case lacquer, paper
card: "Genuine Silverplate," puff and box with
logo, no case identification, case glued mirror,
3⅞"dia x ⅜". $65.00 – $75.00.

*This finish is extremely fragile and held together
only by the case lacquer. Mint finish condition and
the silver plating justifies the price. Fruit motifs are
very unusual — otherwise the workmanship lacks
quality.*

1
2   3

1. Evans — Goldtone, Loose Powder Compact. Flapjack, sunburst design, knife edge, with aqua and blue enameled copper disk lid inset, floral and branch motif, case signed, case glued mirror, 3⅞"dia x ½". $90.00 – $100.00.

2. Evans — Silvertone, Loose Powder Compact. Flapjack, lid and reverse in white enamel with attached carved faux 'Fruit Salad' gemstone spray, bimetal interior and swansdown puff, Saks Fifth Avenue box and puff with logo, case signed, framed mirror, 3⅞"dia x ½". Ref: 1940 ad (var). $250.00 – $275.00.

See page 60, #1 for interior view.

This outstanding example of Evans workmanship borrows from the French jeweler Cartier for the carved gemstone lid ornament style known as "Fruit Salad." Carved rubies, emeralds, and sapphires from priceless Rajah collections mixed with whimsical artistry earned this nickname. Evans hit the top of the line with this classy facsimile.

3. Evans — Goldtone, Loose Powder Compact. Flapjack, aqua enameling over concentric circle lid ribbing, case signed, framed mirror, 3⅞"dia x ⅜". $65.00 – $75.00.

1
3
2

1. Evans. See page 59, #2 for exterior.

2. Evans — Bimetal, Loose Powder Compact. Flap-jack, glossy rose and goldtone broad woven high ribbed case design to knife edge, case signed, case glued mirror, 3⅞"dia x ½". $75.00 – $90.00.

This design also comes in the dimensions of #3, with a value of $150.00 – $175.00.

3. Evans — Sterling, Loose Powder Compact. Flap-jack, brushed rose, silver and goldtone finish, bas-ketweave case motif to knife edge, case signed, framed mirror, 4¾"dia x ½". Ref: 1945. $250.00 – $275.00.

HANDBAG WITH STERLING SILVER FRAME AND FITTINGS BY *Evans*

EVANS CASE COMPANY
NORTH ATTLEBORO · MASS.

Vogue, 1945

1 2
3

1. Elgin American — Goldtone, Loose Powder Compact. Flapjack, "Whirl," brushed case finish with contrasting glossy laurel wreath and star lid border, center circles, box and case signed, framed mirror, 4⅜"dia x ⅜". Ref: 1947 ad. $75.00 – $90.00.

2. Elgin American — Sterling, Loose Powder Compact. Flapjack, "Columbine," brushed finish with glossy goldtone overlay, jonquil and ribbon lid motif, hinged presentation box, case signed, framed mirror, 3⅞"dia x ⅜". Ref: 1948 ad. $150.00 – $175.00.

3. Columbia Fifth Avenue — Goldtone, Loose Powder Compact. Flapjack, heavy chased Greek Key lid border with red enameled center, puff with logo, no case identification, case glued mirror, 3⅞"dia x ⅜". Ref: 1947 ad (var). $50.00 – $65.00.

The generic similarities of the Fifth Avenues are apparent in the lid workmanship of this Columbia. *(See page 56, #2 for the Rex variation.)*

1
2
3
4

1. Rex Fifth Avenue — Enamel, Loose Powder Compact. Flapjack, green enameled case with white enamel contrasting floral lid motif, puff with logo, no case identification, case glued mirror, 4"dia x ⅜". $50.00 – $60.00.

2. Rex Fifth Avenue — Leather, Loose Powder Compact. Flapjack, brown embossed leather clad case with lid cross-hatching, puff and box with logo, no case identification, case glued mirror, 4½"dia x ⅜". Ref: 1945 ad. $65.00 – $75.00.

These two Rex compacts both have the pierced pink vinyl powder screen and the paper instructions for using the "Everlasting Sifter," see page 55.

3. Rex Fifth Avenue — Leather, Loose Powder Compact. Flapjack, brown embossed leather clad case with lid floral display, puff with logo, no case identification, case glued mirror, 4½"dia x ⅜". Ref: 1945 ad. $65.00 – $75.00.

4. Zell — Leather, Loose Powder Compact. Flapjack, red leather clad aluminum case with stamped gilt "D" initial, puff with logo, no case identification, case glued mirror, 4⅛"dia x ½". $45.00 – $55.00.

1   2
             3

1. Unmarked — Goldtone, Loose Powder Compact.
Flapjack, brushed case finish with glossy flat "Pie Wedge" lid indents and monogram cartouche accented by scrolled hand incising, framed mirror, 3⅞"dia x ⅜". $45.00 – $55.00.

The interior and general case design is identical to the Ritz and Trueart compacts on page 57, #1 and 3.

2. Karneé — Silvertone, Loose Powder Compact.
Flapjack, brushed case finish with glossy Art Deco flo-

ral spray border, outline incising, puff with logo, no case identification, case glued mirror, 4"dia x ⅜". $65.00 – $75.00.

3. Rex Fifth Avenue — Goldtone, Loose Powder Compact. Flapjack, "Brocado," embossed rococo lid with concentric circle background, puff with logo, no case identification, case glued mirror, 4"dia x ⅜". Ref: 1946 ad. $50.00 – $65.00.

1   3

2

1. Volupté — Goldtone, Loose Powder Compact. Flapjack, brushed case with glossy goldtone coiled rope lid motif in high relief, case signed, framed mirror, 4"dia x ⅜". $75.00 – $85.00.

2. Zell — Goldtone, Loose Powder Compact. Flapjack, brushed case finish, cast pewter scrolled lid attachment in high relief, maroon enamel reverse, puff with logo, no case identification, case glued mirror, 4"dia x ⅜". $50.00 – $65.00.

3. Rex Fifth Avenue — Goldtone, Loose Powder Compact. Flapjack, glossy case finish with embossed ribboned spray inset with collet mounted faux emeralds, puff with logo, no case identification, case glued mirror, 4"dia x ⅜". $65.00 – $75.00.

1   3
2

1. Rex Fifth Avenue — Goldtone, Loose Powder Compact. Flapjack set, brushed silvertone lid, reverse with pink and blue floral accents, goldtone capped plastic comb, puff and box with logo, no case identification, case glued mirror, 3⅞"dia x ¼". $75.00 – $90.00.

2. Dorset Fifth Avenue — Goldtone, Loose Powder Compact. Flapjack, high gloss red metallic lid finish, "Blanche" block engraved, sample powder packet,

string crocheted pouch, logoed puff, no case identification, case glued mirror, 3⅞"dia x ⅜". $65.00 – $75.00.

3. Rex Fifth Avenue — Silvertone, Loose Powder Compact. Super, engine-turned "Bubbles & Feathers" case design with mock tortoise shell attached lid plate, inlay sterling floral spray, puff with logo, no case identification, case glued mirror, 3¾"sq x ⅝". Ref: 1946 ad. $75.00 – $90.00.

"*Powder and Smoke*"

Rex FIFTH AVENUE

Proud pursemates dedicated
to beauty and duty . . .
adorned with inlaid sterling.
At fine stores.

REX PRODUCTS CORPORATION · 302 FIFTH AVENUE · NEW YORK

Copyright 1945, Rex Products Corp.

Vogue, **1946**

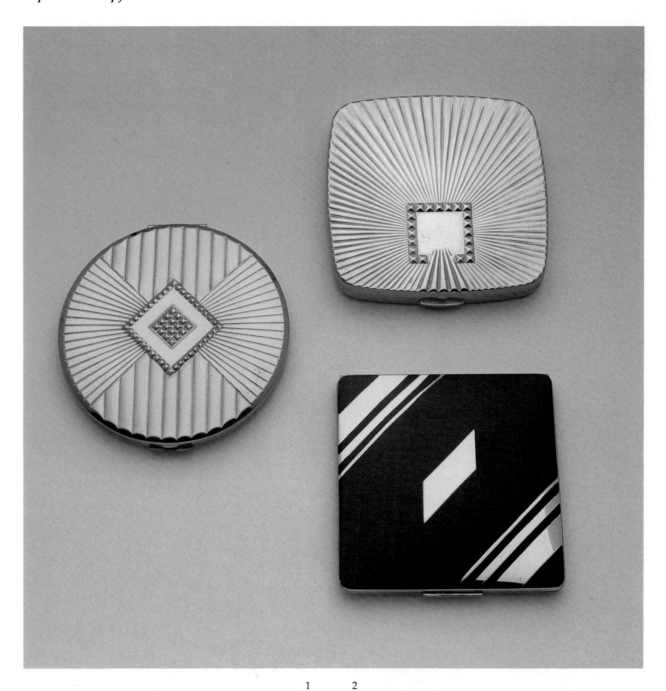

1

2
3

1. Max Factor — Goldtone, Loose Power Compact. Flapjack, "Hollywood Vanity," contrasting glossy and brushed goldtone lid design with broad lateral and diagonal ribbing, embossed center square, box and case signed, framed mirror, 3¾"dia x ⅜". Ref: 1948 (var). $75.00 – $90.00.

2. Max Factor — Goldtone, Loose Powder Compact. Super, "Hollywood Vanity," glossy case with high relief lid sun rays and square monogram cartouche, case signed, framed mirror, 3¾"sq x ⅜". $75.00 – $90.00.

Max Factor noted mainly for the Hollywood movie star endorsed full page ads touting the trademark

"Pan Cake" makeup — which eventually killed the loose powder industry — did have a few very elegant compacts usually in gift packaging. The soubriquet: "Hollywood Vanity" used in the ads is misleading, it is a powder compact only. The word 'Vanity' apparently had more class.

3. Elgin American — Goldtone, Loose Powder Compact. Super, black enameled cushion case with glossy goldtone diagonal lid bands and center monogram cartouche, case signed, framed mirror, 3½"sq x ½". $90.00 – $100.00.

1
2
3

1. Rex Fifth Avenue — Goldtone, Loose Powder Compact. Super, engine-turned "Bubbles & Feathers" case design with mock tortoise shell attached monogramed "M" lid plate, puff and pouch with logo, no case identification, case glued mirror, 3¾"sq x ⅝". Ref: 1945 ad. $65.00 – $75.00.

2 Rex Fifth Avenue — Goldtone, Loose Powder Compact. Super, engine-turned "Feathers" case design with clear lucite lid plate with oval cameo superimposed on faux goldtone hammered background, no case identification, case glued mirror, 3¾"sq x ¾". Ref: 1945 ad. $65.00 – $75.00.

3. Unmarked — Metal/Lucite, Loose Powder Compact. Super, goldtone encased Lucite, with multi floral and bows lid transfer, no case identification, case glued mirror, 4"sq x ½". $75.00 – $90.00.

This marriage of materials was the direct result of WWII metal restrictions and luxury taxes. The workmanship and artistry is excellent with two different case designs. (See page 70, #2 for reverse display.)

1   3
2   4

1. Columbia Fifth Avenue — Silver Plated, Loose Powder Compact. Super, white damask transfer motif, paper label information, no case identification, case glued mirror, 4"sq x ½". Ref: 1946 ad. $75.00 – $90.00.

2. Reverse of page 69, #3.

3. Rex Fifth Avenue — Goldtone, Loose Powder Compact. Super, all-over engine-turned case scrolling, puff with logo, no case identification, case glued mirror, 3¾"sq x ½". $50.00 – $65.00.

4. Rex Fifth Avenue — Silvertone, Loose Powder Compact. Super, all-over engine-turned case "Feathers & Mirrors" case motif, puff with logo, no case identification, case glued mirror, 3¾"sq x ½". $50.00 – $65.00.

The Rex all-over case model was very versatile and pops up in various disguises. Page 69 has two with pinned lid plates. The problem was that the case pins were too small for the usually very heavy lid attachments and came loose, or the drilled holes caused fracture-prone corners. The design also was unable to deter condensation, therefore fogging sometimes occurs under the lid plate. Examine these cases carefully before buying as repairs are not acceptable.

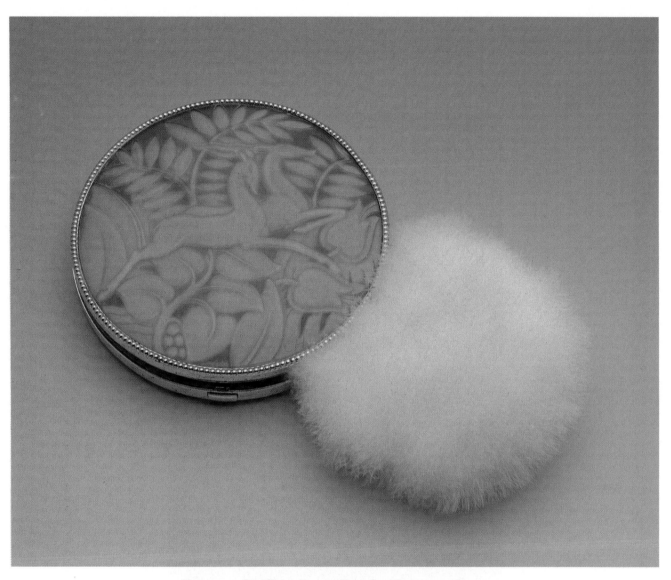

Evans — Sterling, Loose Powder Compact. Super flapjack, Sterling Silver case with rim beading, molded Lucite lid with frosted finish of Post Deco leaping gazelles and fronds, swansdown puff, signed case, case glued mirror, 5⅞"dia x ¾". Very rare. This model also has a Sterling Silver lid — very, very rare.

Chapter Two

VANITY CASES, PURSE KITS & PENDANT VANITIES

1   4
2   5
3   6

1. Coty Presentation Box — Loose Powder Triple Vanity Case. Flying Colors; see #2 & #3.

2. Coty — Goldtone, Loose Powder Triple Vanity Case. Flying Colors, see #3, closed.

3. Coty — Goldtone, Loose Powder Triple Vanity Case. Spread wing lid motif; Flying Colors with red, white and blue accents, exterior lipstick, puffs, box and lipstick have logo, "Air Spun," powder sample packet, case signed, artist: Arthur R. Botham, framed mirror, 4" x 2⅜" x 1". Ref: 1942 ad. $225.00 – $250.00.

4. Coty Presentation Box — Loose Powder Vanity Case. Sleigh Bells, goldtone with red accents, puffs and box with logo, case signed, framed mirror, 3¾" x 3" x ⅜". Ref: 1942 ad. $150.00 – $175.00.

5. Coty Presentation Box — Loose Powder Vanity Case. Wishbone; see #6.

6. Coty — Goldtone, Loose Powder Vanity Case. Embossed lid motif: Wishbone with faux gemstone accent, puffs and box with logo, case signed, framed mirror, 3¾" x 2¼" x ⅜". Ref: 1942 ad. $100.00 – $125.00.

"...A WOMAN DROPPED HER HANDBAG...AND THAT'S HOW IT ALL BEGAN. OUT TUMBLED ONE KIND OF FACE POWDER, ANOTHER BRAND OF ROUGE, A LIPSTICK THAT DIDN'T MATCH IT — A JUMBLE OF MAKEUP."

RICHARD HUDNUT, 1936

Vanity cases have several natures, each one a solution to a specific need or design. Starting out as a way for cosmetic houses to sell more products by combining rouge and powder in one container, the vanity case made a large space for itself but did not survive. Requiring the finest of engineering, case designers, skilled craftsmen and an unending need for a wide assortment of materials, it became too expensive to produce. Although refillable, it also cleverly confined the user to only those products that fitted the case. This gave the cosmetic house a steady customer, and the customer got a superbly made case literally at cost.

However, those cases that were crafted as an independent accessory — and could use loose powder or standard pressed or creme rouge — were usually expensive to refill and own. All the care and artistry the industry could muster were lavished on these cases. Jewelers hallmarked them; enamelers embellished, and silver and gold artisans reached for perfection.

The French first called vanity cases: "necessaires de dame," and when public make-up became a social gambit in the twenties, it followed that a variety of designs were sought for a variety of occasions. Silk cords and chains extended their visibility, interior fittings expanded to include perfume flacons, combs, lipstick tubes, pencils, pads, money holders, and finally the ubiquitous cigarette and its holder were added. Time also dictated design; cases for daytime were sturdier and had more practical fittings, while the evening case, or "sac du soir," gave women the ultimate in conspicuous object d'art display formerly dominated by men's cigar and cigarette cases.

But all this exposure created a demand for inexpensive copies. Like a Dior or Chanel dress copy that would eventually strut the Sears catalogue pages, vanity cases also came down to catalogue levels. From the beginning with only pressed powder and rouge, the cases asserted their multipurpose role. Devising different uses for rouge, such as a nail tint, and using creme rouge for lip color, makeup could be incorporated into the earlier carriers with ease. This worked temporarily until older features were dropped to include tubes for lipsticks and solid perfume wands. When eye makeup moved into the case and loose powder needed restraints, vanity cases exhausted viable design.

Patent numbers clutter vanity cases as the design war raged. Sometimes accommodation was lost as form failed to follow function. Richard Hudnut's stunning Deauville vanities have so much spring action that catching flying puffs might have been a team sport. The Mondaine beauty kits have loose brushes, pencils, and puffs that require constant positioning or the case won't close. Others are so well secured that a tool should have been included for accessory extraction.

Another fascinating feature of vanity case design was size. Miniaturization was the challenge, reversing the design trend of expanding for expansion's sake. The "glove" double vanities that slipped into the palm of a gloved hand were bested by a match box size triple vanity. Containing a tiny lipstick tube, the case defiantly ignores an easier use of double purpose creme rouge.

Compact conversion was a favorite route for vanity case designers. Elgin American adapted the powder door into a triple vanity by adding double compartments for creme and pressed rouge. Others had lids cut out for lipstick tubes that were too high for the case lid. A popular way out was attaching exterior tubes to standard compacts, or ignoring attachment completely and assembling the items in a purse kit masquerading as a vanity case.

Evans used their small round vanity cases as lids for cloth bags, mesh carriers, and cigarette case insets. The Tap-Sift model was a work horse with a myriad of lid designs from Art Deco classic to pseudo Fabergé enameled work. It had its respected place but did not seem to survive World War II. The designs were losing their contemporary edge, and costs and workmanship in a declining market were worrisome. Evans had never been committed to plastics and for a brief period pulled the industry back to metals but not to vanity cases. The fitted Evans purses all featured metal compacts, and the massive carryall could not be considered a true vanity case — merely a box of compartments.

The aristocrat of women's accessories, the vanity case in its numerous roles has not lost its beauty or sense of humor. The vanity is always amusing in its surprises and ingenuity, unlike its stodgy cousins the compact and the carryall. Its very nature of elasticity was to jump and hop as each new cosmetic line needed a gimmick, an image, or logo enforcement. Some houses used certain vanity designs for years without change to maintain a popular line identity. Houbigant and Bourjois/Evening in Paris rarely made major changes, although Houbigant was one of the first with a deco contemporary case. Other houses sought new ideas every few years to shock and startle. Hudnut covered all bases. The DuBarry line remained unchanged, Three Flowers stayed put with Art Nouveau, while Deauville and LeDebut tried a faster dance step.

The compact after nearly ninety years survives in almost the same primitive form in which it started — still serving up powder. The vanity case, however, was doomed, needing a clientele who took pride in quality appearance. The restrictions of WWII so debased this pride that it was never again achieved, proving the artistic temperament of the vanity case too fragile to survive in an age of humorless obsolescence.

NEW COMPACTS BY *Coty*

Add a liberal seasoning of style and humor to careful Coty craftsmanship —and you get these so-smart compacts that are "jewels" to own, a joy to use. Each holds "Air-Spun" Rouge, compartment for loose powder.

"SLEIGH BELLS"

A cheerful little eyeful and earful. The tiny bells tinkle discreetly. Gold color, with a flash of red. Marvelous mechanism. Large, clear mirror. $5.00 plus tax

"BUCKLE"

Sleek and chic and militarily simple. Creamy-white "belt," gold-colored "buckle." Detailed with Coty skill and smartness. $2.95 plus tax

Compounded and Copyrighted by Coty, Inc. in U. S. A.

```
1       4       6
2       5       7
3               8
```

1. Lanchère — Goldtone, Pressed Powder Vanity Can. Double access, intaglio rose lid motif with faint blue shading, case signed: "Blue Rose," single framed mirror, 2½"dia x ⅝". Ref: Pat. 1917. $45.00 – $60.00.

The vanity cans should have all the interior powder and rouge clamps as they usually lack patent and date information on the case. A few tiny case dents can be tolerated as these avant-couriers are rarely in fine to mint condition.

2. Luxor — Goldtone, Pressed Powder Vanity Can. Double access, incised rose spray center circle and lid border, reverse case signed, single framed mirror, 2½"dia x ¾". Ref: 1927 ad. $50.00 – $65.00.

3. Richard Hudnut — Goldtone, Pressed Powder Vanity Can. Double access, engine-turned sun ray reverse and lid with circle logo initial cartouche, case signed: "Three Flowers," double framed mirrors, 2½"dia x ¾". Ref: Pat. 1922/1923. $65.00 – $75.00.

4. Luxor — Goldtone, Pressed Powder Vanity Can. Lid engraved logo signature, reverse signed: "Vanity Box — Armour & Co. Chicago, U.S.A.," framed mirror, 2¾" x 1½" x ⅝". $40.00 – $50.00.

5. Colgate — Goldtone, Pressed Powder Vanity Can. Greek Key incised lid border, case signed, framed mirror, 2¾" x 2½" x ½". Ref: 1920 ad. $65.00 – $75.00.

6. Nylotis — Goldtone, Pressed Powder Vanity Can. Double interior with hinged framed single mirror, bas-relief Art Nouveau peacock with logo, reverse signed, 2½"dia x ¾". $75.00 – $90.00.

7. Unmarked — Goldtone, Pressed Powder Vanity Can. Double interior with hinged framed single mirror, Art Nouveau stylized peacock tail engine-turned lid motif, case interior identical to #6, 2½"dia x ¾". $50.00 – $65.00.

8. Melba — White Metal, Pressed Powder Vanity Can. Double access, framed mirror and case metallic mirror, hammered finish case with stylized "M" border motifs, logo on reverse, 2½"dia x ¾". Ref: Pat. 1924. $65.00 – $75.00.

The silvertone vanity cans are hard to find and are usually dent free. The plating must make for a sturdier case as opposed to the thinner brass cans.

1   4
2   5   7
3   6   8

NORIDA VANITIES FOR LOOSE POWDER
CANNOT SPILL

Just a Twist and Loose Powder

Filled with Loose Powder— It Cannot Spill

Easily and quickly refilled

Norida, the most ingenious and practical vanitie ever invented. And now, you can use your favorite loose powder wherever you go.

Buy one at any drug or department store. Be sure you ask for

The loose powder cannot spill

Single, for loose powder. Double, for loose powder and rouge. Gilt and Silver. Noridas come filled with Wildflower powder and rouge.

Norida Parfumerie 630 S. Wabash Ave. Chicago

Canadian Office 145 Adelaide St. West Toronto

Just a twist and the powder comes forth

Norida

The Vanitie for Your Favorite Loose Powder

Women's Home Companion, **1926**

1. Unmarked — White Metal, Pressed Powder Vanity Case. Shield shape with engine-turned damask lid pattern, hinged metallic mirrors — one magnified, 1⅞" x 1⅞" x ½". $45.00 – $50.00.

This vanity case has been removed from its carrying case. To see it closed and with combined price, refer to page 228, #3.

2. Djer-Kiss — White Metal, Loose Powder Vanity Case. Repoussé Art Nouveau nymphs circled by sun ray lid border, reverse hammered design, hinged double framed mirrors, case signed, 2"sq x ⅝". Ref: 1925 ad. $175.00 – $200.00.

3. Djer-Kiss — White Metal, Pressed Powder Vanity Case. Engine-turned geometric Art Moderne lid motif, case signed, hinged double framed mirrors, 2"sq x ⅝". Ref: 1929 ad. $150.00 – $175.00.

The two Djer-Kiss vanities reflect the radical change in design influences between 1925 and 1929. The 1925 Paris Exposition Des Arts Decoratifs introduced Art Moderne, and those cosmetic houses who wanted to be part of this style rushed to the drawing boards for the new image also called Art Deco but not by the French at first.

4. Norida — White Metal, Loose Powder Vanity Case. Engine-turned concentric circle lid design with center monogram cartouche, revolving powder sifter. Refill instructions, case and box signed, (shown) framed swivel mirror, 2"dia x ⅝". Ref: 1925 ad. $50.00 – $65.00.

Norida spent a fortune advertising their "Cannot Spill" patent. It was a loose powder control that worked and was an alternative to the cake powder and powder bags.

5. D.F.B.Co. — White Metal, Pressed Powder Vanity Case. Book, case with bark-like finish, center attached crest on monogram cartouche, case signed, hinged double metallic mirrors, 2" x 1½" x ½". $50.00 – $65.00.

6. Lanchère — White Metal, Pressed Powder Vanity Case. Double access, intaglio roses lid motif, blue shading, case signed: "Blue Rose," hinged double metallic mirrors, 1½"sq x ½". $40.00 – $50.00.

7. Norida — White Metal, Pressed Powder/Rouge Vanity Case. Repoussé eighteenth century femme figure lid motif, signed on reverse, framed swivel mirror, 2"dia x ⅝". Ref: 1925 ad. $65.00 – $75.00.

8. Poudre L'Peggie — White Metal, Pressed Powder Vanity Case. Double access, embossed Art Deco femme figure and 'Leaping Gazelle' lid design, hinged double framed metallic mirrors, 1¾"dia x ½". $65.00 – $75.00.

<pre>
1   3   5
2   4   6
</pre>

1. Richard Hudnut — White Metal, Pressed Powder Vanity Case. Engine-turned lid design with Acanthus border and monogram cartouche, case and box (shown) and signed: Deauville, hinged framed mirror, shown open — see #4 closed, 2"dia x ⅝". Ref: Pat. 1924. $65.00 – $75.00.

2. Richard Hudnut — White Metal, "Dainty" Powder Sifter. Pierced lid, side lever and knurled back flange for removal, case signed: "Complimentary," logoed back, 1¾"dia x ½". Ref: Pat. 1921. $40.00 – $65.00.

3. Richard Hudnut — White Metal, Pressed Powder Vanity Case. Blue translucent enamel over engine-turned sun ray lid motif with embellished monogram cartouche, see #1 for identical interior, signed: "Deauville," 2"dia x ⅝". Ref: Pat 1924. $75.00 – $90.00.

4. Richard Hudnut. See #1 open.

5. Richard Hudnut — White Metal, Pressed Powder Vanity Case. "Petite Double Compact," embossed swags and flora lid design, circle monogram cartouche, case and box (shown) and signed: "Three Flowers," hinged framed mirror, see #6 open, 1¾"dia x ¾". Ref: Pat. 1924. $75.00 – $90.00.

6. Richard Hudnut. See #5 closed.

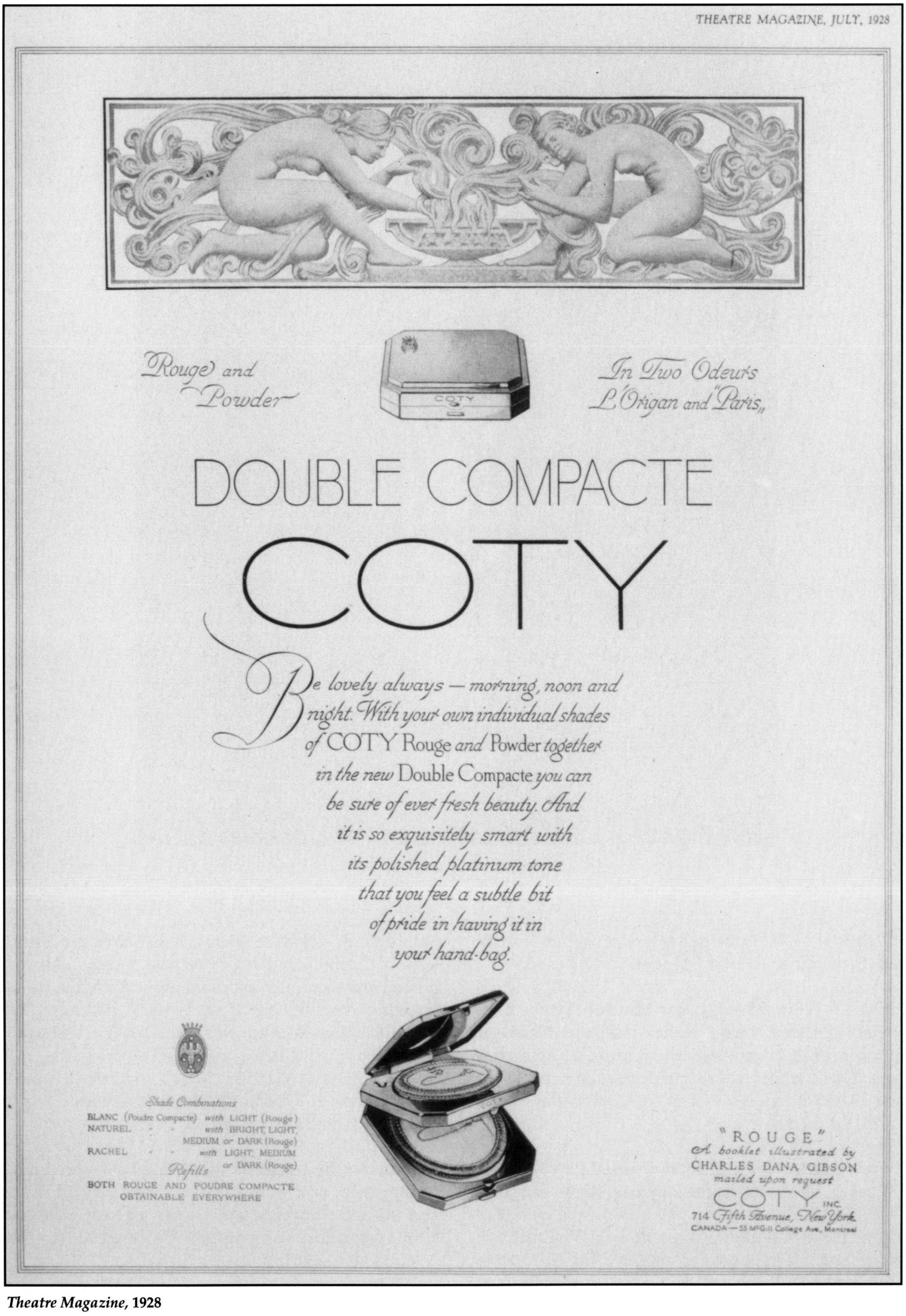
THEATRE MAGAZINE, JULY, 1928
Rouge and Powder
In Two Odeurs L'Origan and "Paris"
COTY
DOUBLE COMPACTE
COTY
Be lovely always — morning, noon and night. With your own individual shades of COTY Rouge and Powder together in the new Double Compacte you can be sure of ever fresh beauty. And it is so exquisitely smart with its polished platinum tone that you feel a subtle bit of pride in having it in your hand-bag.
Shade Combinations
BLANC (Poudre Compacte) with LIGHT (Rouge)
NATUREL - - with BRIGHT, LIGHT, MEDIUM or DARK (Rouge)
RACHEL - - with LIGHT, MEDIUM or DARK (Rouge)
Refills
BOTH ROUGE AND POUDRE COMPACTE OBTAINABLE EVERYWHERE
"ROUGE"
A booklet illustrated by CHARLES DANA GIBSON mailed upon request
COTY INC.
714 Fifth Avenue, New York
CANADA — 55 McGill College Ave., Montreal

Theatre Magazine, 1928

```
        1       3       6
        2       4       7
                5
```

1. Langlois — Goldtone, Pressed Powder Vanity Case. Case signed: Duska, see page 81, #7 closed.

2. Fitch — White Metal, Loose Powder, Triple Vanity Case. Pressed rouge, lipstick tube, Art Nouveau femme profile lid motif with framing by two peacocks, Niello effect, case signed, framed mirror, see page 81, #6 open, 2¾" x 2⅝" x ½". Ref: Pat. 1926. $125.00 – $150.00.

3. Woodworth — White Metal, Pressed Powder Vanity Case. Case signed: Karess, see page 81, #4 closed.

4. Vanstyle — Goldtone, Loose Powder Vanity Case. Horse shoe, black enameled accented lid with triple coiled borders, case signed, case mounted metallic mirror, see page 81, #3 open, 2½" x 2⅜" x ¼". $65.00 – $75.00.

5. Langlois — White Metal, Loose Powder Vanity Case. Cushion, cut-out flower basket triangular logo lid on cream and blue celluloid ground, engine-turned scrolling, case signed: "Cara Nome," hinged double metallic mirrors, 2"sq x ½". Ref: 1932 ad. $50.00 – $65.00.

6. Djer-Kiss — Goldtone, Pressed Powder Vanity Case. See page 81, #2 closed.

7. Woodworth — Goldtone, Pressed Powder Vanity Case. Shield, with blue accented Greek Key lid border and stylized floral blooms, case signed: "Karess," framed mirror, see page 81, #1 open, 2¼" x 2¼" x ½". $45.00 – $55.00.

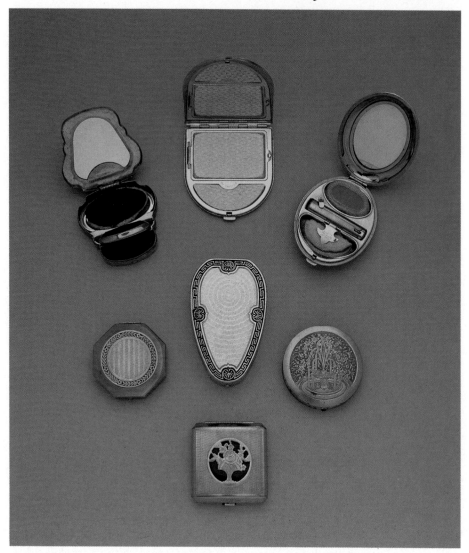

```
1     3     6
2     4     7
      5
```

1. Woodworth — Goldtone, Pressed Powder Vanity Case. See page 80, #7 closed.

2. Djer-Kiss — Goldtone, Pressed Powder Vanity Case. Brushed finish with intaglio green accented laurel wreath lid border and engine-turned vertical lines, case signed, hinged double framed mirrors, see page 80, #6 open, 1⅞"octagon x ⅝". Ref: 1928 ad. $50.00 – $60.00.

3. Vanstyle — Goldtone, Loose Powder Vanity Case. See page 80, #4 closed.

4. Woodworth — White Metal, Pressed Powder Vanity Case. Arrowhead, case with engine-turned sun ray lid motif with blue accented Greek Key lid border and stylized floral blooms, case signed: "Karess," framed mirror, see page 80, #3 open, 3¼" x 2" x ⅝". $75.00 – $90.00.

5. Langlois — White Metal, Pressed Powder Vanity Case. Cushion, cut-out flower basket circular logo lid with blue celluloid ground, engine-turned vertical lines, case signed: Cara Nome, hinged double metallic mirrors, 2"sq x ½". Ref: 1930 ad. $50.00 – $65.00.

6. Fitch — White Metal, Loose Powder Triple Vanity Case. See page 80, #2 closed.

The clamped puff acts as a stopper for the loose powder stored beneath the interior fittings. The success of this primitive non-mechanical powder control remains a puzzle. This case is unused. The top value depends entirely on a completely fitted interior as well as a fine to mint exterior.

7. Langlois — Goldtone, Pressed Powder Vanity Case. Orange coloring accents the bas-relief lid design of a fountain surrounded by floral sprays, red enamel accents the boxed sides, case signed: "Duska," reverse paper label, hinged double metallic mirrors, see page 80, #1 open, 2"dia x ½". Ref: 1930 ad. $125.00 – $150.00.

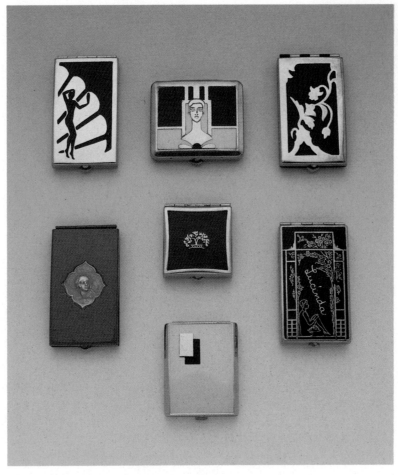

1   3   6
2   4   7
     5

1. Le Chic — White Metal, Pressed Powder Glove Vanity Case. Black champlevé enamel Art Deco femme figure with raised glossy silvertone fan, embossed powder with logo, framed mirror, 2½" x 1½" x ⅜". $75.00 – $90.00.

This case also comes in red enamel.

2. Vashé — White Metal, Pressed Powder Glove Vanity Case. Gray enameled case with Repoussé Art Deco turbaned femme head medallion affixed to lid, logo on powder and rouge cakes, framed mirror, 2½" x 1½" x ⅜". $75.00 – $90.00.

3. Unmarked — White Metal, Pressed Powder glove Vanity Case. Black and white champlevé enamel, Art Deco femme bust with silvertone border relief, strong geometric reverse, framed mirror, 2⅛" x 1¾" x ⅜". $90.00 – $100.00.

4. Vashé— White Metal, Pressed Powder Glove Vanity Case. Brown enameled case with lid embossed bonsai tree, embossed logo on powder and rouge, hinged double metallic mirrors, 1½"sq x ⅜". $50.00 – $60.00.

To justify these values the logo imprint must be visible on either the pressed powder or rouge.

5. Bourjois — White Metal, Loose Powder Glove Vanity Case. White enameled lid with glossy silvertone monogram cartouche superimposed on black enameled cartouche, case signed, hinged double metallic mirrors, 1⅞" x 1⅝" x ½". Ref: 1936 ad. $65.00 – $75.00.

6. Unmarked — White Metal, Pressed Powder Glove Vanity Case. Champlevé black enamel case with Art Deco embossed silvertone bordered floral branch, framed mirror, 2½" x 1½" x ½". $65.00 – $75.00.

7. Unmarked — White Metal, Loose Powder Glove Vanity Case. Champlevé black enamel lid with Art Deco femme figure in raised wisteria trellis motif, "Lucinda" engraved on lid, framed mirror, 2½" x 1½" x ⅜". $75.00 – $90.00.

The carnival-flavor engraved name on this fine Art Deco case is intrusive and is a depreciation factor. Monograms and initials do not usually affect values. On some cases exceptional engraving can be ornamental and enhance the design. Page 16, #4 is a good example. If this case is found "unnamed" the value should be increased by $15.00.

```
    1     4
    2     5
       3          6
                  7
```

1. Unmarked — Goldtone, Loose Powder Vanity Case. Black enameled lid with attached fraternal crest, fine engine-turned sun ray reverse, hinged double metallic mirrors, 2"sq x ⅜". $45.00 – $55.00.

2. Dorothy Gray — White Metal, Loose Powder Vanity Case. Four tone blue enameled lid, mechanical features: exterior powder door and interior "Cheese Grater" sliding powder dispenser, case signed, hinged double metallic mirrors, 2" x 1⅝" x ½". $50.00 – $65.00.

3. Coty — White Metal, Loose Powder Vanity Case. Cushion, case with engine-turned cross hatching and Coty crest on blue enamel lid diamond, mechanical feature: "Scissors" powder door with blue enameled button spring activator, case signed, hinged double metallic mirrors, 2½"sq x ¾". Ref: Pat. 1925 and 1928. $65.00 – $75.00.

4. Richard Hudnut — White Metal, Pressed Powder Vanity Case. Black enameled lid with sun and moon in silvertone contrast, case signed, hinged double metallic mirrors, 2"dia x ½". $40.00 – $50.00.

5. Lanchère — White Metal, Pressed Powder Vanity Case. Double sliding access, engine-turned fine lateral lineation, lid center oval logo flower pot cartouche, puffs with logo, no case identification, separate hinged double metallic mirrors, 2½" x 1⅝" x ½". Ref: Pat. 1928. $90.00 – $100.00.

6. Evans — White Metal, Loose Powder Vanity Case. Black enameled case with silvertone sides, cloisonné stylized flower urn attached to lid, case signed, hinged double metallic mirrors, 2⅛"sq x ⅜". $50.00 – $65.00.

7. Unmarked — Tan Enameling, Loose Powder Vanity Case. Box with brown luggage strap accent, mechanical feature: exterior push piece for interior powder door release, hinged double metallic mirrors, 1¾"sq x ⅝". $50.00 – $65.00.

The mechanical features on these cases served two purposes: the usual losing battle of powder containment, and fingernail friendly door release. Nail biters and those with nail polish had a difficult time with some stubborn powder doors. More than one case has ugly scars from metal fingernail files used as inept openers by frustrated owners.

```
1        4        6
2        5        7
      3        8
```

1. Max Factor — Goldtone, Loose Powder Vanity Case. Black enameled lid with comedy mask in goldtone relief, mechanical feature: sliding powder compartment which dispenses powder into an adjacent well, inscribed instructions — case signed, hinged double metallic mirrors, see page 102, #3 (Prince Matchabelli) for identical interior, 2¼" x 1¾" x ½". Ref: 1938 ad. $60.00 – $70.00.

2. Richard Hudnut — White Metal, Loose Powder Vanity Case. Blue enameled lid with twin cornucopias and center disk in silvertone relief, case has spring pop-up opener, case signed, hinged interior double framed mirrors, 2¼"dia x ⅝". Ref: Pat. 1926. $45.00 – $55.00.

3. Unmarked — Goldtone, Loose Powder Vanity Case. Hammered case finish with femme profile faux cameo mounted vertically, on white enameled square lid inset, framed mirror, 2¼"sq x ⅜". $45.00 – $55.00.

4. Richard Hudnut — Goldtone, Loose Powder Vanity Case. Champlevé blue enamel lid, with stylized tulip motif in goldtone relief, engine-turned shoulders and swirl reverse, spring opener, case signed, hinged double framed mirrors, 2⅝"dia x ⅝". Ref: Pat. 1927. $65.00 – $75.00.

5. Houbigant — Goldtone, Pressed Powder/Rouge Triple Vanity. Strong Art Moderne black and blue to gray shaded triangles with glossy goldtone similar accents, case and lipstick signed, framed mirror, 3¼" x 2" x ⅜". Ref: 1932 ad. $75.00 – $90.00.

Houbigant welcomed the forceful Art Moderne geometrics as their signature not only in compacts and vanity cases but also used the same force in their highly original advertising.

6. Bliss Bros — Bimetal, Loose Powder Vanity Case. Black enameled case with studded rhinestones on cushion reverse and an attached fraternal lid crest, the ultra slim case has a silvertone lid sheet, enameled on the top and interior polished to mirror quality, gold foil sticker: "24K. Gold Electro Plated" on elaborate engine-turned doors, case signed: "BBCO," paper refill instructions and address, 2¾" x 2¼" x ¼". $75.00 – $90.00.

7. Evans — White Metal, Loose Powder Vanity Case. Sky blue all-over case enamel with glossy silvertone relief, lid center with Art Deco carved blue Pâte de Verre attachment, case signed, hinged double metallic mirrors, 2¼"sq x ½". $90.00 – $100.00.

8. Mondaine — Black Enamel, Loose Powder Triple Vanity Case. All-over case enamel with faux femme portrait transfer on domed oval celluloid lid inset, compartment for both creme and pressed rouge, case signed, framed metallic mirror, 2¼" x 2⅛" x ⅜". $45.00 – $55.00.

MAKE-UP REQUISITES FOR
THE PURSE . . . . TRIPLE
VANITY PRESENTATIONS
BY HOUBIGANT

HOUBIGANT TRIPLE VANITIES are fitted with Compact
Powder in three shades, Lipstick in three shades and
Compact Rouge in six shades, including the two latest
tones: "Mat" (medium) and "Moderne" (raspberry).

A platinum-toned Triple Vanity with enlivening stripes
of French Enamel. In Gray, Blue, Green or Red.

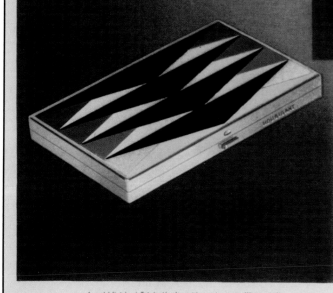

HOUBIGANT COMPACTS retain the fine texture,
the smooth-spreading and adherent qualities of loose
powder, because they are loose powder, compressed
by an exclusive process. The rubbing of the puff will
instantly revert them to loose form. Refills are 50c.

A gold-finished Triple Vanity with modernistic "Triangle"
designs of French Enamel in Green, Blue, Red or Yellow.

HOUBIGANT

PARIS

Vogue, 1932

```
1      3      6
2      4      7
       5
```

1. Unmarked — Goldtone, Loose Powder Vanity Case. Two-tone champlevé blue lid enamel, with trifids and stars in a diamond cartouche, cloisonné Maltese Cross affixed crest, fine engine-turned linear reverse with laurel wreath borders, hinged double metallic mirrors, 2" x 1⅞" x ⅜". $50.00 – $60.00.

2. Vashé — Goldtone, Loose Power Vanity Case. Black enameled case with lid design of wood veneer panel in vertical cartouche, accents of embossed goldtone pine cones and branches, case signed, framed mirror, 3" x 1¾" x ½". $40.00 – $50.00.

3. Rothley — Goldtone, Loose Powder Vanity Case. Black enameled case with goldtone diagonal lid overlays, cushion reverse has belt "Money Clip" affixed, Elgina refill information, case signed, interior identical to #4, framed mirror, 2⅛"sq x ½". $75.00 – $85.00.

4. Elgin American — Goldtone, Loose Powder Vanity Case. Cushion, brushed finish with black enameled lid bands and Eastern Star crest affixed, Elgina refill information, case signed, interior identical to #3, framed mirror, 2⅛"sq x ½". Ref: 1937 ad. $45.00 – $55.00.

5. Richard Hudnut — White Metal, Pressed Powder Triple Vanity Case. Champlevé black, white and blue enameled Art Moderne lid, with diagonal connecting circles, creme rouge compartment, case signed: "Du Barry," framed mirror, 3" x 2½" x ⅜". $75.00 – $90.00.

Two prominent cosmetic houses lost their original identity because of very successful lines. The Du Barry name swallowed up Hudnut as Evening In Paris eventually digested Bourjois.

6. Richard Hudnut — White Metal, Pressed Powder Vanity Case. Champlevé black and white enamel lid with stylized Art Deco tulip, black enameled reverse, spring opener, case signed: "Le Debut," hinged double framed mirrors, 2¼"octagon x ⅜". $75.00 – $90.00.

Hudnut introduced Le Debut in 1928 when he opened his Paris salon at 20 Rue de la Paix. He became one of the first to incorporate the Art Moderne designs in all facets of his cosmetic business. Influenced by the artist, Georges Barbier, the Le Debut line is truly premier design.

7. Mondaine — Goldtone, Pressed Powder Vanity Case. Cushion, with brushed finish and black celluloid lid cartouche bearing gilt stamped coat of arms, interior compartments are lidded, loose powder can be substituted, embossed logo initial "M" on powder and rouge, highly embossed decorative interior, case signed, framed mirror, 3" x 2" x ½". Ref: 1935 ad. $50.00 – $65.00.

```
1       3       6
2       4       7
        5
```

1. Vashé — Blue Leather, Pressed Powder Triple Vanity Case. Book, white metal case with stamped lid of red and gilt accented by circled Art Deco femme figure, recessed lipstick tube, hinged double metallic mirrors, no case identification, logoed box, 2" x 1¾" x ½". $90.00 – $100.00.

2. Mondaine — Goldtone, Pressed Powder Vanity Case. Book, embossed red leather case with stamped Art Deco green and ivory flora/linear zig-zag lid motif, goldtone edgings, case signed, framed mirror, 2¾" x 2" x ½". $65.00 – $75.00.

3. Evans — White Metal/Wood, Loose Powder Vanity Case. Blond wood with inset circle maroon enameled Art Moderne vanity case, white metal embossed banding, case signed: Tap-Sift, rouge embossed: Mayfair/Evans, hinged double metallic mirrors, 2⅝"sq x ½". $75.00 – $90.00.

4. Marhill — Goldtone, Loose Powder Vanity Case. Padded white leather lid with stamped gilt rococo decor, brushed goldtone reverse, no case identification, box and pouch with logo, case glued mirror, 2¾" x 2⅜" x ½". $35.00 – $45.00.

5. Unmarked — Goldtone, Loose Powder Vanity Case. Mock tortoise shell enameled case with lid border of incised dotted floral trailings, case framed mirror, 2½"sq x ⅜". $45.00 – $60.00.

6. Mondaine — Goldtone, Loose Powder Triple Vanity Case. Book, Moroccan leather case with goldtone edgings, hinged octagonal green enamel accented creme lipstick lid well, fitted with metallic mirror, case signed, case framed mirror, 2¾" x 2" x ⅝". $45.00 – $60.00.

7. Mondaine — Goldtone, Pressed Powder Vanity Case. Book, tan Moroccan leather case with gilt and two-tone accents, hand tooling, goldtone edgings, spine with logo, framed mirror, 2¾" x 1¾" x ⅜". $40.00 – $60.00.

```
1    4
2    5
3         6
          7
```

1. Rex — Goldtone/Mesh, Loose Powder Vanity Case. Champlevé green enamel bordered lid with tapestry inset, mesh powder pouch with kid lining, no case identification, puff and embossed rouge with logo, hinged double metallic mirrors, 2⅞"dia x ¾". $45.00 – $55.00.

2. Mondaine — Goldtone, Loose Powder Vanity Case. Cushion, blue silk wrapped lid with multicolor silk thread floral basket petit point embroidery, metallic blue enameled reverse, case signed, framed mirror, 2½" x 2¼" x ⅝". $75.00 – $90.00.

3. Allwyn — Goldtone, Loose Powder Vanity Case. Floral enameling on copper with blue enameled reverse and lid ground, deep lid concavings, foil label on framed mirror: "Black Eyed Susans," puff with logo, no case identification, 3" x 2½" x ½". $45.00 – $55.00.

A good example of outstanding outer case workmanship and almost total inaccessibility (with or without fingernails) into the powder and rouge compartments. Latches are very stiff. It is no wonder this case is unused.

4. Mondaine — Goldtone/Mesh, Loose Powder Vanity Case. Green Pearloid celluloid lid inset, mesh pocket pouch with coated paper lining, embossed logo initial "M" on powder and rouge, puff with logo, no case identification, hinged double metallic mirrors, 2⅜"dia x ¾". $45.00 – $55.00.

5. Milrone — White Metal, Pressed Powder Glove Vanity Case. Red Moroccan leather lid and reverse insets, lid has attached cloisonné plaque, no case identification, puffs with logo, hinged double metallic mirrors, 1⅝" x 1¼" x ½". $75.00 – $90.00.

This miniscule vanity wins the teeny-tiny prize. It is only good for one eye, one eyebrow, small lips, petit nose, etc. at a time. Could it be a gift from Tom Thumb to his bride?

6. Bradley — Goldtone/Mesh, Loose Powder Vanity Case. Lid inset of black silhouette of child and mother gardeners, reverse transfer on clear plastic with gold foil ground, mesh powder pouch with coated paper lining, no case identification, puff with logo of Bradley De Luxe, hinged double metallic mirrors, 2⅜"dia x ¾". Ref: 1940 ad. $50.00 – $65.00.

The case is identical to #4 Mondaine — lid inset excepting.

7. Bliss Bros — Bimetal, Loose Powder Vanity Case. Mock tortoise shell enameled case, cushion reverse, silvertone lid sheet with interior polished mirror, engine-turned quality interior gold-washed doors, ultra thin, logo of Bliss, embossed rouge, case signed: "BBCO," 2¾"sq x ¼". $65.00 – $75.00.

```
1        3        6
2        4        7
         5
```

1. Bliss Bros — Goldtone, Loose Powder Vanity Case. M.O.P. sliding lid with black enameled reverse, gold-washed engine-turned interior, logo of Bliss, embossed rouge, case signed: "BBCO," framed mirror, 3" x 2½" x ⅝". $65.00 – $75.00.

2. Marie Earle — Goldtone Pressed Powder Vanity Case. Faux carved ivory shoulders with rayed quatrefoil lid inset, case signed, framed metallic mirror, 2¾" x 2¼" x ⅜". Ref: 1933 ad. $50.00 – $65.00.

3. Houbigant — White Metal, Pressed Powder Vanity Case. Cushion, six-sided case with plastic coated lid inset, flower basket logo, case signed, hinged double metallic mirrors, 2¼" x 2" x ⅝". Ref: 1934 ad. $45.00 – $60.00.

4. Lampl — M.O.P., Loose Powder Triple Vanity Case. Pavé case with chromed interior, lidded creme and pressed rouge compartments, engine-turned powder well and lid interior, mechanical powder dispenser — see page 102, #2 open, hinged framed mirror lid compartment, 3"sq x ¾". $150.00 – $175.00.

5. Cordray — Goldtone, Loose Powder Vanity Case. Flattened oval case with two heavy incised lid bars, faint lavender shading, case signed, Art Deco femme head on powder door, paper enclosed: "Orchide Bleue," framed mirror, 3" x 2¼" x ¼". $65.00 – $75.00.

6. Coty — Goldtone, Pressed Powder Vanity Case. Aqua bakelite shoulders and lid inset with center incised crest, case signed, papers: "L'Origan," framed metallic mirror, 2¾" x 2¼" x ⅜". Ref: 1934 ad. $45.00 – $55.00.

This case and #2 are from the same manufacturer with variations only in color and lid insets. The cosmetic houses did not make their own cases, so occasionally this duplication occurred. Regardless of Marie Earle splashy advertising on their new look with this case, the Coty case proliferated and became somewhat of a Coty symbol.

7. Bonita — Goldtone, Loose Powder Triple Vanity Case. Glossy goldtone case with rhinestone pavé broad bar opener, lidded creme and pressed rouge compartments, case signed, framed mirror, 3½" x 2¼" x ⅜". $50.00 – $65.00.

```
            4
  1      2  5     7
         3  6
```

1. Elgin American — White Metal, Loose Powder Vanity Case. Shield, blue shaded matte enameled case, chromed interior, case signed: "EA," puff with logo of Elgin Vanity, creme rouge case: "Clarice Jane/Elgin IL.," oval framed mirror, 2½" x 1¾" x ⅜". $25.00 – $40.00.

2. Elgin American — Glossy Green Enamel. See #1.

3. Elgin American — Glossy Cream Enamel. See # 1.

4. Elgin American — Glossy Ivory Enamel. See #1.

5. Elizabeth Arden, White Metal, Loose Powder Vanity Case. Wood veneer lid and reverse insets, wood/burned legend: "Rotary Club — London, O. — 1937," chromed interior with engine-turned powder door, creme rouge lidded pocket in lid, powder sam-

ple puff with logo — see example, no case identification, framed mirror, 3⅛"dia x ½". $45.00 – $60.00.

6. Clarice Jane — White Metal, Vanity Case. Shield, glossy blue enameled case, puff has Elgin added on ribbon logo, otherwise identical to #1 — #4, case signed: "Clarice Jane," oval framed mirror, 1¾" x 2½" x ⅜". $40.00 – $50.00.

The lack of Elgin American case signatures and the over-stamp on the puff ribbon, may indicate that this is a transition case before Elgin assumed dominant identity over Clarice Jane.

7. Vashé — Goldtone, Loose Powder Vanity Case. Diagonal wood veneer lid and reverse, woodburned initials: "M E L" on lid, helmeted crest logo on powder door, case glued metallic mirror, 2⅞"sq x ⅜". $45.00 – $60.00.

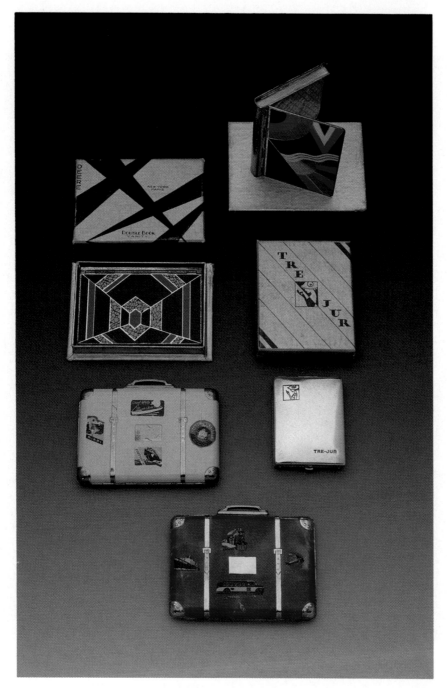

```
      1                4
      2        3       5
```

1. Deere — Goldtone, Pressed Powder/Rouge Vanity Case. Book, case with black, red and Art Moderne faux eggshell lid enameling, floral and lace tracings on reverse, spine and box with logo, framed mirror, box lid shown, 3" x 2" x ¼". Ref: 1932 ad. $175.00 – $200.00.

2. Cara Mia — Goldtone, Loose Powder Vanity Case. Suitcase, ivory enameled case with goldtone hardware, travel sticker decals, case signed, framed mirror, 3¼" x 2¼" x ½". $150.00 – $175.00.

3. Cara Mia — Goldtone, Loose Powder Vanity Case. Suitcase, cerise enameled case with marbled pattern

and goldtone hardware, transportation sticker decals, framed mirror, 3¼" x 2¼" x ½". Ref: 1940 paper. $150.00 – $175.00.

4. Deere — Goldtone, Pressed Powder Vanity Case. Book, case with black, red and Art Moderne enameling with stylized sun rise and geometrics, see #1 for interior information. $175.00 – $200.00.

5. Tre-Jur — Goldtone, Pressed Powder Glove Vanity Case. Glossy case with "Little One" lid logo, paper: Charvai, embossed powder with logo, hinged double metallic mirrors, signed box shown, 2" x 1⅝" x ⅜". Ref: 1929 ad. $125.00 – $150.00.

1   2   4
             3   5

1. Bliss Bros — Goldtone, Loose Powder Vanity Case. Black enameled lid and reverse — see page 99, #1 closed.

2. Mondaine — Goldtone, Loose Powder Vanity Case. Glossy finish with Art Deco creme rouge hinged lid compartment, femme head with cocktail glass motif, tiny metallic mirror, engine-turned interior, no case identification, framed mirror, see page 99, #2 open, 3¼"dia x ½", 1935 ad. $75.00 – $90.00.

3. F J Co. — Goldtone, Loose Powder Vanity Case. Venice canal scene lid inset with plastic shield, black enameled reverse, heavy chased floral sides, case signed, hinged double metallic mirrors, 2¼"dia x ½". Ref: Pat. 1934. $50.00 – $65.00.

4. Elgin American — Goldtone, Loose Powder Vanity Case. Scalloped Case — see page 99, #4 closed.

5. Haywood — Goldtone, Loose Powder Vanity Case. Glossy finish with incised lid cartouche and borders, case signed, case glued mirror, 2¼" x 2⅛" x ¼". $35.00 – $50.00.

2   4
1   3   5

1. Bliss Bros — Goldtone, Loose Powder Vanity Case. Black enameled lid and reverse with diagonal Niello lid band, sides embossed with floral wreathing, engine-turned gold-washed interior, case signed: "BBCO," framed mirror, see page 98, #1 open, 2⅞"dia x ⅜". $65.00 – $75.00.

2. Mondaine — Goldtone, Loose Powder Vanity Case. See page 98, #2 closed.

3. Nymfaun — Goldtone, Pressed Powder Vanity Case. Brushed finish with incised linear borders, elaborate logo embossed powder and rouge, paper refill insert, signed case, framed mirror, 4" x 2½" x ½". $75.00 – $90.00.

4. Elgin American — Goldtone, Loose Powder Vanity Case. Scalloped domed case with incised lid tracings, Elgina creme rouge and powder door compartments, case signed, framed mirror, see page 98, #4 open, 3"dia x ½". Ref: 1937 ad. $65.00 – $75.00.

5. La Mode — Goldtone, Loose Powder Vanity Case. Brushed finish with incised lid monogram cartouche, scroll and floral hand-tinted embellishment, sides embossed with laurel wreathing, puff and rouge foil with logo, no case identification, hinged double metallic mirrors, 2½"sq x ⅜". $65.00 – $75.00.

```
1     3     5
2     4     6
            7
```

1. Richard Hudnut — Goldtone, Loose Powder Triple Vanity Case. Silvertone lid overlay with engine-turned chevrons and circles on black enamel, cut-out for lipstick, case signed, framed mirror, 3⅜" x 2⅜" x ½". $60.00 – $75.00.

2. Richard Hudnut — Goldtone, Loose Powder Triple Vanity Case. Champlevé white enamel with bas-relief lid filigree, recessed lipstick, case signed, framed mirror, 3¼" x 2¼" x ½". $75.00 – $90.00.

3. Bourjois — Goldtone, Loose Powder Triple Vanity Case. See page 101, #4 closed.

4. La Mode — Goldtone, Loose Powder Triple Vanity Case. See page 101, #6 closed.

5. Yardley — Goldtone, Loose Powder Triple Vanity Case. White enamel embossed feathers on lid with red tipped spring release attached lipstick, case signed, hinged double framed metallic mirrors, see page 101, #1 open, 2¾" x 2" x ¾", Pat. 1940. $90.00 – $100.00.

6. Yardley — Goldtone, Pressed Powder Triple Vanity Case. Brushed finish with black enameled lid band and bas-relief logo, white enameled case accents, Heraldic Ermine, hinged lipstick tube, case signed, hinged double framed metallic mirrors, 2½" x 2" x ½". Ref: 1937 ad. $65.00 – $75.00.

7. Langlois — Goldtone, Pressed Powder Triple Vanity Case. Green enameled lid with geometric center accent, engine-turned reverse and interior, case signed: Shari, framed mirror, see page 101, #3 open, 3¾" x 2" x ⅜". $90.00 – $100.00.

now—
compacts that are just as lovely inside as out!

"inside story"

by

VOLUPTÉ

Just look at the outside . . . see the charming
flower design! Then flip it open and behold . . .
the inside is a colorful twin of the cover!
So original, so delightful—and who else
but Volupté would think of such a thing?
Colored enamel compacts and carryalls . . .
golden engraved designs, too . . . $5. to $15.

VOLUPTÉ Inc. • 347 Fifth Avenue • New York 16

compacts • carryalls • lighters • cigarette cases • atomizers • pill boxes

a genuine
Collector's Item
by
VOLUPTÉ

SOPHISTICASE
Holds powder,
cigarettes,
lipstick,
comb, mirror.

LIP-LOCK Compact and lipstick holder in one.

Harper's Bazaar, 1951

1
2
4
5
3

1. Helena Rubinstein — Goldtone, Loose Powder Vanity Case. See #4 closed.

2. Helena Rubinstein — Goldtone, Loose Powder Vanity Case. Diagonal ribbed lid motif with attached lipstick, faux emerald lid clasp, case and lipstick signed, case glued mirror, 2⅝" x 2¼" x ⅜". $50.00 – $65.00.

3. Majestic — Goldtone, Loose Powder Vanity Case. M.O.P. lid with attached lipstick and perfume, case signed, case glued mirror, 3" x 2" x ⅝". $45.00 – $60.00.

4. Helena Rubinstein — Goldtone, Loose Powder Vanity Case. Baroque case with black enameled lid accent, lipstick attached on lid clasp, case and lipstick signed, framed mirror, see #1 open, 3¼" x 2¾" x ½". Ref: 1947 ad. $125.00 – $150.00.

5. Dorothy Gray — Goldtone, Loose Powder Vanity Case. Modern Design case with quatrefoil lid accents, attached lipstick which acts as spring lid release, enclosed paper instructions, all items signed, framed mirror, 3½" x 2¾" x ⅜". Ref: 1948 ad. $75.00 – $90.00.

beauty

grows on

Christmas Trees

trimmed by

helena rubinstein

1. **COMMAND PERFORMANCE**
great new French fragrance. 1 oz.,
12.50. Also 2.00, 3.75, 6.75, 45.00

2. **HEAVEN-SENT STAR—**
one dram of angelic perfume,
1.25. Also 4.50, 7.50, 8.50

3. **LIPSTICK FOUR-CAST—**
the four best lipsticks for your
color type in costume-colored
cases, 3.50

4. **BAROQUE VANITY—**
black and gold-colored
with lipstick clasp, 5.00

5. **WHITE FLAME PERFUME—**
heady, haunting, electric.
1 dram, 2.50. Also 9.50, 18.50

6. **PERFUME TRIO—**
1 dram each of Heaven-Sent,
Town, Apple Blossom, 3.50   *plus tax*

655 FIFTH AVE., N. Y. 22 • PARIS • LONDON • TORONTO

Vogue, 1947

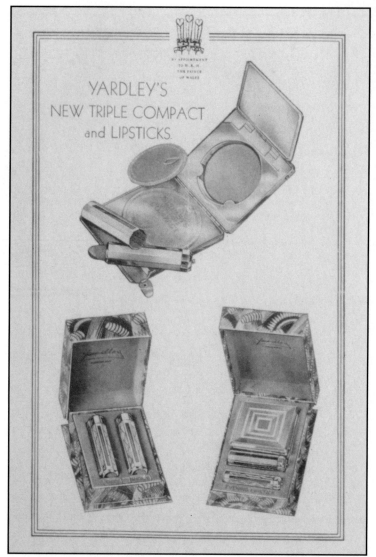

Ad, 1930

1. OLFA — Goldtone, Loose Powder Vanity Case.
Black enameled case with engraved scenes of Paris, faux lipstick lid ornament, black enameled lipstick tube in interior recess, case signed, framed mirror, 3¾" x 2⅞" x ½". $100.00 – $125.00.

2. Zell Fifth Avenue — Goldtone, Loose Powder Vanity Case. Brushed finish with affixed goldtone and iridescent rhinestone lid bijou, attached lipstick and perfume, puff with logo, no case identification, case glued mirror, 3½" x 2¼" x ¾". $50.00 – $65.00.

3. Majestic — Goldtone, Loose Powder Vanity Case. Ribbed lid cross banding with lipstick attached on lid clasp, bottom compartment, case signed, case glued mirror, 3½" x 2¾" x ⅝". $75.00 – $90.00.

The bottom section has a paper liner with a sketch of a row of cigarettes. However, standard cigarettes don't fit. English Ovals maybe?

4. Yardley — White Metal, Pressed Powder Triple Vanity Case. Engine-turned lid borders with green enameled accents, hinged lipstick tube, additional tube for Evening, paper ad, case and box signed, hinged double framed metallic mirrors, 2½" x 2" x ½". Ref: 1930 ad. $125.00 – $150.00.

5. Helena Rubinstein — Goldtone, Loose Powder Vanity Case. Baroque case with ivory enameled lid, lipstick attached on lid clasp, case and lipstick signed, framed mirror, 3½ x 2¾" x ¼". $90.00 – $100.00.

1   4
2   5
3

TREES

Sparkling Trees for
Gay Holidays

COMPACT, LIPSTICK, KIT
COMBINATION

PAUL FLATO
ORIGINALS

$16.50 PLUS TAX *At Smart Shops Everywhere*

1950

1. Ciner — Goldtone, Loose Powder Vanity Kit.
Passementerie needlework on compact lid, lipstick
top accented with faux jade and coral in black faille
fitted kit; kit, compact and lipstick signed, framed
mirror, compact — 2¾"sq x ½", case — 4" x 3" x 1".
Ref: 1951 ad. $150.00 – $175.00

If these kits are missing any of the original compo-
nents, the prices change drastically. They must be
complete and the cloth cases fine to mint condition.

2. K & K — Goldtone, Loose Powder Vanity Kit.
Black enameled lid and lipstick with pavé rhinestone
banding, black faille slipcase, attached lipstick which
activates lid spring release, puff with logo, no case
identification, framed mirror, 3" x 2¼" x ¾". $100.00 –
$150.00.

3. Flato — Goldtone, Loose Powder Vanity Kit.
Glossy case with lid and lipstick affixed faux emerald
fir tree bijoux, green leather slipcase, all items signed,
framed mirror, compact — 2½" x 2¼" x ½", case — 3" x
2¾" x 1". Ref: 1950 ad. $175.00 – $200.00.

4. Wand Art — Goldtone, Loose Powder Vanity Kit.
Brushed finish with lid and lipstick "Original Hand
Art Work" (glued spangles), padded black suede kit,
paper enclosed, puff and case with logo, no case identification, framed mirror, compact — 2¾" x 2½" x ⅜",
case — 3¾" x 2½" x 1¼". $75.00 – $90.00.

5. Ciner — Goldtone, Loose Powder Vanity Kit. Lid
and lipstick handset with prong mounted semi-pre-
cious gem stones: Jade, Lapis, Amethyst, etc., on an
attached Art Nouveau swirled ribbon motif, black
satin fitted kit, all items signed, framed mirror, compact — 2¾"sq x ½", case — 4" x 3" x 1". $175.00 –
$200.00.

6. K & K — Goldtone, Loose Powder Vanity Kit.
Black enameled lid and lipstick with faux cabochon
turquoise and ruby mounted banding, patterned red
satin slipcase, attached lipstick which activates spring
lid release, puff with logo, no case identification,
framed mirror, 3" x 2¼" x ¾". $100.00 – $150.00.

1
2 3 5
4 6

<pre>
              2
    1   3   5
              4
</pre>

1. Zell — Goldtone, Loose Powder Purse Kit. See page 113, #2 closed.

2. Zell — Goldtone, Loose Powder Purse Kit. Ribbed sun burst compact with two lipsticks and comb, gold thread ivory tapestry kit with metallic bordered flap, peach taffeta interior, puff with logo, no case identification, case glued mirror, compact — 2½" x 2¼" x ⅜", case — 4" x 2½" x 1¼", see page 113, #5 open. Ref: 1955 ad. $65.00 – $75.00.

3. Lenel — Goldtone, Loose Powder Purse Kit. Brushed finish with lid, lipstick and perfume affixed rhinestone bijoux, black silk velvet fitted pouch, no

ornamentation, everything signed, labeled or logoed, framed mirror, compact — 2¾"sq x ⅜", pouch — 5" x 3½". $150.00 – $175.00.

4. Coty — Goldtone, Pressed Powder Purse Kit. Fiesta, all items ribbed: compact, lipstick and comb, ecru cloth kit with multicolored flowers and blue stars, everything signed, framed mirror, see page 113, #1 open, compact — 2¾"sq x ½", case — 3¾" x 3¼" x 1". Ref: 1952 ad. $65.00 – $75.00.

5. Dorset Fifth Avenue — Goldtone, Loose Powder Purse Kit. See page 113, #4 closed.

2
1   3   5
4

1. Coty — Goldtone, Pressed Powder Purse Kit. See page 112, #4 closed.

2. Zell — Goldtone, Loose Powder Purse Kit. Diagonal ribbed compact with lipstick and comb, matching ribbed metallic kit with plastic herringbone flap, red satin lining, kit has hinged access, puff with logo, no compact identification, case glued mirror, see page 112, #1 open, compact — 2¼" x 2⅛" x ½", case — 3¼" x 2⅜" x 1". Ref: 1955 ad. $50.00 – $65.00.

3. Harriet Hubbard Ayers — Goldtone, Loose Powder Purse Kit. Fine lined all-over compact with coved black plastic sides, lipstick tube and mascara box, (also comes with perfume), tan leather fitted kit with gold taffeta lining, no case ornamentation, powder sample, everything signed, case glued mirror, compact — 3¼" x 2¾" x ¼", case — 5" x 3" x ¾". Ref: 1940 ad. $150.00 – $175.00.

4. Dorset Fifth Avenue — Goldtone, Loose Powder Purse Kit. Floral compact lid transfer and ribbed reverse, incised lipstick tube, ivory cloth case with stamped multicolor and gilt flora, ribbed metallic sides, ivory taffeta lining, puff and kit with logo, case glued mirror, compact — 2¾" x 2½" x ⅜", case — 4" x 2¾" x ¾", see page 112, #5 open. $50.00 – $65.00.

5. Zell — Goldtone, Loose Powder Purse Kit. See page 112, #2 closed.

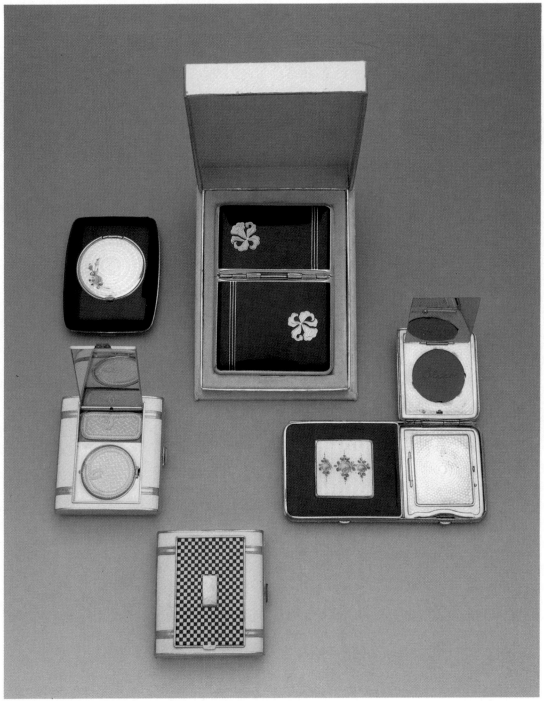

1
2   4
3   5

1. Evans — White Metal, Combination Vanity Case. Cushion, black enameled case with guilloché white enamel vanity inset, loose powder and logo embossed rouge: "Mayfair," engine-turned cigarette compartment interior, signed case, hinged double metallic mirrors, 3¼" x 2½" x ¾". Ref: 1932 ad. $65.00 – $75.00.

2. Unmarked — Goldtone, "Luggage" Combination Vanity Case. See #3 closed.

3. Unmarked — Goldtone, Loose Powder Combination Vanity Case. Luggage, ivory enameled case with raised strap accents, checkerboard lidded vanity inset with monogram cartouche engine-turned cigarette

compartment interior, case glued metallic mirror, 2⅞" x 2⅝" x ⅝". Ref: 1938 ad. $75.00 – $90.00.

4. Richard Hudnut — White Metal, Combination Vanity Case. Black enameled case with white enameled orchids in bas-relief, loose powder, logo embossed rouge and recessed lipstick, chromed interior with cut-out logo cigarette clamps, everything signed, framed mirror, see page 115, #3 open, 4¼" x 3" x ⅜". Ref: 1937 ad (var). $150.00 – $175.00.

5. Bliss Bros — Goldtone, Combination Vanity Case. See page 115, #5 closed.

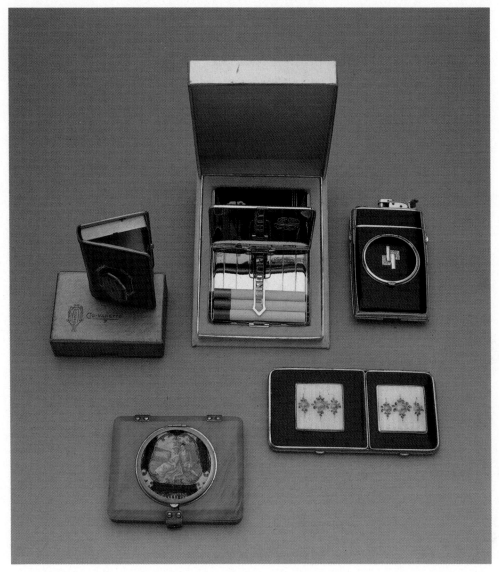

1   3   4
  2   5

1. Mondaine — Goldtone, Combination Vanity Case. Book, red moroccan leather "Cig-Vanette" case, with hinged lid creme rouge cartouche — tiny mirror, logo embossed pressed powder and rouge, case and box signed, framed mirror, 3" x 2" x ¾". $65.00 – $75.00.

2. Unmarked — Bakelite, Combination Vanity Case. Faux amber top and bottom case with goldtone sides and hinges, vanity case lid inset with transfer bucolic pastoral scene, loose powder and pressed rouge, four metallic mirrors all different magnification — two case framed, two hinged, 3¾" x 2¾" x ⅝". Ref: 1938 ad. $125.00 – $150.00.

3. Richard Hudnut — White Metal, Combination Vanity Case. See page 114, #4 closed.

4. Evans — White Metal, Combination Vanity Case. Black enameled front with vanity case inset, embossed Art Moderne lid motif, loose powder and logo embossed rouge: "Mayfair," top side lighter and fuel reservoir, case and box signed, hinged double metallic mirrors, 4¼" x 2½" x ¾". Ref: 1932 ad. $75.00 – $90.00.

5. Bliss Bros — Goldtone, Combination Vanity Case. Black enameled case with guilloché white enamel lid insets, sides embossed with goldtone floral wreathing, both compartments with elaborate engine-turning and gold-washed, loose powder and logo embossed rouge: "Bliss," case signed: "BBCO," double hinged metallic mirrors, see page 114, #5 open, 5" x 2½" x ⅜". $150.00 – $175.00.

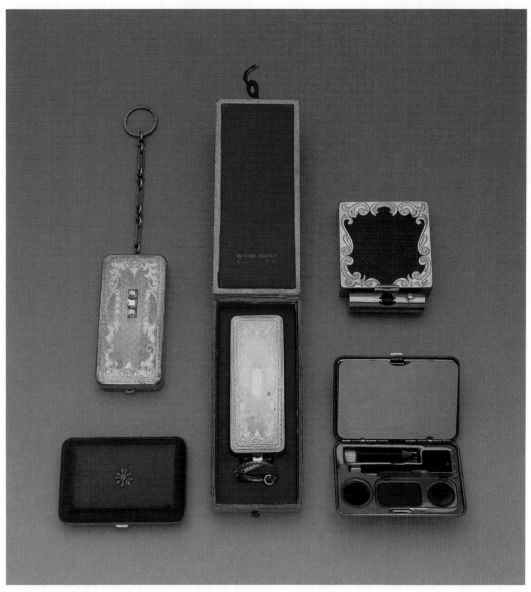

1
2   4

         3   5

1. Richard Hudnut — Pendant Beauty Box. Goldtone with incised case work, monogram cartouche has three square cut mounted faux gemstones, heavy chased broad link chain and finger ring, pressed powder and rouge, combination eye shadow and lipstick wand, papers: "Du Barry Beauty Box," case signed, framed mirror, see page 117, #1 open, 3¼" x 1⅝" x ½". $100.00 – $125.00.

All these beauty boxes must be completely fitted to justify the estimated values.

2. Mondaine — Beauty Box. Cushion, lavender enameled case with affixed marcasite snowflake lid bijou, loose powder, logo embossed rouge: "M," makeup compartment contains: mascara and brush, eyebrow pencil, creme rouge and eye shadow, no case identification, hinged double metallic mirrors, see #5 and page 117, #2 open, 3" x 2" x ⅝". Ref: 1936 ad. $125.00 – $150.00.

3. Richard Hudnut — Pendant Vanity Case. Goldtone with incised case work, heavy chased broad bar link chain and finger ring, pressed powder and rouge, signed case and cerise satin lined Du Barry presentation box, framed mirror, see page 117, #3 for closed box, 3½" x 1¼" x ⅜". $125.00 – $150.00.

4. Helena Rubinstein — Minute Make-Up Vanity Case. Double access, goldtone case with black enameled accents on lid and lipstick tube in chased baroque borders, lipstick attached to lid clasp, vanity top with loose powder and pressed rouge, puffs with logo: "Valaze," double metallic mirrors, bottom hinged compartment with chromed lid/mirror, contains cotton cleansing pads, case signed, see page 117, #5 open, 2⅞" x 2¼" x ⅝". Ref: 1939 ad. $150.00 – $175.00.

5. Mondaine — Beauty Box. See #2 and page 117, #6 closed.

116

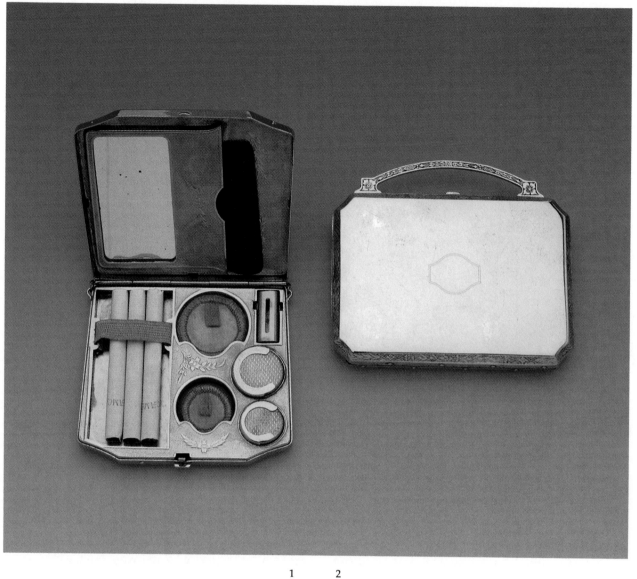

1   2

1. E.A.M. — White Metal, Demi Carryall. See page 128 closed.

2. E.A.M. — White Metal, Demi Carryall. Rigid handled glossy finish case with gold-washed interior, beveled chased floral wreathed borders, pressed powder and rouge, lipstick and solid perfume tubes, misc. compartment, both larger compartments are hinged, the smaller rouge is not, case signed, embossed framed mirror, see page 128 open, 4¼" x 3" x ⅝". $225.00 – $250.00.

THEATRE MAGAZINE, NOVEMBER, 1924

for beauty's sake

A creation of beauty fashioned as an accessory to the beauty of charming women — the TERRI VANITY is a dream of an artist made practicable.

Every service that a woman requires is right at hand in this latest *Terri Vanity.* A mirror large enough to see the full face; containers for lip rouge, face rouge and powder, compartments for cigarettes, keys and coins.

The *Terri Vanity* reflects its aristocracy in its very lines. Distinctively shaped, it is at once a recognized scion of the famous *Terri Vanities.* The entrancing oval effect strikes a particularly new note. And the double mesh wristlet! Like an exclamation point completing an ecstatically beautiful sentence . . .

Terri
VANITY

TERRI, INCORPORATED
4 West 40th Street
New York City

You can get the Terri Vanity at the better shops. Should you have difficulty, send $7.50 to Terri, Inc., 4 West 40th Street, New York City, and you will be enjoying the beauty of your vanity very soon thereafter.

Terri, Incorporated, 4 W. 40th Street, New York City. Gentlemen: I am enclosing $7.50. Please send me the Terri Vanity.

Name _____
Street Address _____
City _____ State _____

Theatre Magazine, 1924

1. Mondaine — White Metal, Demi Carryall. Ivory enameled case with deep yellow oval domed lid cartouche, see #5 for variation.

2. Terri — Goldtone, Demi Carryall. Oval luggage case with faux black Moroccan leather finish, glossy straps, braided black silk wrist cord with band slide, exterior comb recess, pressed powder and logoed embossed rouge, plastic lipstick, coin, or key hinged lid compartment, cigarette well, case signed, hinged framed mirror, 3¾" x 2½" x 1". Ref: 1924 ad. $125.00 – $150.00.

3. Zell Fifth Avenue — Goldtone, Demi Carryall. Black enameled case with deep incised cross hatched lid lines, ribbed reverse, snake wrist chain, double access, embossed faux engine-turning, loose powder, comb clip, lipstick, miscellaneous compartment with clip, cigarette reverse compartment, no case identification, puff with logo and original tag, case glued mirror, 4" x 3" x 1¼". $75.00 – $90.00.

4. Unmarked — White Metal, Demi Carryall. Sides and borders of chased floral wreathing, oval lavender guilloché enamel lid cartouche with enameled embellishments, broad bar wrist chain, engine-turned geometric reverse, loose powder, coin holder, lipstick, hinged framed mirror, lid compartment, 3" x 2" x ¾". $65.00 – $75.00.

5. Mondaine — White Metal, Demi Carryall. Black enameled case with hinged Art Deco femme/cocktail glass lid inset for creme rouge, tiny metallic lid mirror, black braided silk wrist cord, pressed powder and rouge with logo, hinged miscellaneous compartment, case signed, framed mirror, see #1 open, 4" x 3" x ⅜". Ref: 1935 ad. $100.00 – $125.00.

6. Glamour — Goldtone, Demi Carryall. Double access, M.O.P. and Abalone shell checkered case, snake wrist chain, engine-turned interiors, loose powder, comb clip, lipstick, reverse cigarette compartment, puff with logo, no case identification, case glued mirror, 4" x 3" x 1⅛". $75.00 – $90.00.

1   4   5
2
3   6

1
2

4
5

3

1. Lyric — Goldtone, Vanity Carryall. Brushed finish with rhinestone enhanced bolster lid, detachable black silk carrier with lipstick strap sleeve, mock tortoise shell comb in carrier recess, loose powder, lidded white enameled compartment, lid cigarette well, no case identification, puff and lipstick with logo, hinged framed mirror, 3¾" x 1¾" x 1½". $100.00 – $125.00.

The small enameled compartments found in these post WWII carryalls were often used for tiny saccharin tablets to provide an alternative to sugar for coffee. They became a diet fad and a social gesture, as the Dior 'wasp waist' look needed more than a waist cincher.

2. Unmarked — Goldtone, Vanity Carryall. Double access, brushed silvertone case with stenciled femme smoker, incised flora quartered on reverse in both tones, clip-on lipstick, snake wrist chain, loose powder, case glued mirror, 3½" x 2⅜" x ¾". $100.00 – $125.00.

3. Kigu — Goldtone, Vanity Carryall. Double access, engine-turned cross banded case with monogram cartouche on lid, non-detachable black suede casing with sleeves for lipstick and perfume, suede wrist strap, loose powder, case signed everywhere: "England," framed mirror, 5¼" x 2½" x ¾". $175.00 – $200.00.

4. Kigu — Goldtone, Vanity Carryall. Double access, faux engraved case with bevel borders, monogram lid cartouche, snake wrist chain, clip-on lipstick, loose powder, several case signings, "Made in England," framed mirror, 3¾" x 3" x ⅞". $75.00 – $100.00.

5. Zell — Goldtone, Vanity Carryall. Double access, woven basketry case in high relief, snake wrist chain, clip-on lipstick, loose powder, no case identification, puff with logo, case glued mirror, 3¾" x 2¼" x ⅞". $50.00 – $75.00.

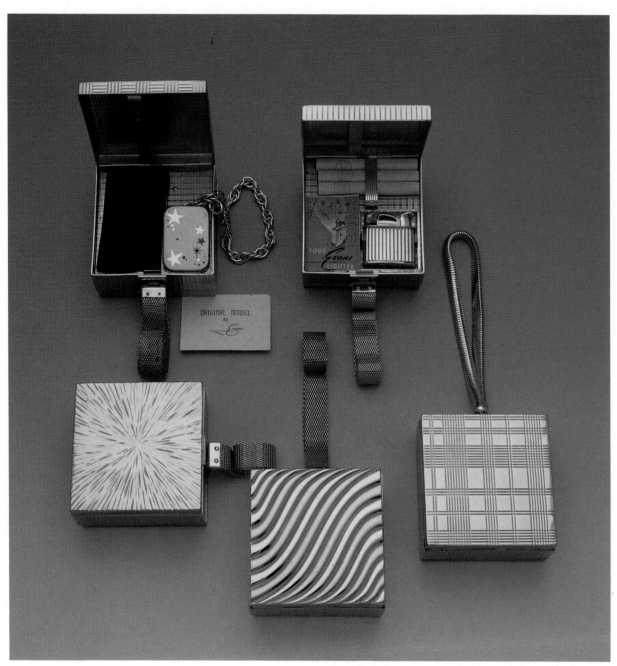

1 4
2 5
3

1. Evans — Goldtone, Petite Carryall. Double access, "Basket Weave" case, with mesh wrist strap, music box charm bracelet on link chain: *Let Me Call You Sweetheart*, loose powder, coin holder, lipstick, mock tortoise comb in clip, black satin coin purse, case signed, case glued mirror, 3¼"sq x 1¾". Ref: 1955 ad. Rare.

All the cases on this plate are depicted in the 1955 catalogue as Evans' new "Petite" carryalls, #1 is a non-smoking model with the substitution of a music box in the lighter well and the addition of a coin purse to fill the remaining space. Many of these impressive cases were Valentine Day gifts — hence the song.

2. Evans — Goldtone, Petite Carryall. "Sunburst," same case as #1 — no lighter. $75.00 – $100.00.

3. Evans — Goldtone, Petite Carryall. "High Tide," same case as #1, lighter. $125.00 – $150.00.

4. Evans — Goldtone, Petite Carryall. "Columns," same case as #1, lighter. $125.00 – $150.00.

5. Evans — Goldtone, Petite Carryall. "Plaid," same case as #1, snake wrist chain, no lighter. $75.00 – $100.00.

1   2   4 5
        3

1. Evans — Silvertone, Standard Carryall. Double access, snake wrist chain, loose powder, puff with logo, large clear plastic comb in clips, square lipstick, coin holder, cigarette bar, case signed, case glued mirror, 5½" x 3⅛" x 1". $150.00 – $175.00.

2. Evans — Goldtone, Standard Carryall. "Waves" — same case as #4. $100.00 – $125.00.

3. Evans — Goldtone, Standard Carryall. "Quilt" — same case as #4, exc: thicker snake chain and round lipstick tube. $100.00 – $125.00.

4. Evans — Goldtone, Standard Carryall. Single access, geometric case with ribbed sides, snake wrist chain, loose powder, puff with logo, black silk coin purse with small comb, square lipstick, case signed, hinged metallic mirror divider to lid compartment, 5½" x 3⅛" x ¾". $100.00 – $125.00.

5. Evans — Goldtone, Standard Carryall. "Sunburst," same case as #1, exc: broad mesh wrist strap. $125.00 – $150.00.

If any of these Evans cases are in original boxes with model numbers and have original pouches, add $25 to values. Also, because of the scarcity of fine to mint silvertone Evans cases, silvertones do have a higher value.

1
    2
    3

1. Evans — Goldtone, Standard Carryall. Double access, M.O.P. case with goldtone ribbed sides, broad snake wrist chain, loose powder, puff with logo, large clear plastic comb in clips, square lipstick, coin holder, case signed, case glued mirror, 5½" x 3¼" x 1⅛". $150.00 – $175.00.

2. Evans — Goldtone, Standard Carryall. Double access, M.O.P. lid with inset faceted faux gemstones, diagonal ribbed reverse, graduated link wrist chain, same interior as #1, 5½" x 3¼" x 1⅛". $175.00 – $200.00.

3. Evans — Goldtone, Standard Carryall. Double access, pearl, faux cabochon emeralds, with attached filigree adornment, weathered bark-like finish, graduated link wrist chain, same interior as #1. Very rare.

How this case survived almost forty years of handling is a puzzle. Although the stones are prong mounted and handset, the pearls go their own way, and the lid ornament has more sharp points than a porkypine. No wonder it is unused — what a clothes snagger!

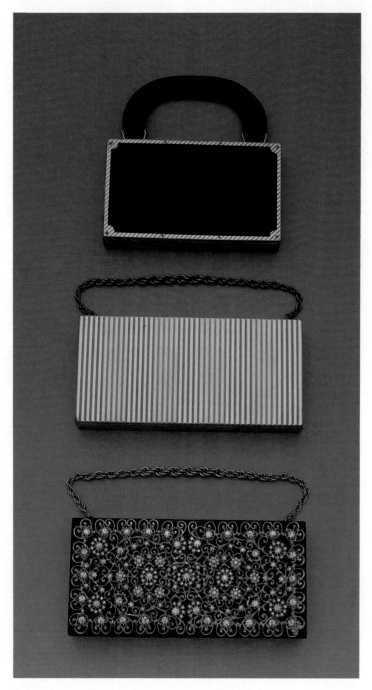

1
2
3

1. Evans — Goldtone, Standard Carryall. Double access, black suede upholstered case with rigid wrist handle, diagonal body with ribbed sides, loose powder, puff with logo, large clear plastic comb in clips, square lipstick, coin holder, case signed, case glued mirror, 5½" x 3⅛" x 1". $200.00 – $225.00.

2. Evans — Goldtone, Oversize Carryall. Double access, rose and goldtone lid ribbing, graduated link wrist chain, loose powder, puff with logo, large clear plastic comb in clips, lipstick tube with green plastic

dome top, coin holder, lighter, case signed, case glued mirror, 6¾" x 3¼" x 1". Ref: 1952 ad. $150.00 – $175.00.

The Evans ad touts this new addition to their collection: "…first of its kind to be fitted with an Evans automatic lighter."

3. Evans — Goldtone, Oversize Carryall. Double access, black enameled case, silvertone filigree lid with handset faceted faux gemstones, graduated silvertone link wrist chain, same interior as #2. $225.00 – $250.00.

Evans is elegance

Cigarette Case about $20; Compact about $20;
Automatic Lighter about $12.50; at depart-
ment stores and leading jewelers.

Photo by H. I. Williams

©**EVANS CASE COMPANY**, *New York City · No. Attleboro, Mass.*

Vogue, 1947

2

1

4

3

1. Evans — Silvertone, Standard Carryall. Double access, sun ray case with affixed faux gemstone star burst lid bijou, broad mesh wrist band, loose powder, puff with logo, clear plastic comb in clips, coin holder, square lipstick, case signed, case glued mirror, 5½" x 3⅛" x 1¼". Ref: 1955 ad. $150.00 – $175.00.

2. Evans — Goldtone, Standard Carryall. Single access, linear bark-like case finish with attached faux marquise gemstone lid ornaments, snake wrist chain, loose powder, puff with logo, lipstick cylinder, black silk coin purse with small comb, case signed, hinged metallic mirror divider to lid compartment, 5½" x 3⅛" x ¾". $100.00 – $125.00.

3. Evans — Goldtone, Standard Carryall. Single access, cross bar lid with faux sapphires mounted at bar intersections, see #2 for interior. $125.00 – $150.00.

4. Evans — Goldtone, Standard Carryall. Double access, diagonal case with attached faux ruby and diamond "Clip" lid ornaments, see #1 for interior. Ref: 1947 ad. $150.00 – $175.00.

All the Evans carryalls in this book have goldtone interiors, regardless of the outer case coloration or ornamentation.

Shirley Temple

A Selznick Star

Starring in

THE STORY OF SEABISCUIT

A Warner Bros. Production

color by TECHNICOLOR

*Finishing Touch to
Evening Glamour...*

EVANS bracelet-handled Coronation Carryall — fitted with after-five indispensables. Brightest rhodium reflects a crown of rhinestones, heralds the elegance within.

EVANS CASE CO.
No. Attleboro, Mass.

Sales Offices:
NEW YORK   LOS ANGELES   CLEVELAND
DALLAS   CHICAGO   BOSTON

Inside, jeweler-designed automatic "pop-up" lipstick, covered powder well, puff, comb and coin holder plus separate space for cigarettes . . . (hanky or keys if you prefer).

At leading jewelry and department stores.

Evans is elegance

EVANS
Coronation Carryall — $36.50*
Other carryalls from $25.*

CREATORS OF FAMOUS EVANS FITTED HANDBAGS,
AUTOMATIC LIGHTERS, CIGARETTE CASES AND POWDER BOXES

*Plus tax

1949

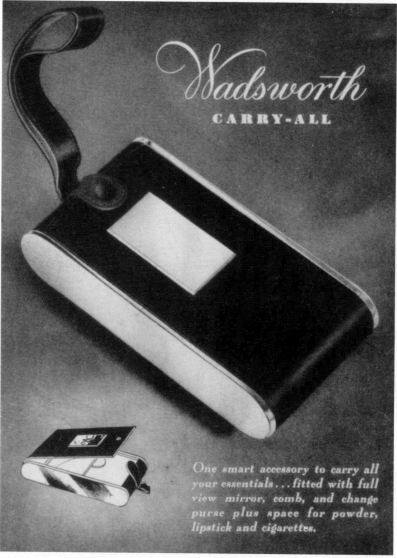

Harper's Bazaar, **1948**

1. Unmarked — Goldtone, Standard Carryall. Double access, brushed case finish with lid affixed rhinestone crown bijou, broad mesh wrist band, loose powder, hinged pop-up lipstick tube, gray flannel coin purse and small comb, case glued mirrors, 5¼" x 3⅛" x 1". $65.00 – $75.00.

2. Unmarked — Goldtone, Standard Carryall. Single access, upholstered leather case, pearl gray lid and brown on reverse, broad mesh wrist band, interior fitted with loose powder, hinged lipstick, glass perfume, plastic-coated flannel snap coin purse and clear plastic comb, pill box, "Made in U.S.A.," hinged mirror, (shown open), 5¾" x 3½" x 1¼". $100.00 – $125.00.

This carryall makes no attempts at Evans cloning, and no maker identification either.

3. Kaycraft — Goldtone, Standard Carryall. Double access, M.O.P. lid with brushed reverse, broad mesh wrist band, engine-turned interiors, loose powder,

hinged lipstick tube, gray cloth coin purse with small mock tortoise shell comb, hinged money clip, no case identification, box signed: "A Genuine Ocean Pearl Creation by Kaycraft," case glued mirror, 5½" x 3⅛" x ¾". $100.00 – $125.00.

4. Wadsworth — Leather, Standard Carryall. Double access, green leather exterior with brushed goldtone sides and lid monogram cartouche, leather strap handle, ivory kid interior with Ivorene framing — no metal — loose powder, puff with logo, coin purse on reverse of compartment lid — all lids are leather, snap closures on exterior lids, goldtone lipstick tube, case signed, case glued mirror, 6¼" x 3¼" x 1¼". Ref: 1948 ad. $75.00 – $100.00.

With its lack of metal, this case seems a prime candidate for WWII metal restriction dates, but the so-called luxury tax was still intact up through the Korean "Police Action," keeping some interest in this ill-conceived mix of leather and tinted loose powder.

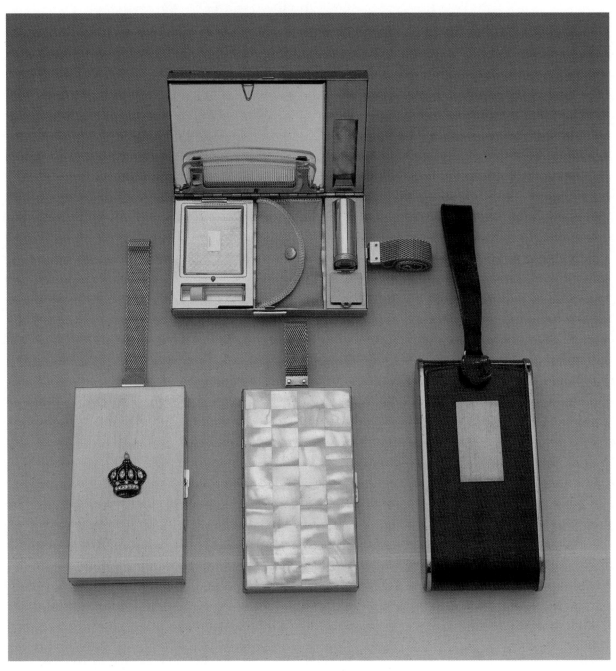

2

1   3   4

1
2

1. Volupté — Silvertone, Purse Carryall. Single access, matte black enameled lid framing with attached rhinestone swag, incised horizontal lines, black silk detachable carrier with wrist band, hinged lid mirror covering two compartments, loose powder, puff with logo, case signed, see page 143, #1 open, 6" x 4" x 1". $150.00 – $175.00.

2. Volupté — Goldtone, Musical, Purse Carryall. Single access, ribbed lid with attached rhinestone musical motif, black silk detachable carrier with wrist band

and reverse snap closure compartment, interior swiss music box: *Let Me Call You Sweetheart*, loose powder, puff with logo, lipstick, case signed, hinged metallic mirror, 5" x 3" x ½". $125.00 – $150.00.

The Volupté purse carryalls have poorly made fabric carriers. However, they are an integral part of the total case design. Without the carriers the cases revert to clutch carryalls and lose about a third of their value. If these cases are in fine to mint presentation boxes add $25 to the value.

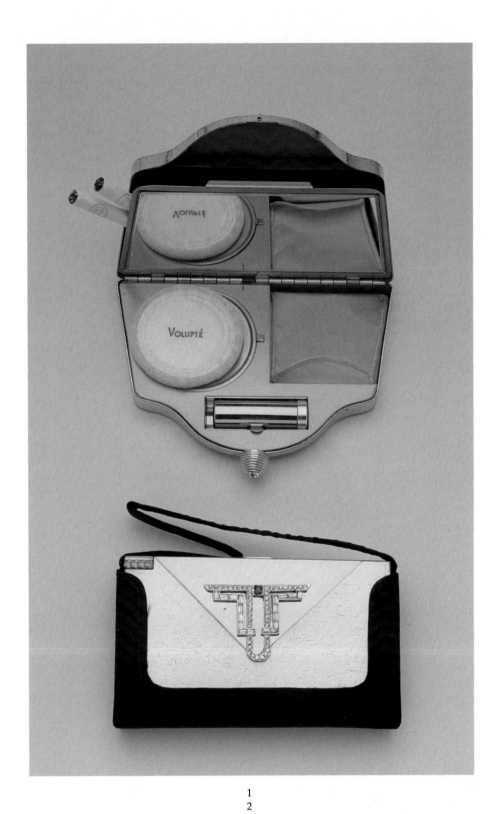

1
2

1. Volupté — Silvertone, Purse Carryall. See page 142, #1 closed.

2. Volupté — Bimetal, Purse Carryall. Single access, brushed silvertone case with chevron glossy goldtone lid motif with affixed faux gemstone 'Clip' bijou in the Art Moderne style, black silk detachable carrier with wrist band and reverse snap closure compartment, loose powder, puff with logo, lipstick, case signed, hinged metallic mirror, 5" x 3" x ½". $125.00 – $150.00.

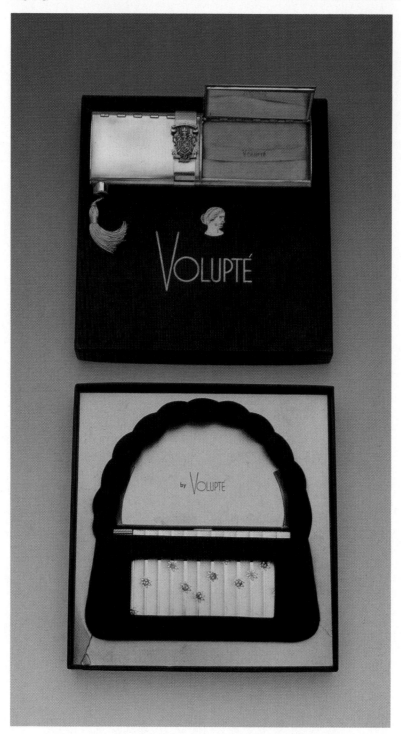

1
2

1. Volupté — Goldtone, Baton Carryall. Double access, brushed oval case with sliding band opener, fraternal crest attached to band, exterior access tasseled lipstick, loose powder, case signed, case glued mirror, 6⅞" x 2⅜" x ⅞". $125.00 – $150.00.

The case designation of Baton is a derivative of the French term — "Baton de Marechal" or Field Marshall's Stick. Designed to fit comfortably into the palm of the hand, this case also comes with a carrier.

2. Volupté — Bimetal, Purse Carryall. Single access, brushed silvertone case with vertical glossy goldtone lid bars, strewn daisies — some with rhinestone centers — lid decor, padded black silk faille carrier with twisted rope handle, loose powder, peach taffeta coin purse, puff with logo, case signed, hinged metallic mirror, 5¼" x 3" x ⅝". $150.00 – $175.00.

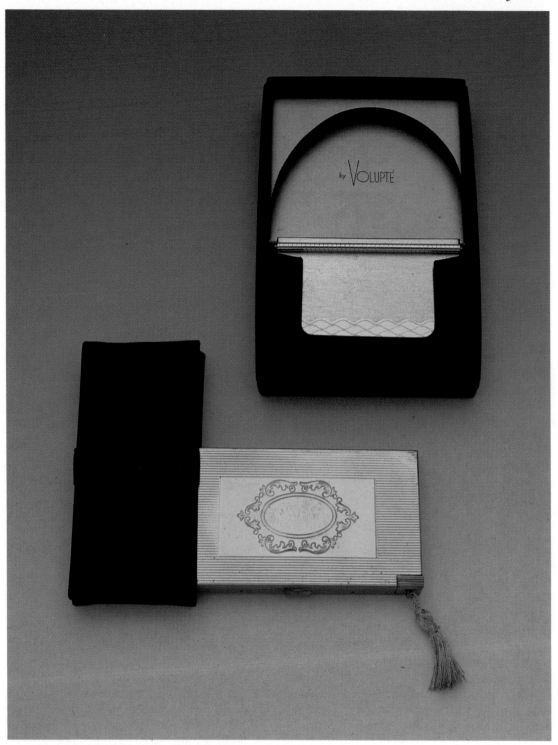

1
2

1. Volupté — Bimetal, Purse Carryall. Single access "Swing Lok" lid bar, brushed silvertone case with glossy goldtone incised wave lid motif, black silk faille detachable carrier with wrist band, reverse snap closure compartment, loose powder, puff with logo, lipstick tube, clear plastic comb in clips, case signed, case glued mirror, 4¼" x 3⅛" x ¾". Ref: 1949 ad. $125.00 – $150.00.

Volupté cases are usually 'nail-friendly' meaning easy entry to powder and other compartments. With

the introduction of this Sophisticase model, they went one more step: both compartments have exterior flanges which only require a thumb lift to open. They are snug and well engineered.

2. Volupté — Goldtone, Clutch Carryall. Single access with exterior access tasseled lipstick, black silk faille slip case, ribbed lid has scrolled monogram cartouche, loose powder, puff with logo, peach taffeta coin purse, case signed, hinged metallic mirror, 5¼" x 3" x ½". Ref: 1951 ad. $75.00 – $100.00.

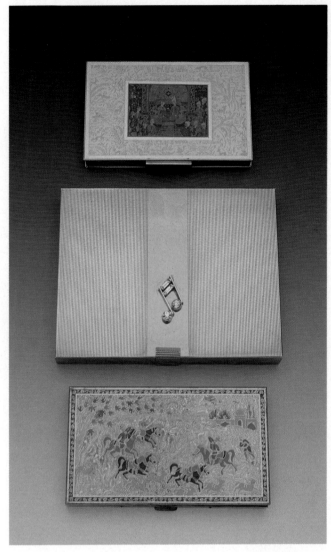

1
2
3

1. Flapjack Production — Goldtone, Clutch Carryall. All-over applied Oriental transfer with Persian scenic lid cartouche, interior vertical rib banding on three hinged compartments and square lipstick, loose black and white plastic round box, loose powder, no case identification, puff with logo, framed mirror, see page 147, #1 open. 4⅞" x 3¼" x ½". Rare.

The design and engineering on this gem is quirky; when the case is opened everything including the lipstick tube jumps to attention. The interior is stunning, borrowing a bit of La Minaudière pizzazz, but the case has no firm closure — major aggravation for a clutch.

2. Volupté — Goldtone, Musical Super Carryall. Single access, vertical incised linear lid with glossy band and affixed bijou of faux gemstone notes, exterior lipstick acting as: Lip-Lock closure, papers, music box plays: *The Blue Danube*, three hinged interior compartments, loose powder, puff with logo, clear plastic comb in clip, case signed, case glued mirror, 6" x 4¾" x ¾". Ref: 1955 ad. $250.00 – $300.00.

A good try at the Minaudière style of French jeweler Van Cleef & Arpels. Impressive and heavy! The music box addition doesn't help the weight. This 1955 ad shows an optional carrier. If available with music box this should move into rare category.

3. Volupté — Goldtone, Portmanteau. Single access, all-over enameled case design of Persian hunt scene with blue borders and sides, glossy interior with hinged creme and pressed rouge compartment, loose powder, puff with logo, white enameled well for coin purse and small comb, case signed, hinged metallic mirror, 5¼" x 3" x ⅝". Ref: 1936 ad. $75.00 – $100.00.

Another ad appeared in 1946 as Volupté recycled pre-WWII stock. "Portmanteau" is their wording, meaning a case that opens in the middle like a book and has no handles.

1
2
3

1. Flapjack Production — Goldtone, Clutch Carryall. See page 146, #1 closed.

2. Volupté — Goldtone, Super Carryall. Single access, incised circled lid with affixed rhinestone bijou, push-piece case opener, glass-topped cigarette compartment, ivory faille comb case and coin purse with recess for small oval lipstick, loose powder, puff with logo, case signed, case glued mirror, 6" x 4¾" x ¾". Ref: 1939. $275.00 – $300.00.

The interior arrangement of this case and the case on page 146, #2 is totally different, beginning with the case closures. This case continued for a time after WWII with a 1946 ad.

3. Volupté — Goldtone, Portmanteau. Single access, incised vertical linear lid bands with affixed rhinestone encrusted winging bird bijou, see page 146, #3 for like interior, 5¼" x 3" x ⅝". Ref: 1946 ad. $100.00 – $125.00.

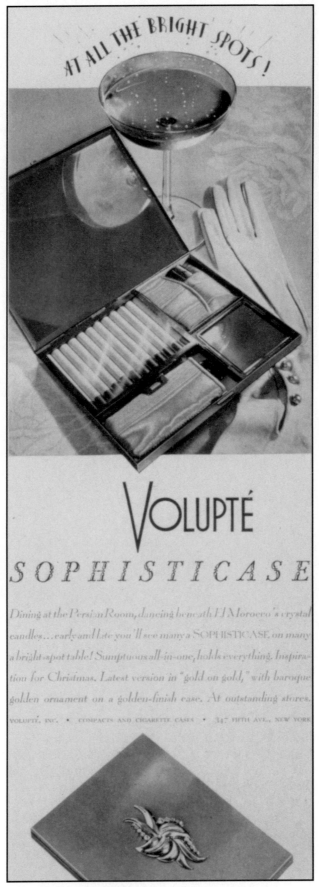

Vogue, 1939

1
2

1. Elgin American — Goldtone, Purse Carryall. Loaf case with all-over embossed Post Deco 'Leaping Gazelles' and fern, black cut velvet carrier: "Ingber" with silk braided and tasseled handle, interior motif repeated in lower relief, double compartments, loose powder, puff with logo, lipstick tube, money clip, hinged framed mirror lid divider, case signed, see example open, 4½" x 2½" x 1½". Ref: 1952 ad. $125.00 – $150.00.

The 'Leaping Gazelles,' competing in the thirties with the Borzoi and Scotty dog animal motifs, for some reason became a very popular motif again after WWII. The Post Deco flavor of these cases is obvious. The sharp angles are softer and the fauna is more realistic. However, art deco in feeling, these later cases must not be confused nor valued with

true Art Deco. A leaping gazelle does not always an Art Deco case make.

The use of evening purses to carry these cases was not uncommon and gave individuality to a rather common fashion accessory of the fifties. Some purses may have been designed to act as a carrier — this example is a perfect fit.

2. Elgin American — Bimetal, Purse Carryall. Brushed silvertone all-over case with glossy goldtone flora lid accents, blue faille detachable carrier with wrist band and snap closure reverse compartment containing comb and mirror, double interior compartments, loose powder, puff with logo, lipstick tube, case signed, hinged framed mirror lid divider, 4¼" x 2½" x 1". $75.00 – $100.00.

1
2
3
4

1. Evans — Fabric, Vanity Pouch. Black satin bag with white guilloché enamel vanity lid, small link wrist chain, rhinestone mesh bib — front and back, ivory taffeta lining, silvertone hinged compartment lid and double hinged metallic mirrors, loose powder, pressed rouge with logo: "Mayfair," case signed, 4" x 4". Ref: 1938 ad. $250.00 – $300.00.

2. Evans — Goldtone, Vanity Mesh Bag. Goldtone mesh with slender woven mesh wrist chain, silk lined, lid vanity case with ivory backed hinged compartment lid and double hinged metallic mirrors, loose powder, puff with logo, papers, pressed rouge with logo: "Mayfair," case signed, 4" x 4½". Ref: 1938 ad. $250.00 – $300.00.

3. Unmarked — Lucite, Compact Canister Carrier. Black Lucite cylinder with goldtone lid and bottom plates, broad link wrist chain, goldtone, engine-turned 1½"dia compact attached to interior lid plate, loose powder, framed mirror, 3" x 3¾". Rare.

4. Evans — Mesh Pendant Vanity Pouch. Ivory enamel pearlized mesh bag with ivory taffeta lining, tandem lipstick, ivory enamel lid with black and silvertone accented Art Moderne center clef, lid inset vanity with hinged double metallic mirrors, Tap-Sift powder well, pressed rouge with logo: Mayfair, case signed, 2½" x 2½". Ref: 1932 ad. $300.00 – $350.00.

1
2
3

1. Pandora — Silk, Clutch Purse. Horseshoe, black silk with silvertone frame, attached faux gemstone and goldtone floral basket front bijou, back wrist strap, ivory taffeta lining, cloth framed and hinged mirror, interior label: "Beauty Bag," lid compartment with large logo puff: "Charm," 4¼" x 4" x ¾". $150.00 – $200.00.

2. Lenor — Taffeta, Clutch Purse. Envelope, black and white check taffeta with loop and button closure, ivory lining, mock tortoise shell plastic framed compact with matching fabric padded lid inset, loose powder, powder screen frame with logo, matching coin purse, double loose mirror, 6" x 4". $65.00 – $75.00.

3. Lin-Bren — Fabric Purse. Multicolor cord fabric purse with broad wrist strap, goldtone lid flap band and snap ornament, blue taffeta lining, interior signed, all-over matching fabric padded compact, signed everywhere, loose powder, framed mirror, lipstick and comb, 6½" x 5" x 2". $75.00 – $100.00.

DISCOVERIES IN BEAUTY

PURSE-WITHIN-A-PURSE? If you wish—but we think this Petitpurse by Dorset could hold its own with this year's fashion for small bags, carry in addition to its compact, lipstick, comb, your daytime needs. Saks Fifth.

Vogue, **1948**

1. Lin-Bren — Cloth, Clutch Purse. Expandable box with ribbed goldtone sides, black faille case with goldtone snap ornament, black taffeta lining with logo, 3"dia compact with loose powder — framed mirror and puff with logo, matching cigarette can with sliding top, lipstick and comb, 6" x 3¾" x 1½". $65.00 – $75.00.

2. Dorset Fifth Avenue — Leather, Clutch Purse. Hunter green leather envelope with oval goldtone lid monogram cartouche and snap closure, brown taffeta with logo lining, goldtone compact 3"sq with loose powder, puff with logo, case glued mirror, lipstick and comb, 6½" x 4¼", clutch. Ref: 1948 ad. $75.00 – $90.00.

1 3
2 4

1
2

1. Unmarked — Faux Leather, Fitted Vanity Carry-ing Case. See page 157 closed.

2. Unmarked — Leather, Fitted Clutch. See page 157 closed.

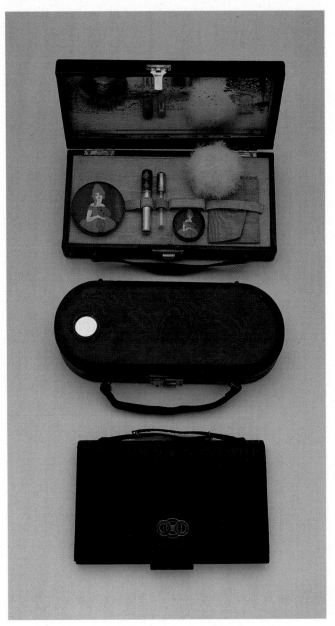

1
2
3

1. Unmarked — Leather, Fitted Vanity Carrying Case. True black patent leather case with wrist strap, greige moiré lining with fittings in slip bands, two hand-painted goldtone cans suitable for powder and rouge, painted topped tube for hairpins, glass perfume flacon, coin purse, hinged bottom, full size compartment, lid glued mirror, case key lock, (shown open) 10" x 5" x 2¼". $200.00 – $250.00.

2. Unmarked — Faux Leather, Fitted Vanity Carrying Case. Damask patterned case with wrist strap, round framed mirror inset in lid, lunette sides, rose Art Moderne damask lining with fittings in slip bands, two hand painted goldtone cans suitable for powder and rouge, lipstick, comb and clothes brush, hinged bottom, full size compartment with coin purse and pocket for double mirror, lid glued mirror, case key lock, see page 156 open, 10½" x 4¼" x 1¾". $250.00 – $275.00.

3. Unmarked — Leather, Fitted Clutch. Black ribbed Moroccan leather case, with adjustable wrist strap, lid flap with cloisonné triple ring motif, cloth label: "Foreign," greige moiré lining, double access, fold-over leather backed mirror, pockets for fittings: Coty rouge, Kissproof creme rouge, lipstick and comb, see page 156 open, 8½" x 5" x 1". $150.00 – $175.00.

Has a U.S. snap identification: Fulco, Prov, R.I.,?

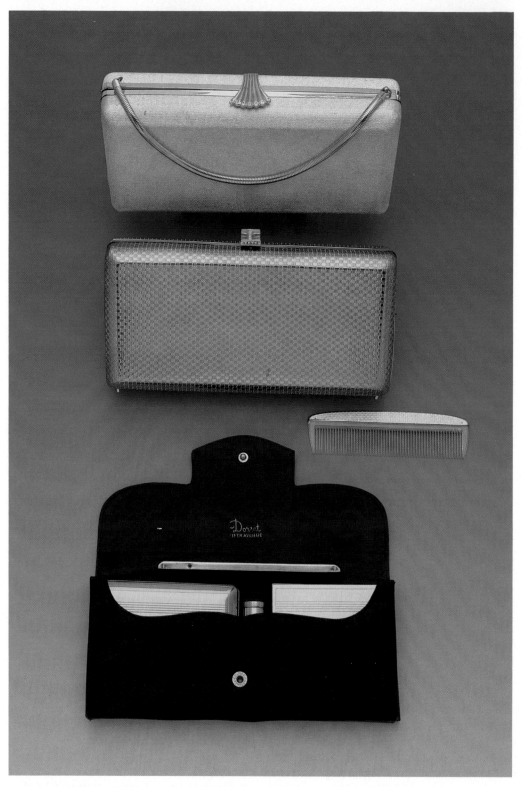

1
2
3

1. Volupté — Goldtone, Rigid Clutch Purse. Brushed all-over finish with snake wrist chain, rhinestone mounted fan lid closure, ivory satin lining with logo, pocket for clear plastic comb, 8" x 4" x 1¾". $65.00 – $75.00.

2. Volupté — Goldtone, Rigid Clutch Purse. Embossed herringbone case design with matching capped plastic comb in pocket, rhinestone mounted lid closure, peach satin lining with logo, no wrist chain, 8" x 4" x 1¾". $65.00 – $75.00.

3. Dorset Fifth Avenue — Fabric, Fitted Clutch Purse. Navy blue faille case with goldtone fittings: square loose powder compact, cigarette cased, lipstick and comb, everything signed, 8" x 3½" x 1". $75.00 – $90.00.

1
2

1. Rex Fifth Ave — Fabric, Fitted Purse. Silver metallic brocade case with silvertone ring handles, snap closure, blue satin interior, pockets for goldtone lipstick tube and square loose powder compact with matching fabric lid inset, clear plastic comb, coin purse, compact and puff signed, framed mirror, 8" x 6½" x 2". Ref: 1948 ad. Rare.

This might have been a display model for Rex. The purse is mounted in a faux black suede box base with a clear plastic domed sleeve. The plastic has a large printed logo which would not photograph.*

2. Pegi Paris — Fabric, Fitted Clutch Purse. Silver metallic brocade case with snap closure, ivory taffeta interior, pockets for goldtone square compact and mock tortoise shell plastic comb, lining and puff signed, case glued mirror, 8¾" x 4½" x 1½". $65.00 – $75.00.

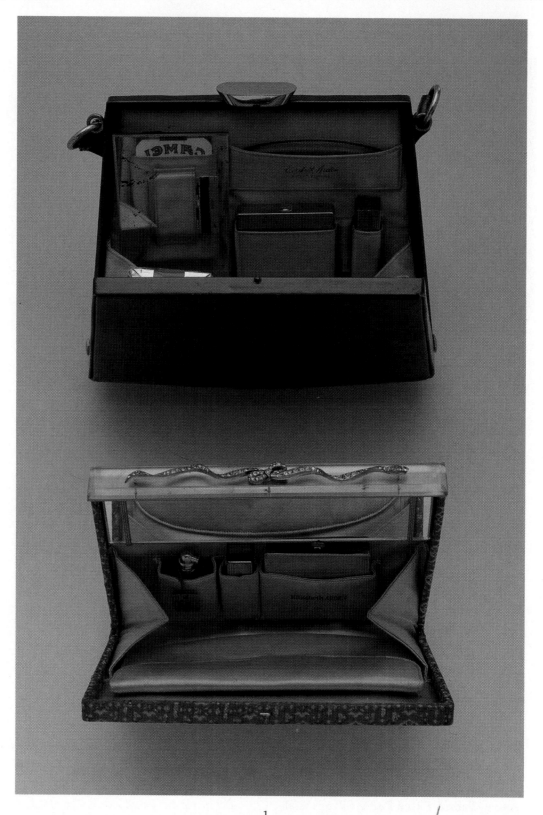

1
2

1. Elizabeth Arden — Leather, Fitted Purse. Pearlized blue kid leather purse with leather wrist strap, ecru silk satin interior with goldtone square lipstick and loose powder compact, coin case, pockets for cigarette pack, matches and clear plastic comb, mirror attached to lining, compact and lipstick signed, 9½" x 7" x 2". Ref: 1948 ad. $150.00 – $200.00.

2. Elizabeth Arden — Fabric, Fitted Clutch Purse. Old rose silk brocade case with rhinestone encrusted trailing ribbon affixed to clear Lucite bar opener, peach silk satin interior with pockets for goldtone square lipstick and loose powder compact, perfume falcon: "For Her," clear plastic comb, snap closure pocket, attached mirror, everything signed, 8" x 5¾" x 1". Ref: 1948 ad. $200.000 – $250.00.

Zell Fifth Avenue — Leather, Fitted Clutch Purse.
Red calf case with back clutch strap, attached front
tab, goldtone frame and leather covered lunette closure, red moiré lining with logo, pockets for: loose
powder compact, cigarette case, lipstick, comb,
lighter and fabric-backed loose mirror, key case and
coin purse are loose in purse, only puff with logo, 9"
x 5¾" x 2½". $250.00 – 300.00.

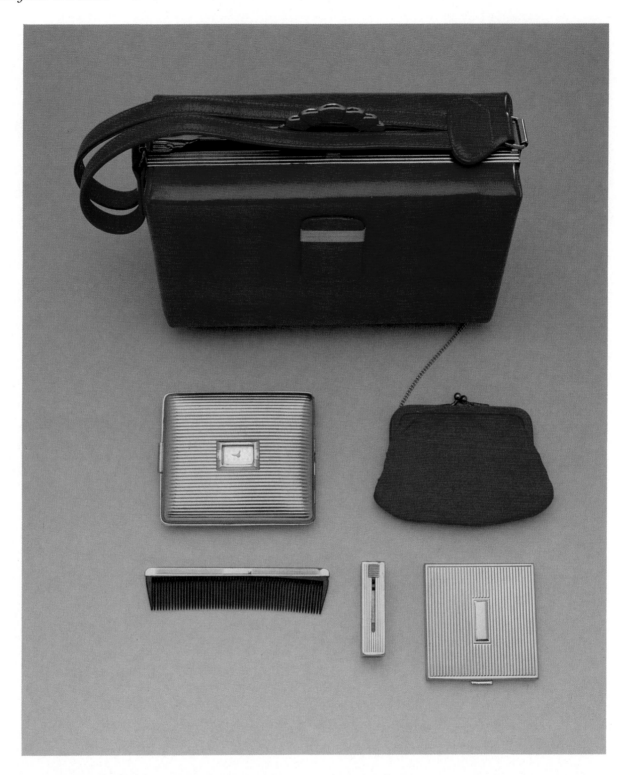

Evans — Leather, Fitted Purse. Red calf leather box with split strap handles, attached front tab, goldtone frame and fan closure, red cord lining with logo with pockets for goldtone fittings: square loose powder compact, lipstick, cigarette case with watch lid inset, capped comb, coin purse has attached chain, lighter is loose, everything is signed, 8" x 5" x 2¾". Ref: 1945 ad. Rare.

This 1945 ad does not show fittings. As with all Evans bags, the fittings must match the framing design, i.e. this case has a ribbed frame, and all the accessories also have this design. There is room in the large cigarette case pocket for the lighter (not shown), but this could have been an added accessory, because it does match in style and came in the coin purse. The rarity of this bag is the watch/cigarette case. Evans watch/compact models are not uncommon, so customizing a cigarette case with a watch for this purse was possible.

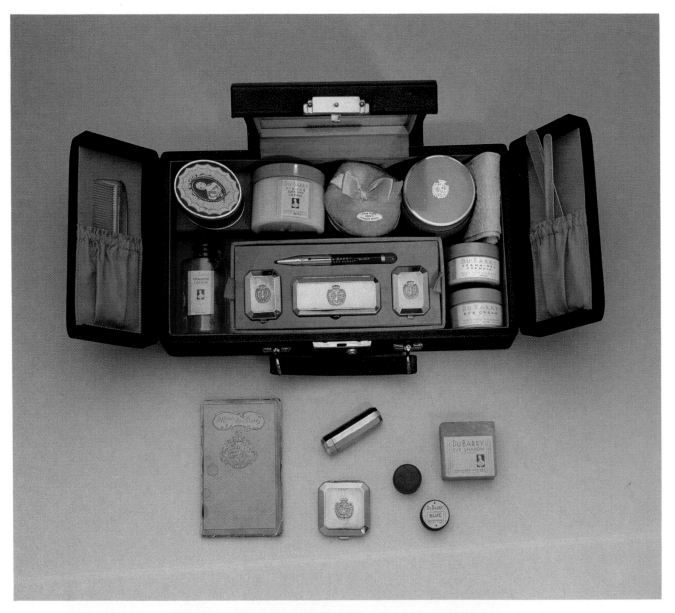

Richard Hudnut — Leather, Fitted Traveling Make-up Kit. Black Moroccan case with pink cotton faille lining, lift-out tray, case signed: Richard Hudnut, All Du Barry fittings, 79 page biography of Mme du Barry — Edited by Richard Hudnut — Published in New York, 1904, fittings include: blue creme eye shadow, creme rouge, mascara case with brush, eyebrow pencil, pressed rouge, pressed eye shadow in box, lipstick tube, tiny red plastic creme rouge samples, compact pressed powder refill box, and assorted jars, boxes, and bottles, 11¼" x 6" x 2¾". Rare.

Chapter Four

MILITARY, PATRIOTICS & NON-METALS

On the set for "THIRTY SECONDS OVER TOKYO" at M-G-M Studio

A Wac* gets an intimate glimpse of this Metro-Goldwyn-Mayer motion picture production and visits with Van Johnson and Phyllis Thaxter, who play Capt. and Mrs. Ted W. Lawson, Mervyn Le Roy, the director, and Hal Rosson, the director of photography.

*Women's Army Corps urgently needs you. Join the WAC now!

PAN-CAKE MAKE-UP originated by MAX FACTOR HOLLYWOOD

Remember, there is only one "Pan-Cake", the original, created by *Max Factor Hollywood* for Technicolor Pictures
and the Hollywood screen stars, and now the make-up fashion with millions of girls and women.

Vogue, 1944

December 8, 1941 was the World War II war date for the United States of America, but France and Britain had been struggling with Hitler since 1940. Cosmetic house entrepreneur and test pilot, Jacqueline Cochran, was encouraging women pilots to join the British Air Transport Auxiliary (ATA). In 1941 "Bundles for Britain" was a popular social charity and volunteers opened a boutique in New York selling purse accessories with British flags or regimental crests to raise war relief funds. Macy's supported the Battle of Britain heroes showing compacts with RAF insignia. The war, when it began in the U.S., caused major upheavals in the cosmetic industry: restrictions against metals and silk for domestic use. In April 1942, the only metal allowed in the production of costume jewelry and compacts was sterling, and on March 8, 1942, the government enacted a ban on silk, channeling all production to the navy for battleship gun powder bags! The silk ban did create a new product for a short time: liquid leg make-up to replace silk stockings. The back leg seams were not always applied successfully with an eyebrow pencil.

Non-metals such as celluloid, pearloid, ivorene, bakelite, and ebonite were early attempts to lower the costs of vanity cases. With the insuing poor results at durability these materials gained a declassé image in compacts that took a war to change. Starting with the "make-do" spirit that personified WWII, the non-metal and silk era of compacts and vanity cases began with the newer resin plastics that were also being hyped in other industry patriotic ads. These new materials, Lucite and Plexiglas, gave designers a freer hand to create different dimensions but instilled a need to conceal inherent flaws.

The silk ban, at first, didn't seem disruptive — other than the death of hosiery, but it proved to have profound repercussions. Silk was the only fabric that worked as a loose powder screen. The substitutes tried to fight the loose powder control problem with poorer weapons: pierce tin plates, plastic with punched out holes (and paper instructions on usage), tulle and other mesh fabrics, and puffs with powder pockets. This final inept battle with portable loose powder may have tipped the user over the the concept of pancake and creme powders. Enough was truly enough after the war.

Plastics as a new material was to prove equally disruptive and fatal. The old materials were tried again and found wanting again. Snakeskin, calf, kid, ostrich, and alligator attempted to stand against tinted powders; cloth assumed different disguises; zippers hung on; snaps and buttons tried; wood, cardboard,

ivory, and tortoise shell all had a last stand. Plastics, however, won the battle and lost the war for the discriminating woman buyer.

Henriette, always innovative, was trying out a new concept in 1939: "Airglass Carryall...Clear As Sparkling Water...New As Tomorrow...Jewel-tinted Lucite..." This was not repeated in 1940 or 1941 ads. It was Volupté who hit the mark running early in 1941 with "Crystalite...new idea...translucent substance shimmering with pearl essence..." Elizabeth Arden used the work "Lucite" in a May, 1951 ad, but it was for a monogram cartouche accent on a fitted purse. Dorothy Gray offered "All Clear Red," a plastic compact and lipstick in a 1941 Christmas gift set and the word, "plastic" was out in the advertising arena as the emperor's new clothes.

It seemed to be a challenge on how many ways the word "plastic" could be disguised in ad jargon. Volupté started off with "Crystalite" and "Pearlglow." Henriette tried "Crystal Clear," and "Feather Light" was predictable. "Non-Priority Plastic" said it all. It became such a patriotic gesture to buy and carry plastic accessories that the more blatant pre-war metallics were put away for the duration, or in a weak moment sacrificed to a boy scout metal scrap drive.

The war also created another market — patriotic vanity cases in all forms of military display. The cosmetic industry, unable to introduce new lines because of alcohol and other ingredient restrictions, recycled and renamed: Bourjois/Courage, and tagged lipsticks Hudnut/Emblem Red, Elizabeth Arden/Winged Victory, Tussy/Fighting Red, and Dorothy Gray/All Clear Red. Bright red lipstick became "...a sudden streak of lipstick across the lips spells courage." But red lipstick was not enough. Like the blue service star in the window, compacts and vanities had to make their own style of patriotic commitment.

Patriotic cases have public and private codes. Intensely personal, the case insignia could identify or remind. Some were bought by servicemen at base PX's for events, sweetheart, family, or special mementos. Some were homemade; some were manufactured. Some were elaborate; some were engraved. Some were never used; some were used to tatters.

In one of the rare instances in American industrial history, patriotic cases were not extolled in advertising. They just appeared. Many today are still treasured as family keepsakes, and collecting them is almost an intrusion into times of death and survival. Contrary to the other compact categories, patriotics stand alone disregarding case materials, design or workmanship. Condition, of course, sets the value, but more important is the theme and emblem. If possible, always try to gather any scraps of history relating to the case, so it can keep its identity. With patriotics the collector should be an archivist as well.

This category of non-metals and patriotics crosses over the previous categories by including all forms of cases (compacts, vanities, carryalls, etc.), because the emphasis is on the material rather than the form, no attempt is made to sort them out other than in a perfunctory way. Many of these cases could be considered limited editions, because of the limited times for which they were designed. Trying to set values on such items which may or may not be unique is perilous. Maybe ten years from now a better picture will emerge for this category.

Life, 1942

1 2 3 4
5   6

1. Unmarked — Plastic, Loose Powder Compact. Hat, U.S. Army khaki and brown with gold foil brim crest, case glued mirror, 2⅞"dia x 1¼". $65.00 – $75.00.

2. Unmarked — Plastic, Loose Powder Compact. Hat, U.S. Navy "Brass Hat" with copper top, embossed crest, case glued mirror, 3"dia x 1¼". $75.00 – $90.00.

3. Henriette — Plastic, Loose Powder Compact. Hat, U.S. Navy blue and black with gold foil brim crest, no case identification, box with logo: #102A-28 Navy, same case as #1.

4. Unmarked — Plastic, Loose Powder Compact. Hat, U.S. Army red, white and blue with gold foil crest, same case as #1.

5. "V For Victory" W.W.II War Stamp Corsage. "4th in a series by American Designers, July's corsage is the victory 'V' by Mainbocher. Nine stamps for one dollar,

without profit." Ref: 1943. This was a gift from a grandparent to the author — and put into a scrapbook. Children, usually receiving these stamps as gifts, put them into books not unlike the ration books and when $18.75 was reached, the books were cashed in for a $25 war bond with a ten year maturity. Not for sale.

6. Revell's Glamour Kit — Plastic, Combination Case. Black plastic case with affixed faux gemstone 'V' bijou, loose powder compact, cigarette compartment, lighter, lipstick brush (?), and "Blackout" flashlight — all contained in screw-top side tubes, puff with logo, case signed: "Revell Plastics Hollywood," case glued mirror, 4½" x 3½" x 1". Very rare.

The blackout flashlight was used for keyhole entry as the West Coast was for some time under blackout conditions fearing a Japanese invasion after Pearl Harbor. The flashlight is not detachable, so it could not be used to illuminate the compact interior.

2   5
1   3   6
4

1. Unmarked — Goldtone, Combination Case. Kamra with deep pink alligator-patterned leather case, lid crest, "Frankfort a/M," loose powder compact, recessed lipstick, cigarette reverse compartment, framed mirror, 4" x 2" x ⅝". $125.00 – $150.00.

Although this does not have a direct reference to the post WWII occupation of South Germany by U.S. military forces, Frankfort was part of the "U.S. Zone."

2. Lady Vanity — Plastic, Loose Powder Compact. Black Moroccan leather lid and reverse with stamped "U S N" on lid, yellow lucite case, no case identification, puff with logo, case glued mirror, 4" x 2¾" x ½". $75.00 – $100.00.

3. Unmarked — Goldtone, Loose Powder Compact. Flapjack, mottled red enameled lid with high embossed sloped scrolled borders and quilted reverse, "U.S. Zone Germany" map lid inset, 7th Army affixed insignia, see #4 for uniform shoulder patch, framed mirror, 4"dia x ⅜". $250.00 – $300.00.

4. 7th Army Uniform Shoulder Patch. See #3, patch legend is as follows: Motto — "Seven Steps To Hell" (Yellow logo). Colors: red — field artillery, blue — infantry, yellow — armored.

5. Unmarked — Goldtone, Combination Case. Kamra, dark blue mottled enameled case with silvertone inlay map: "U.S. Zone," loose powder compact, recessed lipstick, reverse compartment with manicure kit — see #6, framed mirror, 4" x 2" x ⅝". $175.00 – $200.00.

6. See #5

For some reason this map of the U.S. Occupation of Germany has part of the French zone included, along with other odd geographic depictions. Also, this model has one of the non-smoking options for souvenir buying Yanks.

```
        1    4
      2   3   5
```

1. Unmarked — Ivorene, Pendant Loose Powder Compact. Marbled green case with silvertone ball-link dangles, lid and reverse affixed Ivorene branch with rhinestone florets, matching disk link wrist chain, Ivorene interior, case framed mirror, 3" x 2" x ¾". $200.00 – $250.00.

2. Flore-Reale — Cardboard, Pendant Pressed Powder Vanity Case. Blue silk all-over case with hand-applied gold braid and silk flowers, gold wrist cord and tassel with pink glass beads, gold foil interior compartments with pressed rouge, goldtone oval lipstick tube, original stickers and labels (price: $2.25) "Les Dames Exquisites Emploient." Case framed mirror, 3" x 2" x ¾". $150.00 – $200.00.

The interior compartments are tiny boxes assembled to fit each item. The value here is solely based on survivorship, certainly not on precious metals or materials. That this delicate objet d'art made it

intact from the early twenties to today tells how cherished it must have been.

3. Unmarked — Celluloid, Pendant Pressed Powder Vanity Case. Red faux lacquer case with incised lid motif enhanced with red rhinestones, black silk wrist cord and tassel with wood beads, black Ivorene interior, no mirror, 3" x 2" x ¾". $125.00 – $150.00.

4. Rimmel — Tortoise Shell, Pendant Pressed Powder Vanity Case. Case encircled by brown silk cord which acts as wrist cord and tasseled lipstick holder, goldtone French logo lipstick tube is held by a Chinese-Finger-Puzzle casing, framed mirror, 1¾"dia x ¾". $150.00 – $175.00.

5. Unmarked — Celluloid, Pendant Compact. Red case with stencil in black of child applying powder, black and white twisted cotton string wrist handle, case glued mirror, 3⅜" x 2⅝" x 1½". Rare.

Harper's Bazaar, 1943

1. Unmarked — Silk, Vanity Kit Bag. Doubled lavender silk covered case with drawstring closure, exterior mirror bottom, sewn glass beaded ornamentation with overlay gold mesh lace, double velour puff, box #329 — J.C. Penney Co., 2½"dia x 5". $175.00 – $200.00.

Also comes in black silk evening or mourning model.

2. Unmarked — Silk, Petite Vanity Kit Bag. Blue silk with drawstring closure, exterior mirror bottom, hand-stitched with lace applique, cardboard inner frame (bottom of a powder box?), double velour puff, 3"dia x 1½". $150.00 – $175.00.

3. Lizard Brand — Silk, Loose Powder Compact. Padded blue damask Chinese bridge and boat scene on

lid and flora reverse, silvertone frame, string tag identification case framed mirror, 3"sq x ⅝". $25.00 – $40.00.

4. Rex Fifth Avenue — Taffeta, Vanity Kit Bag. "Handy Andy" with black cord drawstring closure, "United Nations Stripe" colors, exterior mirror inset in bottom wood frame, peach taffeta lining, logo on puff and stencilled on interior wood bottom, 4"dia x 3½". Ref: 1943 ad. $75.00 – $100.00.

5. Lizard Brand — Silk, Loose Powder Compact. Padded red damask Chinese Pagoda scene on lid and pastoral reverse, same case as #3.

6. Lizard Brand — Silk, Cigarette Case. Companion to #5. $50.00 – $75.00 set.

1 4
2 5
3 6

1
                3
       2

1. Unmarked — Snakeskin, Loose Powder Compact.
Flapjack, tan case, snap flap closure, case glued mirror, 4½" x 4½" x ¾". $100.00 – $125.00.

2. Dermetics — Leather, Loose Powder Compact.
Green case with stamped gilt gazelle/sunrise Art Deco lid motif, puff with logo, case glued mirror, 3½"sq x ⅝". $75.00 – $100.00.

3. Marcee — Leather, Loose Powder Compact.
Horseshoe, red case with stamped gilt Art Nouveau tendrils, puff with logo, case glued mirror, see page 183, #4 open, 3¾" x 3½" x ¾". $125.00 – $150.00.

1   4
2   5
3   6

1. Unmarked — Leather, Loose Powder Compact. Horseshoe, embossed tan ostrich skin patterned case, zipper closure — stamped: "Lightning," Ivorene interior with pierced powder screen and framed mirror, 4" x 3⅞" x ¾". $125.00 – $150.00.

Very interesting use of Ivorene as total interior framing, so shown open only. Maybe European — purchased in Bath, England.

2. Marcee — Leather, Loose Powder Compact. Cushion, tan case with stamped gilt cross-hatch lid motif, tab and button closure, puff and box with logo, case glued mirror, 3½"sq x ¾". $75.00 – $100.00.

3. Stratton — Leather, Loose Powder Compact. Padded Wedgwood blue mottled case, thumb lift flanges and metallic guard, ivory kid interior with hinged powder well cover and stamped gilt logo, mirror mounted with four metallic clips, 3¾" x 3" x ⅝". Rare.

4. Marcee — Leather, Loose Powder Compact. See pages 180, #3 and 182, #3 closed.

5. Unmarked — Snakeskin, Loose Powder Compact. Padded natural snakeskin case with goldtone rolled edges, zipper closure — stamped: "Royal," ivory kid interior with pink and blue polka dot powder screen, attached mirror; see page 182, #4 open, 3½" x 2¾" x ¾". $100.00 – $125.00.

6. Rex Fifth Avenue — Leather, Loose Powder Compact. Faux alligator patterned calf case with mock tortoise shell backing and sliding tray mirror, plastic mirror lip acts as closure, folded interior has ivory damask lining, puff with logo; see page 182, #5 partially open, 4"sq x 1". Ref: 1945 ad. $150.00 – $175.00.

Instantly Recognized!

The Mock Tortoise Shell Compact features the new Jeweler's chasing, and is about **$5.00.**

The genuine Leather Compact below, is available in Alligator grains of brown, green, red, black or blue, with Mock Tortoise Shell back, about **$7.50.**

At better stores everywhere, or write to

COMPACTS by
Rex
FIFTH AVENUE

REX PRODUCTS CORP · 302 FIFTH AVE · NEW YORK
Made in the "Queen City"—New Rochelle

Harper's Bazaar, 1945

1 3
2 4

1. Lee Products — Ebonite, Loose Powder Compact. Flapjack, black case with attached "Stork Club" lid insignia, no case identification, papers, case glued mirror, 4½"dia x ¾". Rare.

2. Unmarked — Plastic, Loose Powder Compact. Flapjack, tri-shaded gray mottled lid with pale gray reverse, case glued mirror, 4½"dia x ⅝". $75.00 – $90.00.

Oysters on the half shell is an apt description for this one.

3. Lady Louise — Plastic, Loose Powder Compact. Octagon flapjack, red case with vertical ribbed lid band, case glued mirror, 4¼"dia x ½". $75.00 – $100.00.

4. Rho-Jan — Plastic, Loose Powder Compact. Flapjack, black case, quilted lid with inset rhinestones, case glued mirror, 5"dia x ¾". $125.00 – $150.00.

Case warping is a common problem with these large flapjacks. If the mirror is intact and the case closes, side 'gapitis' should be tolerated and not affect the value by much. The design and overall condition is the deciding factor.

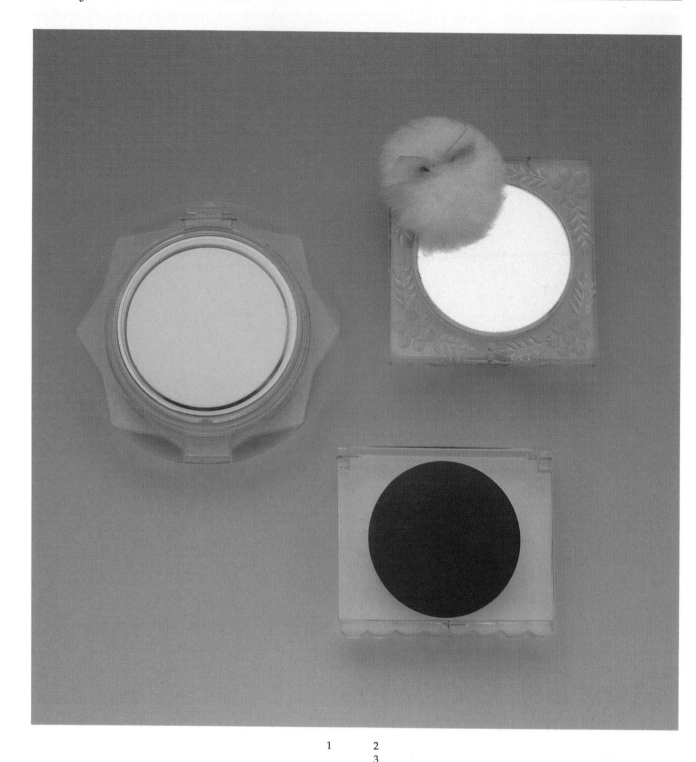

1

2

3

1. Belle Ayre — Plastic, Loose Powder Compact.
Flapjack, clear faceted case with blue mirror lid inset, no case identification, puff with logo, case glued mirror, 5"dia x ¾". $100.00 – $125.00.

Blue and peach tinted glass was very popular during the high deco period and adds a pleasant accent but doesn't do much for the complexion! Almost all double or triple mirrors used in vanity cases had some difference in magnification. Since eye glasses were definitely not a fashion statement, these cases had a clientele regardless of make or style.

2. Unmarked — Lucite, Loose Powder Compact.
Super, clear etched case with mirrored lid inset, case glued mirror; see page 188, #3 variation, 4"sq x 1". $75.00 – $100.00.

3. Unmarked — Lucite, Loose Powder Compact.
Super, clear case with scalloped lower case closure, dark blue lid circle is reverse of interior case glued mirror, 3⅞" x 3¼" x ⅝". $75.00 – $100.00.

1
2
3

1. Rho-Jan — Plastic, Loose Powder Compact. Flapjack, purple marbled case, high domed, no case identification, puff with logo, case glued mirror, 5"dia x 1". Ref: 1947 ad. $100.00 – $125.00.

2. Unmarked — Plastic, Loose Powder Compact. Flapjack, purple marbled case with hand painted dogwood lid display, gilt borders, case glued mirror, 5"dia x ¾". $50.00 – $65.00.

3. Mavco — Lucite, Loose Powder Compact. Flapjack, mock tortoise shell case with hand painted flowers and rhinestone lid decor, spiral lined reverse, no case identification, puff and box with logo, case glued mirror, 3⅞"dia x ¾". Ref: 1944 ad. $65.00 – $90.00.

1

2
3

1. Unmarked — Plastic, Loose Powder Compact.
Flapjack, mock tortoise shell case, swirl band lid design, case glued mirror, 4¾"dia x ½". $100.00 – $125.00.

Some great designs never die. The industrial designer, Raymond Loewy, who shook up post-war Detroit and the American public with the audacious Avanti and Studebaker automobiles, decided in 1932 that hub caps were too complicated. He used this swirl band motif on the then very sporty Hupmobile hub cap. Which vanity case designer in the mid for-

ties, who might have owned a 1932 Hupmobile, reused Loewy's concept?

2. Pilcher — Lucite, Loose Powder Compact. Super, red case with etched flora lid square motif, metallic pushpiece closure, no case identification, puff with logo, case glued mirror, 4½"sq x ½". $125.00 – $150.00.

3. Unmarked — Plastic, Loose Powder Compact. Super, mock tortoise shell case with affixed faux black cameo lid ornament, case glued mirror, 4"sq x ¾". $125.00 – $150.00.

Facial Forecasting WITH REFLECTIONS BY Mavco

Mavco

COMPACTS AND
CIGARETTE CASES
CREATED OF
GLAMOROUS LUCITE

14 East 38th St. · New York 16, N. Y.

Vogue, 1944

1   3

2   4

5

1. Saravel — Lucite, Loose Powder Compact. Super, clear case with reverse transfer lid floral motif, no case identification, puff with logo, case glued mirror, 4½"sq x ⅝". $100.00 – $125.00.

2. Unmarked — Lucite, Loose Powder Compact. Super, clear lid with reverse silver foil backing for orchid transfer, green base, case glued mirror, 3¾"sq x ½". $150.00 – $175.00.

A perfect example of design ingenuity under the WWII metal restrictions. By using the green base as a dimensional ploy, and incorporating the interior powder gasket as a frame for the lid motif, the case takes on master craftsmanship quality. The use of metallic hinges and rivets and the hinged closure are the only use of metal and gives the case stability.

3. Miahati — Lucite, Loose Powder Compact. Clear case with reverse lid inset of shell flowers, puff with logo, case signed, case glued mirror, 3"sq x ¾". $65.00 – $80.00.

4. Unmarked — Lucite, Loose Powder Compact. Flapjack, clear case with reverse lid transfer of nosegay on ivory ground, case glued mirror, 4½"dia x ⅝". $75.00 – $90.00.

Another example of design ingenuity in a difficult medium. The closure is a hinged latch which swings up from the bottom and clasps the lid. Works surprisingly well.

5. Unmarked — Plexiglas, Loose Powder Compact. Clear case with reverse lid transfer of fruit, foil mirror sticker: "Genuine Plexiglas — Hand Painted" case glued mirror, 3"sq x ⅝". $50.00 – $65.00.

Both Lucite and Plexiglas are resin based plastics and are trademark names. Like other names that became generic because of common usage, Lucite became the tag name for the hard, crystal clear plastic used for objects like compacts, while Plexiglas is associated with fighter aircraft canopies and windows. There is no easy differentiation between the two, short of a test tube. So, why bother? Enjoy the innate beauty of both.

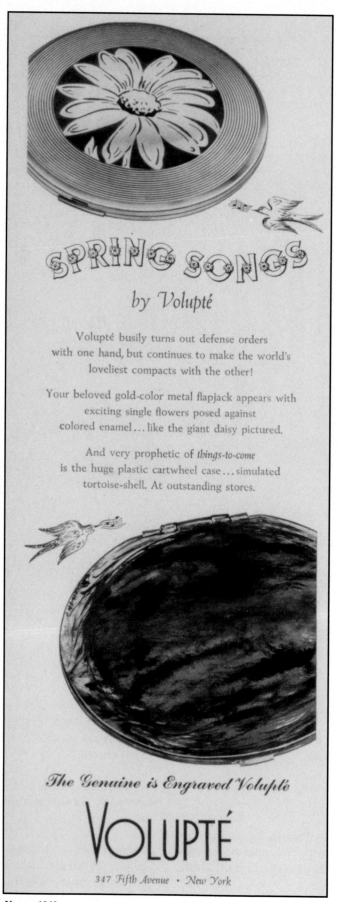

SPRING SONGS

by Volupté

Volupté busily turns out defense orders
with one hand, but continues to make the world's
loveliest compacts with the other!

Your beloved gold-color metal flapjack appears with
exciting single flowers posed against
colored enamel...like the giant daisy pictured.

And very prophetic of *things-to-come*
is the huge plastic cartwheel case...simulated
tortoise-shell. At outstanding stores.

The Genuine is Engraved Volupté

VOLUPTÉ

347 Fifth Avenue · New York

Vogue, 1942

1
2
3
4
5

1. Revlon — Plastic, Pressed Powder Compact. Flapjack, orange case with turtle (?) lid motif, foil label on reverse, coin purse closure, case glued mirror, 4"dia x ⅝". Ref: 1964 ad. $25.00 – $50.00.

The ad proclaims that this case was designed by "Van Cleef & Arpels."

2. Ziegfeld Glorified Girl — Plastic, Loose Powder Compact. Clear base with purple lid, goldtone accent bands, scalloped flange sides, no case identification, puff with logo, case glued mirror, 4½" x 3¾" x ⅝". Ref: 1946 ad. $65.00 – $80.00.

3. Ziegfeld Show Girl — Plastic, Loose Powder Compact. "Wild Raspberry" case, ribbed lid with goldtone wire accents, no case identification, puff with logo, case glued mirror, 3½"sq x ⅝". Ref: 1946 ad. $50.00 – $65.00.

4. Ziegfeld Show Girl — Plastic, Loose Powder Compact. "Lollipop Yellow" opaque case; see #3 for case.

5. Hampden — Lucite, Loose Powder Compact. Raspberry faceted domed case, mirrored lid effect with interior double mirror, coin purse closure, no case identification, puff with logo, case glued mirror, 4"dia x ¾". Ref: 1945 ad. $50.00 – $65.00.

Ziegfeld Girl

PRESENTS

Show girl

Showgirl...streamlined, metal-banded compact whose design and impressive beauty mark it so definitely a creation of Ziegfeld Girl— color stylists and fine craftsmen in plastics. At better stores everywhere, in Oriental Sapphire, California Gold, Mint Frappe, Tortoise, Lollipop Yellow, Wild Raspberry, Jet. $2.95.*

*Slightly higher in Canada, and other countries.
© 1946, ALLIED PLASTICS COMPANY

Vogue, 1946

1
2
3

1. Revell Plastics — Plastic, Loose Powder Compact. Flapjack, mock tortoise shell case, no case identification, puff and box with logoes: "Soubrette," box also has "Revell," case glued mirror, 5"dia x ½". $75.00 – $100.00.

2. Patricia Page Fifth Avenue — Lucite, Loose Powder Compact. Mock tortoise shell case, no case identification, interior puff and box with logos, model: #1300 — Shell, case glued mirror, 4" x 3¼" x ½". $125.00 – $150.00

Another example of high style design in a difficult material. Using the intrinsic best of Lucite the case has a skillful marquetry effect framed with a darker scalloped border. A touch of metal in the hinge and pushpiece gives the case deserved quality.

3. Unmarked — Lucite, Loose Powder Compact. Mock tortoise shell case, case glued mirror, 3¼"sq x ⅝". $65.00 – $90.00.

Eleanor Hamlin

designs her new compacts in the most precious of plastics—Plexiglas. She gives you your choice of jewel colors—aquamari
coral, topaz, amethyst. Three dollars at your favorite store or write Mavco, Fourteen East Thirty-Eighth Street, New York City. Jewels by Tri

Vogue, 1945

1   3
2

1. Mavco — Plexiglas, Loose Powder Compact. Flapjack, aquamarine mottled case, no case identification, puff with logo, case glued mirror, 5"dia x ½". Ref: 1944 and 1945 Ads. $65.00 – $80.00.

The provenance on this case gets a little confusing. Mavco had the 1944 ad. However, in the 1945 ad designer Eleanor Hamlin's name is featured over Mavco with her "new" compacts. There is no discernable difference in the cases. Also Hamlin's signature is prominently featured in #3, but #1 has no identification. A good guess is this is the 1944 model.

2. Unmarked — Lucite, Loose Powder Compact. Petticoat, apricot case with affixed goldtone filigree circle framing lid mounted faux faceted sapphire, red backing of interior mirror acts as exterior ground, case glued mirror, 4½" x 4" x ¾". $150.00 – $175.00.

3. Mavco — Plexiglas, Loose Powder Compact. Flapjack, yellow translucent faceted case, double interior mirror acting as exterior lid accent, case and puff signed: Eleanor Hamlin/Mavco, framed mirror, 4"dia x ¾". $75.00 – $90.00.

Another quirk — see page 196, #5 for a near double to this case by Hampden. The difference is the flattened case of the Mavco and all-around edge faceting. Also the Mavco has a spring operated pushpiece — Hampden has a coin purse closure.

Mavco's

AMERICAN BEAUTY
COMPACTS IN CLOUD LIGHT PLEXIGLAS

In the vanguard of Fall's most provocative beauty accomplices are these to-be-treasured, mammoth, wafer-thin compacts.

Cloud-light, they're fashioned of Plexiglas* valiantly seeing active service in the gun turrets of our glorious air force.

In Mavco's American Beauty compact, Plexiglas also proves of enduring quality — catching and returning endless reflections of your loveliness. . . .

About $3 — at finer stores everywhere. Complete with leakproof sifter; lake-clear beveled mirror; "air-borne" puff. Plain or monogrammed at additional cost.

*Plexiglas is a Rohm & Haas product

Mavco COMPACTS...CIGARET CASES

14 EAST 38TH STREET • NEW YORK 16, N. Y.

Vogue, 1944

1   2
          3

1. Ziegfeld Petticoat Girl — Plastic, Loose Powder Compact. Mock tortoise shell scalloped case, puff with logo, case signed, case glued mirror, 4"sq x ⅜". Ref: 1945 ad. $65.00 – $80.00.

See the ad for all the various "Girls" cases. Florenz Ziegfeld died in 1932, but Hollywood continued to revive him until 1945 when MGM reeled out the final all-singing, all-dancing "Follies" film. These cases might have been an attempt to ride the movie's publicity coat tails. Nobody had better publicity coat tails than MGM.

2. Mavco — Plexiglas, Loose Powder Compact. Flapjack, clear case with gold foil snowflake interior mirror backing, case, pouch and box signed: "Eleanor Hamlin/Mavco, Model: #902 — Gold," case glued mirror, 5"dia x ½". Ref: 1945 ad (var). $100.00 – $125.00.

3. Unmarked — Plastic, Loose Powder Compact. Flapjack, amber domed case with molded sunburst and floral lid design, ribbed border, blue and silver foil sticker on mirror: "Sterling Silver Catches," case glued mirror, 4"dia x ¾". $125.00 – $150.00.

Liberty, 1926

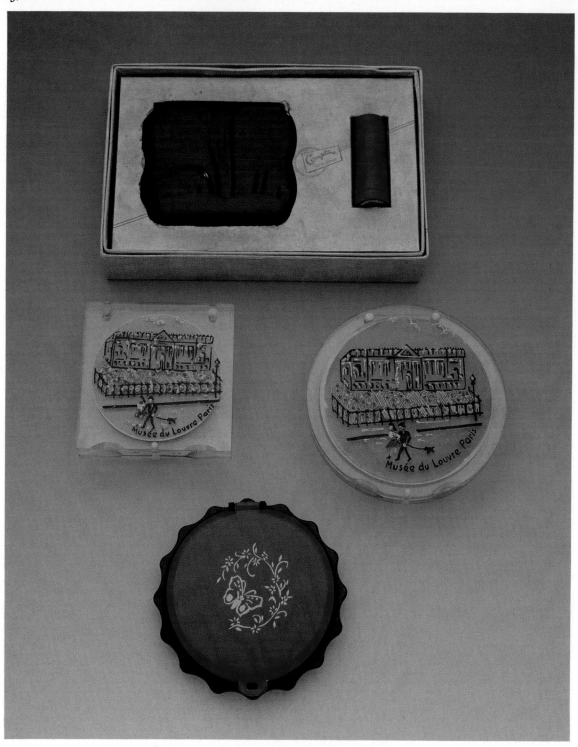

1
2   4
3

1. Comptone Fifth Avenue — Plastic, Boxed Set.
Blue loose powder compact with ruffled purse-like lid, red plastic/cardboard lipstick tube, no case identification, box and puff with logos, paper label on lipstick, case glued mirror, 3¼" x 2¾" x ⅝" (compact). $100.00 – $125.00.

2. Bell Deluxe — Lucite, Loose Powder Compact.
Clear case with hand-painted Paris scene on interior mirror aqua backing, puff with logo, case glued mirror, 3"sq x ½". $65.00 – $80.00.

3. Zell — Plastic, Loose Powder Compact. Blue case with cog wheel rim, red lid with transfer butterfly and floral spray, no case identification, puff with logo, case glued mirror, 3¼"dia x ¾". $50.00 – $65.00.

4. Bell Deluxe — Lucite, Loose Powder Compact.
Clear case with hand-painted Paris scene on interior mirror, blue backing, puff with logo, case glued mirror, 3⅞"dia x ½". $75.00 – $90.00.

```
1       3       5
2       4       6
                7
```

1. Avon — Plastic, Pressed Powder Vanity Case.
Green marbled "Cigarette Box" case with slide-out
bottom compartment, pop-up case glued mirror,
pressed rouge, brush with logo, case label, 3¼" x 2½" x
¾". $45.00 – $60.00.

2. Unmarked — Plastic, Loose Powder Compact.
Flattened bolster, ivory case with blue lid inset, hand
painted lid — palm trees and surf, "Daytona Beach,
Fla," case glued mirror, 3¼" x 2¼" x ¾". $25.00 –
$40.00.

*These cases (see #7) are almost always badly warped.
Be very careful of mirror on opening. The low end in
WWII non-metal quality and included for total
range of collection plastics.*

3. N
LOC — Bakelite, Loose Powder Compact.
R
Screw top, black case, red etched lid with circle motif
of hansom cab with horse and driver, case signed,
metallic mirror, 2½"dia x ½". $75.00 – $100.00.

4. Unmarked #3 with Domed Cushion Case. (No flat
surface for logo in bottom of powder well,) white
femme Art Deco lid silhouette. $125.00 – $150.00.

5. Same as #3 with all black case.

*Inspect carefully before buying, the lids have a ten-
dency toward cracks or hairline splits.*

6. Polly Bergen — Plastic, Pressed Powder Compact.
Purple faint marbled case with affixed goldtone turtle
lid bijou, gilt foil back label, puff with logo, case
framed mirror, 3¼" x 2½" x ⅝". $25.00 – $40.00.

*The turtle lid ornament was the Polly Bergen cos-
metic line's logo: La Tortue.*

7. Same as #2 with reverse case coloring and no paint-
ing. $20.00 – $35.00.

1
2   4
           3   5
                      6

1. Langlois — Plastic, Loose Powder Boudoir Compact. Clear case with ribbed flanged flat bottom, blue spangled interior mirror backing for lid accent, interior powder well paper backing — shown: "Cara Nome," case glued mirror, 3½"dia x ¾". $40.00 – $60.00.

With its bottom flanges and sharp points, this case was obviously not meant to be carried in a purse. Langlois was a big promoter of Christmas gift sets, and this might have been part of one featuring dressing table items.

2. Mavco — Lucite, Loose Powder Compact. Clear case with blue pearlized embossed interior mirror backing for lid accent, no case identification, box and pouch with logo, case glued mirror, 3⅞"dia x ½". Ref: 1944 ad (var). $65.00 – $80.00.

Mavco used both Lucite and Plexiglas in their advertising, labeled as "Cloud Light Plexiglas" and "Lovely Lucite." The surprise is both examples are very 'plastic' looking — not much quality, thin, and no clarity.

3. Victoria Vogue — Plastic, Loose Powder Box. This was either a container for just a puff, or was a craft item for individual workmanship (see #6).

4. Unmarked — Plastic, Loose Powder Compact. Clear case, with pale yellow marbled interior mirror backing for lid accent, case glued mirror, 3" x 2½" x ½". $25.00 – $40.00.

5. Fuller — Celluloid, Loose Powder Compact. Green Pearloid case with Ivorene interior, comb compartment on reverse, case signed, framed mirror, 2¼" x 2¼" x ½", Pat. 1925. $50.00 – $65.00.

6. Victoria Vogue — Plastic, Loose Powder Compact. Clear case, double velour puff with hand crocheted Eastern Star insignia, case signed, loose celluloid backed oval mirror, 3"dia x ¾". Rare.

Someone took care to assemble this little one of a kind item. Totally impractical with no powder control, maybe it was meant to be cherished, not used.

206

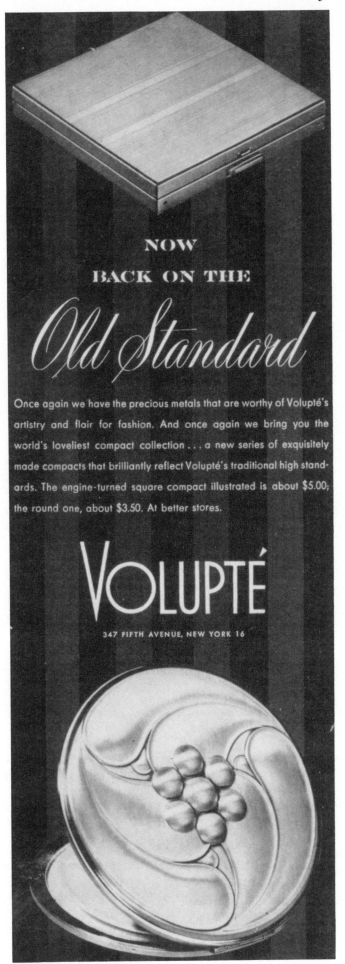

NOW
BACK ON THE
Old Standard

Once again we have the precious metals that are worthy of Volupté's artistry and flair for fashion. And once again we bring you the world's loveliest compact collection . . . a new series of exquisitely made compacts that brilliantly reflect Volupté's traditional high standards. The engine-turned square compact illustrated is about $5.00; the round one, about $3.50. At better stores.

VOLUPTÉ

347 FIFTH AVENUE, NEW YORK 16

Vogue, 1946

Chapter Five

SOUVENIRS, NOVELTIES & WHIMSIES

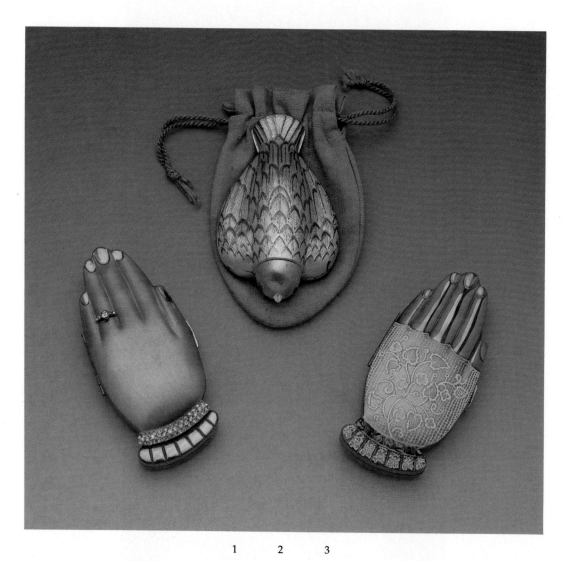

1   2   3

1. Volupté — Goldtone, Loose Powder Hand Compact. Brushed finish, Golden Gesture, case with faux gemstone "engagement" ring and bracelet, puff with logo, case signed, case glued mirror, 4⅝" x 2" x ¾". Ref: 1946 Ad. Rare.

2. Elgin American — Silvertone, Loose Powder Vanity Case; Bird-In-Hand. Case signed by Dali, brushed finish with goldtone highlights, aqua faille drawstring pouch, lipstick, pill compartment, puff with logo, case signed, framed mirror, 4½" x 2½" x 1¼". Ref: 1951 Ad. Very rare.

3. Volupté — Goldtone, Loose Powder Hand Compact. Brushed finish, Nineties Mitt, case with white enameled faux lace mitt with multicolor enameled bracelet, puff with logo, case signed, case glued mirror, 4⅝" x 2" x ¾". Ref: 1947 Ad. $225.00 – $250.00.

The Volupté Hand compact is truly a whimsy — a totally different and unexpected use of design for a compact. The ad does not mention the artist/designer; however, patent papers do: Ruth Warner Mason. The case had one major problem; it dents easily, and dents severely affect the value. As a collection matures in quality, adding a dented case should not be considered.

"...POTENTIAL PURCHASERS MAY INCLUDE DOWAGERS AND CHORUS GIRLS, DEBUTANTES AND STENOGRAPHERS. IT IS IMPOSSIBLE TO PLEASE THEM ALL WITH ONE DESIGN OF COMPACT...WE MUST PRESENT THEM WITH A WIDE VARIETY OF CONTAINERS."

THE AMERICAN PERFUMER
MAY 1931

In 1931 the prophet who wrote the above quote could not have conceived to what reaches of imagination compact case designers eventually achieved. Some were gems of inventiveness and very successful and some were just plain dumb. This chapter attempts to sort out three basic categories of the non-conforming case: souvenirs, novelties, and whimsies.

The souvenir cases are obvious and self-explanatory, namely, a case that was bought to sustain good or bad memories of a visit, event, or commemoration. Some cases were made for souvenir sales, and others were created by using decals, attached emblems or insignia, and maybe something as simple as a scratched in or painted on name. Scenes of places are the most popular. With the completion of the Empire State Building in New York City and the opening of its observation deck, it became a favorite subject for the souvenir compact.

Means of transportation merited special emphasis. The mighty ocean passenger liners are featured on cases, probably purchased in the ship gift shops, and proudly flashed to envious friends on landing. Trains, buses and planes were not able to supply such souvenirs, unless there was some adjunct reason for the case being offered. The world's fairs dominated the souvenir market and lured the top manufacturers, such as Evans and Elgin, into the game. These cases are very well made, but the majority are from unknown makers and are more miss than hit on quality. The value is regulated by other collectors who might be interested in the event depicted rather than the case itself.

The second category of novelties is wide open and truly full of wit and ingenuity. The key is — they usually *do* something. From music boxes, time keepers, and mirror cleaners to hidden compartments and piggy banks, each one is a surprise. Some surprise by a different shape, others like to camouflage their tricks. Most of the novelties, however, were serious workers with a purpose. The Volupté Whisk-er brush, the Lin-Bren coin purse, the powder control cases, all had functions to perform.

Others have intrinsic uses that combine features giving the case a double life. Chains that convert cases to necklaces or bracelets and clip backings for clothing attachment move the case into an article of jewelry. And finally the coy ones that hide their true nature either with a twist in materials or hand-made adaptations, or play at pretend: a cue ball, a game, a pocket watch, a flower basket. Each time one of these pixies is given a smile, listen in return for a ghostly tee-hee.

Some whimsy cases have notoriety. Mention the Bird, or the Hand, and recognition is immediate. One or two companies made a habit of offering bizarre designs. Volupté tried to market a design line in the fifties called "Collector's Items." They deliberately ignored the cosmetic aspects and attempted to create a collectible — ahead of their time, little did they realize how successful these avant-garde cases would become.

Whimsies are defined as "An odd fancy, curious, quaint or fanciful, a whim." This applies to those compact cases that assume a different appearance or shape, defying the conventional. Unlike the novelties, they do not have a sense of humor and are rather smug in their position of collecting eminence. This smugness is skin deep as they suffer from forced design. Finishes and skilled enameling were not a priority; and casework on the Hand, for example, lacks structure and tempts dents. The Bird has timorous springs, and Volupté's Vanity top is mirrored metal that also reflects fingerprints and scrapes. But like a glittering pop star, they are now a status symbol in any compact collection.

Not all whimsies are this over refined, Dorothy Gray's lovely Picture Hats are sturdy and have survived the years with grace. Coty gave case quality, but shaved it a bit on interiors. The truly two-faced manufacturer is Richard Hudnut. The stunning double profile and portrait Art Deco vanities personify this company's commitment to contemporary art. Noted for their Art Nouveau Three Flowers logo, they abruptly turned as the times turned to cubism. It must have been a fast turn, since the face cases lack any semblance of quality both in case structure and enameling. But Hudnut continued to market the highest quality in their more conventional cases by giving them showcase boxes and signed artist ads, apparently using double standards, did not feature the faces. The faces should be included in any serious collection for their bold art — warts and all.

All three categories in this chapter stand tall; each has collecting merit. Novelties will continue to expand as more documentation occurs, and who knows what undiscovered compact a nameless designer on a good day conjured up for his company. Or what event was so important — locally — that a hot shot souvenir seller made it immortal on a lowly compact. The Bird will continue to fly out of the reach of many, and the Hand will halt some collectors on price, but as Scarlett said: "Tomorrow is another day..." and another compact collectible show.

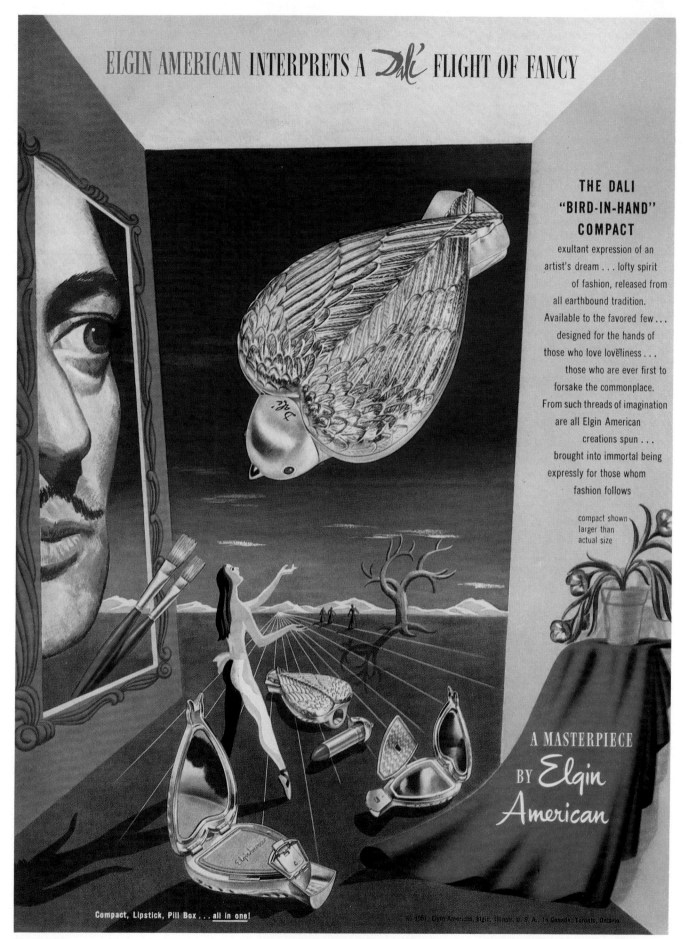

Golden Gesture

Pure phantasy, inspired by the fabulous art of the East.
Volupté creates unique Hand Compacts—
unusual fashion accessories, unadorned or jewel-studded.
Compacts shown from about 5.00 to 30.00.*
Others to 14 karat gold at 500.00.*

*SUBJECT TO FEDERAL TAX

Hand Compacts by VOLUPTÉ

Harper's Bazaar, 1946

Vogue, 1943

1. Unmarked — Silvertone, Pressed Powder Compact. Engine-turned case with attached shield of Ohio: State Capitol, Columbus, Ohio, State House depicted, framed mirror, 1⅞"octagon x ½". $50.00 – $65.00.

2. Unmarked — Silvertone, Pressed Powder Compact. Celluloid topped lid with view, of Old Faithful, Yellowstone National Park, framed mirror, 1⅞"dia x ⅜". $35.00 – $50.00.

3. Unmarked — Silvertone, Loose Powder Compact. Celluloid topped lid with view of Washington Mansion, Mount Vernon, Virginia, red enameled border, metallic mirror, 2"sq x ½". $35.00 – $50.00.

4. Pilcher — Goldtone, Loose Powder Compact. Celluloid attached lid plaque with Empire State Building-New York City decal, no case identification, signed box, framed mirror, 3½" x 2⅜" x ⅜". $100.00 – $125.00.

5. Unmarked — Silvertone, Loose Powder Compact. Celluloid topped lid with view of Empire State Building, New York and Skyline, black enameled border, metallic mirror, 2"sq x ½". $50.00 – $75.00.

6. Chez Re Lew — Goldtone, Pressed Powder Vanity Case. Affixed insignia of Deshler Wallick Hotel, Columbus, Ohio, engine-turned border, case signed, framed mirror, 2"dia x ½". Rare.

The enameled crest of this souvenir case is incorrect. The wording reads Deshler & Wallick Hotels. There was only one hotel and no "&." The rouge compartment is part of the mirror framing.

7. Unmarked — Goldtone, Pressed Powder Compact. Rivet attached blue opaque plastic disk with inset rhinestones, "Empire State Building NY," framed mirror, 2"dia x ½". $50.00 – $65.00.

This case and #6 have the same exterior case. However, this case has adaptions for a wrist chain and tassel and is unsigned.

8. Unmarked — Silvertone, Loose Powder Compact. Celluloid topped lid with view of Grand Canyon National Park, with plains Indian in bonnet headdress, white enameled border, metallic mirror, 2"sq x ½". $50.00 – $65.00.

1
2   6
3   4   7
  5   8

```
1        3        5
2        4        6
```

1. Unmarked — Goldtone, Pressed Powder Compact. Brushed finish with lid inset: Comprimette Oriental Gouraud — Ferd. T. Hopkins & Son, New York, Paris, Montreal, no date, lotus wreath border, framed mirror, 2½"dia x ⅜". $100.00 – $125.00.

2. Unmarked — Ivorene, Loose Powder Compact. Ivory case with celluloid topped lid paper, eighteenth century couple and legend: Gallipolis 1730 – 1940 — Sesqui-Centennial, goldtone laurel wreath border, reverse has a large dimple (?), case framed mirror, 2½"sq x ⅜". $125.00 – $150.00.

Gallipolis is an early Ohio town on the Ohio River.

3. Unmarked — Silvertone, Loose Powder Vanity Case. Champlevé white enamel lid with bas-relief Chicago skyline, lid legend: World's Fair Chicago 1933 – 1934, hinged double metallic mirrors, 2½" x 1⅝" x ⅜". $125.00 – $150.00.

4. Elgin American — Goldtone, Loose Powder Vanity Case. Spearhead, maroon enameled case, affixed lid bijou of Washington D.C. Cherry Blossom Festival, pink surround capitol building inset with rhinestones, creme rouge, puff with logo, case signed, framed mirror, 4½" x 2" x ¾". $150.00 – $175.00.

5. Girey — Goldtone, Loose Powder Vanity Case. Kamra with green Pearloid case and champlevé green lid enamel, bas-relief scene: Hall of Science — A Century of Progress — Chicago World's Fair 1933, powder puff with logo, case signed, framed mirror, 2¾" x 1¾" x ⅜". $100.00 – $125.00.

6. Evans — Silvertone, Loose Powder Vanity Case. Black enameled case with champlevé enamel inset lid scene in bas-relief of comet tails encircling globe, legend: World's Fair — A Century of Progress 1934, rouge embossed: Mayfair, case signed, hinged double metallic mirrors, 2¼"sq x ⅜". $125.00 – $150.00.

It is unusual to find a Fair design without a featured building or skyline. However, the Fair had no one motif or logo similar to the 1939 – 40 New York World's Fair Trylon and Perisphere icons.

The Chicago World's Fair of 1933-34 was comparable to the 1851 Great Exhibition of London and the 1925 Paris Exposition Des Arts Decoratif in which all three events changed the way the world looked. From locomotives to jewelry each exhibit forced new thinking in artistic and industrial design. We are still being shaped by the Chicago legacy.

```
        1       3       6
        2       4       7
                5
```

1. Elgin American — Goldtone, Loose Powder Compact. Multi-enameled map of Arizona lid motif, puff with logo, case signed, framed mirror, 2¾"sq x ¼". $45.00 – $60.00.

2. Unmarked — Bi-Tone, Loose Powder Compact. Silvertone case with goldtone lid accents: New York City scenes and buildings, (U.N. Building/Post WWII), case glued mirror, 2¾" x 2⅜" x ½". $30.00 – $45.00.

3. Elgin American — Goldtone, Loose Powder Compact. American Passenger liner: S.S. Constitution, engraved on ribbed lid, pouch and puff with logo: American Beauty, case signed, framed mirror. 2¾"sq x ¼". Rare.

On April 4, 1956, the American passenger liner S.S. Constitution left New York harbor for Monaco carrying 66 members of Grace Kelly's wedding party. Arriving in Monte Carlo on April 12th, the ship was circled by the royal yacht, Deo Juvante, piloted by His Serene Highness Prince Rainier III of Monaco. The liner was mothballed in the late sixties.

4. Stratton — Goldtone, Loose Powder Compact. British Passenger liner: R.M.S. Franconia, white enameled lid with black silhouette, scrolled case edging with star motif on reverse, black pouch, puff and box with logo, case signed, framed mirror with automatic powder door opener instructions, 3"dia x ½". $65.00 – $80.00.

5. Van-Ace Fifth Avenue — Goldtone, Loose Powder Compact. Embossed case with attached rhinestone enhanced Statue of Liberty New York on lid, floral embellishments, puff with logo, case signed, framed mirror, 3½" x 2¼" x ½". $50.00 – $75.00.

6. Zell Fifth Avenue — Goldtone, Loose Powder Compact. Black and white photo paper glued to lid, legend: "The Waltz By Arthur Murray Dancers," ribbed reverse, no case identification but Zell Acanthus motif on powder door and pearlized liner, puff with logo, case glued mirror, 2¾"sq x ⅜". $150.00 – $175.00.

Arthur Murray and his wife as his partner were a very popular ballroom dance act. They were more famous as dance studio entrepreneurs. Their students also became an act. The paper lid scene on this case has no protective coating, hence the high evaluation. Condition not rarity calls this figure.

7. Wadsworth — Goldtone, Loose Powder Compact. Brushed silvertone lid finish with highlighted map of West Virginia, with some surrounding cities, reverse engraved: State Convention Morgantown, WV 1950, puff with logo, case signed, case glued mirror, 3"sq x ⅜". $35.00 – $50.00.

1	3
2	4
	5

1. Rex Fifth Avenue — Goldtone, Loose Powder Compact. Novelty cartoon lid design signed by Hilda Terry, no case identification puff with logo, case glued mirror, 3½"dia x ⅜". $75.00 – $100.00.

Artist Hilda Terry in the fifties had a very popular magazine cartoon series on American teenagers.

2. Lady Vanity — Goldtone, Loose Powder Compact. Horseshoe, novelty cartoon lid design signed by artist Annette Honeywell, slight pebble case finish, talon zipper closure, snakeskin hinge, Ivorene interior, no case identification, puff with logo, case glued mirror, 3¾" x 3¼" x ½". $75.00 – $100.00.

The connection between the chasing and chased chickens and the Hollywood & Vine sign must be a local Los Angeles joke.

3. Lady Vanity — Goldtone, Loose Powder Compact. Dolly on a carousel horse (same as #2).

4. Columbia Fifth Avenue — Goldtone, Loose Powder Compact. Novelty lid transfer drawings of the Dior Look wasp-waist mannequin and assorted umbrellas, case signed, case glued mirror, 2¾"sq x ⅜". $50.00 – $75.00.

The waist and hemline tells it all. It is post WWII.

5. Rex Fifth Avenue — Goldtone, Loose Powder Compact. Novelty cartoon lid design of teenagers in a jalopy signed by artist Hilda Terry, celluloid shield, no case identification, puff with logo, case glued mirror, 2¾"dia x ⅝". $75.00 – $100.00.

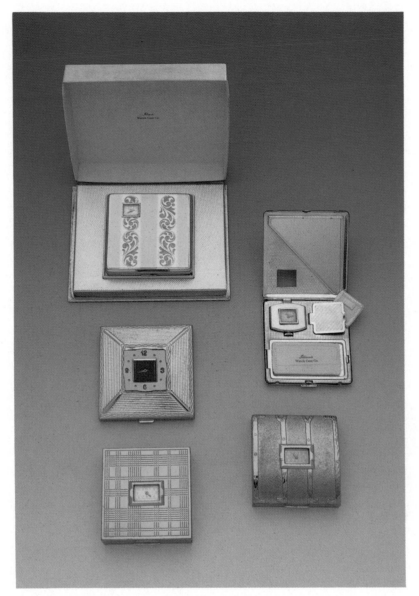

1 4
2 5
3

1. Illinois Watch Case Co. — Goldtone, Loose Powder Vanity Case. Hand chased scrolled lid bands with cut out case for viewing interior Weldwood watch, gold foil and ivory presentation box with guarantee and instructions, puffs and pouch with logos, signed case, triangular framed mirror, see #4 open, 2¾"sq x ½" (case). $175.00 – $200.00.

2. Amere — Bimetal, Loose Powder Compact. Travel clock case with hinged black clock face with logo, numerals on clock frame, ribbed silvertone stepped lid shoulders, incised goldtone borders, and ribbed reverse, case signed: Made in Switzerland, framed mirror, 3"sq x ¾". $150.00 – $175.00.

3. Evans — Goldtone, Loose Powder Compact. Embossed plaid case: The Patrician, with watch lid inset, ribbed sides, puff with logo, case signed, double

hinged metallic mirrors, 2½"sq x ¾", 1948 ad (var). $125.00 – $150.00.

The use of the double hinged metallic lid mirrors is an odd design for access to the watch. As opposed to Elgin's slim case, with its boxy mid case opening, this Evans remains one of the rare examples of wasted space in a compact. The watch is centered in the lid compartment, and there is no interior catch on the hinged mirror divider.

4. Illinois Watch Case Co. Silvertone, Loose Powder Vanity. See #1 for goldtone closed case.

5. Evans — Goldtone, Loose Powder Compact. Luggage styled case with embossed straps and watch lid inset, domed top and ribbed reverse; see #3 for interior information, 2½"sq x ¾". $150.00 – $175.00.

1

2   4

3   5

1. Volupté — Goldtone, Loose Powder Vanity Case. Music box, brushed case finish with attached flying pegasus lid ornament, plays: *In My Merry Oldsmobile*, exterior lipstick acts as Lip-Lock closure, puff and box with logos, case signed, framed mirror, 3¼" x 2¼" x ¾", 1949 ad. $150.00 – $175.00.

2. Elgin American — Goldtone, Loose Powder Compact. Music box, contrasting finishes with lid incised musical instruments, paper mirror sticker: *Brahms Waltzer* (typo), puff and pouch with logos, case signed, case glued mirror, 2¾" x 1¾" x ¾", 1953 ad. $125.00 – $150.00.

3. Elgin American — Goldtone, Loose Powder Compact. Music box, Rococo case with musical lyre clo-

sure, plays *The Anniversary Waltz*, black faille slipcase, puff with logo, case signed, case glued mirror, 2¾" x 1¾" x ⅝", 1953 ad. $125.00 – $150.00.

4. Clover — Goldtone, Loose Powder Compact. Music box, damascene oriental landscape scene with water wheel and artist signed, Sankyo musical movement, unidentified tune, puff and box with logos, case signed, framed mirror, 3⅜" x 2⅜" x ¾". $150.00 – $175.00.

5. AGME — Goldtone, Loose Powder Compact. Music box, silvertone engine-turned lid inset, plays: *La Vie En Rose,* case signed: "Made in Switzerland," framed mirror, 3¼" x 2¼" x ⅝". $150.00 – $175.00.

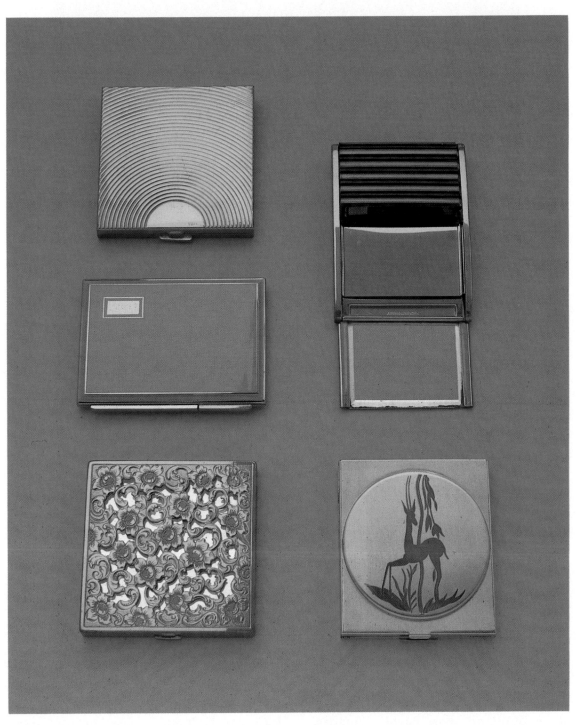

1
2
3
4
5

1
2
3
4

1. Volupté — Goldtone, Loose Powder Compact. "Turnabout" powder control case; see #2 closed.

2. Volupté — Goldtone, Loose Powder Compact. "Turnabout" powder control case, with revolving mirror lid, and ribbed framing, puff with logo, case signed; see #1 nopen, 2⅞"sq x ½". Ref: 1950 ad. $100.00 – $125.00.

3. Coty — Goldtone, Loose Powder Compact. See page 223, #3 closed.

4. Unmarked — Goldtone, Loose Powder Compact. Tambour case opener with black and gold plastic slats, tray mirror, flip-up goldtone interior powder well cover, case signed: "Made in Germany," side framed mirror; see page 223, #4 open, 3¼" x 2⅜" x ½". $125.00 – $150.00.

Now!

THE COMPACT THAT TURNS ITSELF

INSIDE-OUT... FOR BEAUTY'S SAKE!

TURNABOUT
by VOLUPTÉ

Closed, the mirror-top beautifies your compact . . . then

merrily whirls inside as you open the compact . . .

and gives you a clear, clean view to beautify *you!* And the

merry-go-round mirror *never becomes clouded with powder!*

This exciting talk-maker is Volupté's

newest idea . . . in a host of lovely designs, $5 to $7.50.

a genuine
Collector's Item
by
VOLUPTÉ

Volupté Inc.
347 Fifth Avenue
New York 16

| COMPACTS
| CIGARETTE CASES
| LIGHTERS
| CARRYALLS
| PILL BOXES
| ATOMIZERS

Vogue, 1950

1
2

3
4
5

1. Lin-Bren — Leather, Loose Powder Compact.
Black Moroccan leather case, lid coin purse with black moiré logo on liner, chevron goldtone flap snap, case slide closure, puff with logo, case signed, framed mirror, 3½"sq x ¾". $75.00 – $100.00.

2. Nite-Glow — Goldtone, Loose Powder Compact.
Flashlight case; see #4 and #5 closed.

3. Henriette — Goldtone, Loose Powder Combination Case. Double access, black enameled lid with circular engine-turned motif, case has bottom drawer with hinged flap opener, case signed, framed mirror, 3"sq x ¾". $65.00 – $90.00.

Henriette cases always seem to need just one more step to make their designs work, i.e., the 'bellows'

case, and this one. The drawer has no closure and gaps open with ease. It could hold cigarettes, keys, matches, or currency (no lipsticks or lighters) but keeping anything in the drawer is the rub. The only safe bet would be a folded handkerchief.

4. Nite-Glow — Goldtone, Loose Powder Compact.
Flashlight, red enameled case, thumb-lift lid has interior reflective mirrored surface, slot for interior light beam from tiny lightbulb, battery and mechanics recessed in case with powder well, case signed; see #2 open, 2¾" x 2" x ⅝". $75.00 – $100.00.

5. Nite-Glow — Goldtone, Loose Powder Compact.
Flashlight case, green enameling; see #2 and #4.

```
1   3   5  6
  2    4    7
```

1. Dorothy Gray — Silvertone, Loose Powder Compact. See #3 closed.

2. Nildé — Silvertone, Loose Powder Compact. Mechanical, Art Moderne lid motif (view in #1 mirror), metallic mirrored spring plate interior lid and spring mounted knurled puff well, thick felt puff acts as gasket, sliding interior panel exposes powder well, case signed: "Nildé Paris," world patent information on reverse, 2¼" x 2" x ½". $150.00 – $175.00.

Too difficult to describe the amazing mechanics of this case. The powder control is absolute with not a wisp of roaming loose powder.

3. Dorothy Gray — Silvertone, Loose Powder Compact. Mechanical, black and ivory enameled lid striping with horizontal deep ribbing, case has lid activated powder grater that moves vertically to release powder, case has bottom door for loose powder refills, case signed, metallic mirror, see #1 open, 2" x 1¾" x ½". $75.00 – $90.00.

Most compact designers assumed that every woman had a metal nail file which could be used as a vanity case or compact handy-dandy maintenance tool. Mainly used to ladle loose powder from box to case, the nail file was also needed to gain access to powder

storage such as #3. Many compacts bear the scars and scratches of a carelessly wielded metal nail file.

4. Myrra — Silvertone, Loose Powder Compact. Mechanical, blue enameled case with exterior blue silk tasseled ring mounted on lever which activates an interior rotating powder well lid, case signed: "Myrra Paris, Made In France," metallic mirror, 2"sq x ½". $125.00 – $150.00.

5. Unmarked — Silvertone, Loose Powder Dress Clip Compact. Black enameled lid with engraved: "KKK," attached dress clip on reverse, metallic mirror, 1⅝"dia x ¼". Very rare.

6. Unmarked — Silvertone, Loose Powder Compact. Etched lid design of flower basket in the Langlois & Houbigant style, blue and gray silk tassel attached to exterior flange for sliding tray compartment, wire mesh powder screen, case signed: "Made In Japan," spring hinged mirror, 2¼" x 1¾" x ½". $65.00 – $80.00.

7. Kigu — Goldtone, Loose Powder Portrait Compact. Mechanical, hinged blue metallic lid heart with Marcasite bow knot bijou, (view in #6 mirror), heart opens by sliding pressure, framed oval portrait with logo, contrasting lacquer lid design, puff with logo, no case identification, framed mirror, 3"dia x ¾". $50.00 – $65.00.

1
2

3
4

5

1. Unmarked — Goldtone, Loose Powder Mesh Compact and Black Beaded Ivory Kid Lined Pouch with Snap Flap Carrier. Embossed compact lid design of Minstrel and His Lady, framed mirror. Compact — 2½"dia x ½". $45.00 – $60.00. With pouch — 4" x 3¾", set. $75.00 – $100.00.

All the items on this page are arranged marriages, joined as gifts or combined for a special occasion. The pairing of the dissimilar pouches and compacts enhances both, and in these examples the marriage was a happy one. The values are only for suitably mated sets — the cases must be a perfect fit and compatible design.

2. Quinlan — 24KT Goldplate, Loose Powder Compact and White Beaded Rayon Lined Pouch with Snap Flap Carrier. Embossed compact lid fleur de lis design, case signed, framed whimror. Compact — 3"dia x ⅜". $75.00 – $100.00. With pouch — 4"dia. Set: $125.00 – $150.00.

3. Unmarked — Silvertone, Shield Vanity Case and Rose Brocade Chinese Silk Covered Case with Crocheted Handle. See page 76, #1 for vanity case. Fabric case has ivory silk interior with framed mirror and pocket for vanity case, slip thong closure of ivory, fabric case — 3½" x 3¼" x 1¾". Set: $100.00 – $125.00.

4. Cheramy — Silvertone, Pressed Powder Vanity Case and Beaded "Pansy" Gold Silk Lined Pouch with Wrist Strap. Engine-turned case, puffs with logo, case signed, sliding framed mirror, compact — 2"dia x ⅝", $45.00 – $60.00. With pouch — 3¼"dia, set: $75.00 – $100.00.

5. Helena Rubinstein — Minute Make-Up Vanity Case and Black Beaded Pouch with Embroidered Flowers. Black satin lined and label: "Made In Belgium," large snap flap closure; see page 116, #4 for vanity case, beaded case — 3" x 2¼" x 1". Set: $175.00 – $200.00.

228

```
        1    3
        2    4
             5        6
```

1. F. Uhrey & Co. — Cardboard, Pressed Rouge Compact. Lavender box with gilt legend: De Luxe Parfumerie De Paris, handmade fleece puff with blue silk and Ivorene cap/ring, paper framed mirror, 1⅝"octagon x 1". Rare.

This is not a refill but a compact, since it is fitted with a small mirror. It leans towards the "Boudoir Compact" category.

2. Unmarked — Beaded, Powder Puff Pouch. Glass beaded "Pansy" pouch with ivory kid lining, goldtone backed hand mirror, handmade fleece and pink silk puff, 3"dia. $100.00 – $125.00.

These pansy pouches were a commercial item and used for a quick touch at a shiny nose after an active dance. They were not made to hold powder.

3. Unmarked — Ivory, Loose Powder Compact. Solid block of ivory with lid carving of cherry blossoms, goldtone interior fittings and mirror framing, 2¾" x 2" x ⅝". $125.00 – $150.00.

4. Houbigant — Tortoise Shell, Pressed Powder Vanity Case. Tortoise shell case, powder well with logo: France, lipstick compartment, case glued mirror, 2¼ x 2⅛" x ⅝". $125.00 – $150.00.

5. Herbert Roystone Co. — Brass, Loose Powder Compact. "Sport" model with lid transfer of eighteenth century pair, reverse has logo: L'Amé — La-May Compact, "Pat. Aug. '23, '21," and touting more expensive case of German silver, framed mirror, 2½"dia x ½". Ref: 1927 ad. $40.00 – $60.00.

6. The Cupid Puff — Brass, Loose Powder Tin. Crimped edged case made from spent ammo cartridge with highly embossed lid design of cupid and rococo border, powder filled blue silk topped puff, pin and black ink stenciled box lid, case has no mirror, case — 1¾"dia x ⅝", box — 2"sq x ⅞". Set: Very rare.

Legend on this set says it was made by WWI German prisoners of war and interned in France for souvenir sale to the newly arriving American Expeditionary Forces. Making souvenir items out of munition shells, or anything else that was salvageable, has a long wartime tradition.

1		5
2	4	6
3		7

1. Pitman & Keeler — Goldtone, Combination Set. Wine velvet and gold foil presentation box with expansion bracelet and vanity case, monogrammed heart motif, case has engine-turned interior with hinged double metallic mirrors, no case identification, bracelet and box signed, case — 2½" x 2¼" x ½", box — 7" x 3½" x 1⅜". Set: $150.00 – $175.00.

Unmarked vanity case has strong La Mode design flavor.

2. Elgin American Lipstick Case. See #3.

3. Elgin American — Silvertone, Combination Set. "Family Tree" glossy goldtone lid and lipstick accent, compact has papers, lipstick case has pop-up mirror and aqua faille drawstring pouch, puff and pouches with logos, presentation box and cases signed, framed mirror, compact — 2¾"sq x ⅜". Ref: 1951 ad, lipstick — 2¼"sq x ⅝". Set: $100.00 – $150.00.

4. Evans — Goldtone, Loose Powder Bracelet Compact. M.O.P. lid with broad link bracelet, puff with logo, case signed, framed mirror, 2"dia x ⅝". $150.00 – $175.00.

5. Harriet Hubbard Ayers — Goldtone, Loose Powder Bracelet Compact. M.O.P. lid with affixed rhinestone bijou, snake chain bracelet, papers: "Golden Chance," puff with logo, case signed, framed mirror, 1⅛"dia x ½". $175.00 – $200.00.

6. Richard Hudnut — Goldtone, Combination Set. Faux gemstone affixed ornament on lid with sun ray motif and lipstick circlet, puff with logo, signed cases, framed mirror, case — 2½" x 2¼" x ½", lipstick — 2¼"dia x ⅜". Set: $75.00 – $100.00.

7. Richard Hudnut — Goldtone Lipstick. See #6.

```
1   5
2   6  7
3  4   8
```

1. Anselme — Goldtone Cased Comb. See #2.

2. Anselme — Goldtone Combination Set. Bas-relief Rococo case motif, pressed powder compact with French papers, puff with logo, no case identification, framed mirror, goldtone cased tortoise shell comb. compact — 2¾"dia x ½", comb — 5" x 1⅜". Set: $65.00 – $75.00.

3. Coty — Silvertone Combination Set. Double access vanity case with logoed crest on lid, pressed powder and rouge, papers, puff with logo, case signed, framed metallic mirrors, cased glass perfume bottle with case logo and foil sticker: "L'Aimant." Ref: 1928 ad, vanity — 1⅞"sq x ½", perfume — 2½" x ¾". Set: $75.00 – $100.00.

4. Coty — Silvertone, Cased Perfume. See #3.

5. Volupté — Goldtone Combination Set. Presentation box with Lip-Lock vanity case and matching lighter, loose powder case with exterior lipstick clo-sure, affixed enameled stylized smoking cigarette holder, papers, puff with logo, signed cases and box, framed mirror. Ref: 1952 ad, vanity — 3¼" x 2¼" x ¾", lighter — 2⅝" x 1⅜" x ⅜". Set: $125.00 – $150.00.

A lapse in design — a matching lighter but no room in case for cigarettes? She lit his cigarette!!

6. Emerich — Goldtone, Cased Glass Perfume. See #7.

7. Emerich — Goldtone Combination Set. Fine cross-hatch case design with affixed Marcasite bow and arrow bijou, loose powder compact signed: "Made In Germany, Emerich," spring release lid, framed mirror, tortoise shell spring release cased comb, signed: "Germany," cased glass perfume with dauber, compact — 3"sq x ¼", comb — 4⅛" x 1", per-fume — 2" x 2" x ½". Set: $125.00 – $150.00.

8. Emerich — Goldtone Cased Comb. See #7.

a **COMPACT** *that's a real conversation piece*

Petite Boudoir

by

VOLUPTÉ

Have you seen the compacts that Hollywood stars and fashionable women collect as a hobby? Write for "Collector's Items by Volupté"—free, illustrated booklet . . . tells how to decorate your home with compacts!

Collector's items

from $2 to $25

Compacts · Pillboxes · Cigarette Cases · Carryalls · Atomizers

VOLUPTÉ

347 Fifth Ave · New York 16

Look for this emblem!

Volupté brings you an exquisite little compact that actually stands on its own legs! Imagine the excitement when you pull it out of your purse in a restaurant—at a party—in a cocktail lounge. (The legs snap back for neat, easy carrying.) Or keep it on your dressing table! Petite Boudoir is a perfect miniature of the carved golden dressing table Marie Antoinette loved in her boudoir . . . and the newest in Volupté's series of Collector's Items. About $5 . . . wherever fine compacts are sold.

pat. pend.

Harper's Bazaar, 1950

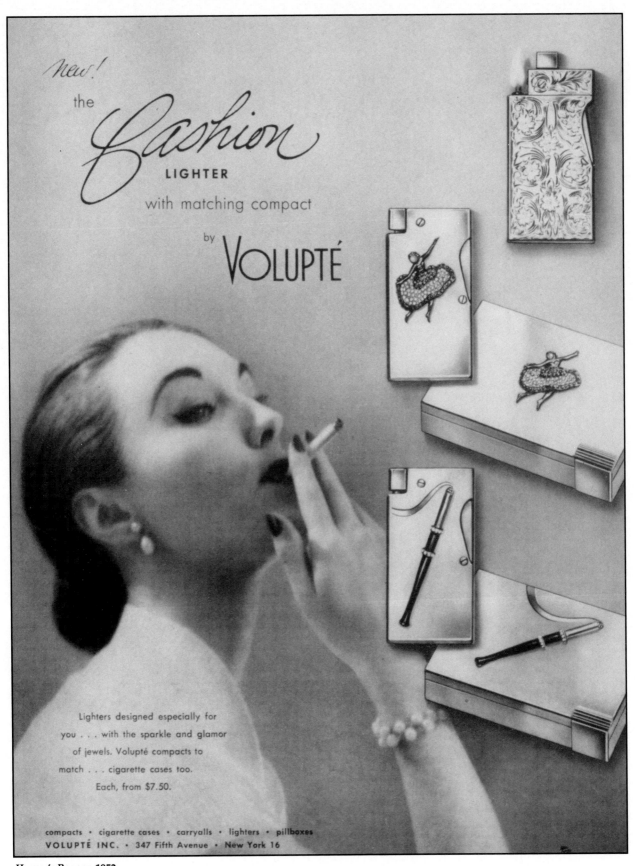

new!

the

Fashion

LIGHTER

with matching compact

by VOLUPTÉ

Lighters designed especially for
you . . . with the sparkle and glamor
of jewels. Volupté compacts to
match . . . cigarette cases too.
Each, from $7.50.

compacts • cigarette cases • carryalls • lighters • pillboxes
VOLUPTÉ INC. • 347 Fifth Avenue • New York 16

Harper's Bazaar, 1952

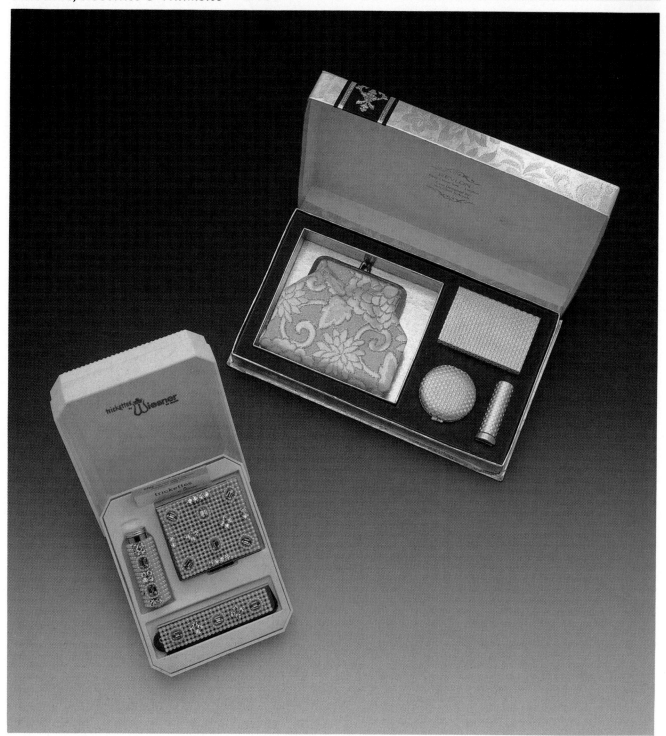

1   2

1. Wiesner of Miami — Goldtone, Presentation Set.
Three piece Trickette ensemble: loose powder compact, comb case and lipstick with all-over Pavé faux pearl and gemstone ornamentation, signed ivory plastic box, loose powder compact with protective paper with logo on reverse, no other identifications, case glued mirror, compact — 2⅞" x 2½" x ¾". Ref: 1953 ad, comb — 4" x 1", lipstick — 2⅜" x ¾", box — 6½" x 5⅛" x 2". Set: $200.00 – $225.00.

2. Revlon — Goldtone, Presentation Set. Four piece gift set: Goldenweave Evening Entourage of pressed powder and rouge compact — with brush, lipstick,

white and gold thread brocade bag, gold foil box, all items have bold foil labels, box signed: "Case Designed By Van Cleef & Arpels," case glued mirrors, powder compact — 3" x 2" x ⅝", rouge compact — 2"dia x ½", lipstick — 2¼" x ⅝", bag — 4¾" x 4¼", box — 10" x 6" x 1¼". Set: $175.00 – $200.00.

The allure of owning anything remotely touched by the world renowned French jeweler Van Cleef & Arpels may have made this the major enticement for Revlon customers. The advertising union of these two names with their divergent clientele was short lived.

1
2

3
4

1. Richard Hudnut — Plated, Loose Powder Vanity Case. Red enameled accented lid with Art Deco Phoenix birds, presentation box, puff and embossed pressed rouge with logo, case signed: "Gold & Platinum Plated," peach moiré pouch, sample Gemey powder packet, framed mirror. Vanity case — 3¼" x 2½" x ½", box — 5½" x 4¼" x 1". Set: $250.00 – $275.00.

The presentation box has a storage compartment under the black velvet vanity case framing. It is a stiffened lid, note the small access tab. The compartment contains the pouch and powder sample packet.

2. Richard Hudnut — Goldtone, Loose Powder Vanity Case. See #1 closed. Vanity case. $175.00 – $200.00.

3. Coty — Goldtone, Loose Powder Vanity Case. Maroon and red enameled Art Moderne lid motif, presentation box, puffs and embossed pressed rouge with logo, revolving powder door, case signed, hinged double metallic mirrors. Vanity case — 2¼"sq x ½", $125.00 – $150.00. Box — 3¾"sq x ¾". Set: $150.00 – $175.00.

4. Rex Fifth Avenue — Goldtone, Loose Powder Compact. Flapjack, engine-turned lid with affixed blue enameled seal of Ohio, faux gemstone enhanced, puff with logo, no case identification, case glued mirror, 4"dia x ¾". Very rare.

The lid ornament is a First Lady Of Ohio pin, which was given as gifts by the wives of Ohio Governors.

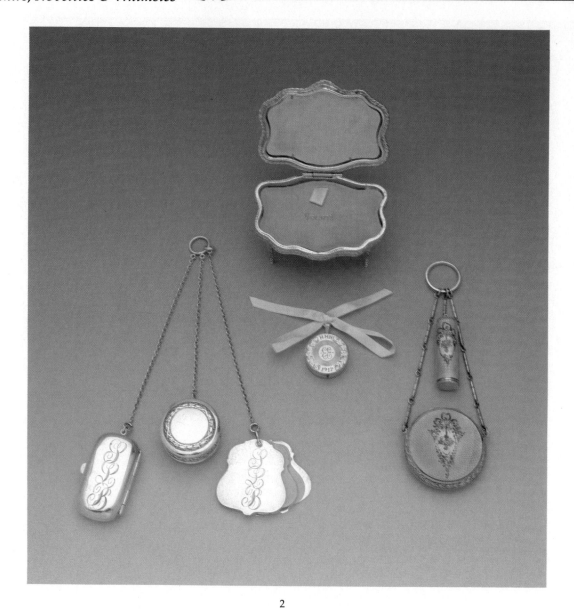

2
1   3   4

1. Unmarked — Sterling, Loose Powder Chatelaine.
Three piece set: compact with embossed borders, coin holder (5¢ and 10¢), writing tablet with Ivorene leaves (7), all items signed: "Sterling," fleece puff, metallic mirror. Compact — 1½"dia x ¾", coin holder — 2" x 1¼" x ½", writing tablet — 1⅞" x 1¾". Set: $400.00 – $450.00.

2. Volupté — White Metal, Loose Powder Compact.
"Petite Boudoir" case with folding legs, mold casted body, puff with logo, case signed, two metallic mirrors, 3⅜" x 2⅜" x ½", open — 1½" high. Ref: 1950 ad. $350.00 – $400.00.

Volupté's ad campaign to encourage women to buy compacts as a collectible prompted these "…Conversation pieces" which were part of the "Genuine Collector's Item" line. Usually copied from some pseudo historical objet d'art, this supposedly is a copy of Marie Antoinette's dressing table.

3. HFB — Gold Filled, Loose Powder Locket Compact. Hand chased lid design with two sets of engraved initials and date — 1917, handmade felt puff, framed mirror, 1⅛"dia x ¼". $250.00 – $300.00.

4. Thomae Co — Sterling, Loose Powder Pendant Vanity Case. All items have pale blue guilloché enameling with ivory, pink and gold enhancement, hand chased compact rim, baton link chain with finger ring, lipstick bottom screws off, vermeil interior with revolving powder door, case hallmarked framed mirror, compact — 2"dia x ½", lipstick — 1¾" x ½". Rare.

The Thomae Co. of Attleboro, MA was founded in 1920 and specialized in fine jewelry. The hand artisanship on this case (#3398) is so outstanding that it rivals any Fabergé work. If it had been done in gold, rather than sterling, the price would surely be in the thousands.

the GIFT of IMAGINATION

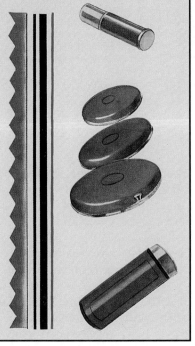

BLESSED are men and women possessed of imagination, for they shall give Christmas gifts important beyond mere cost ... charming trifles that prove treasures because of their exquisite rightness.

Such are the Christmas conceits suggested by Dorothy Gray. The new Dorothy Gray Vanity Case is a unique and lovely thing, for it conveniently holds every make-up requisite: rouge, powder, puffs and an ample mirror, lipstick, Eye Shadow, Lashique, tiny eyebrow brush and tweezers. This novel Vanity is slim enough to slip in a small handbag, and comes in a variety of leathers and colors to match favorite costumes. (Priced from nine to eighteen dollars.)

To tuck in the toe of a feminine stocking there are smart cases of sea-green metal which hold compact powder, rouge, lipstick, lip rouge, and Lashique. (The first three named are but one dollar each, the latter two are one dollar and a quarter.)

Little jars and bottles of the essential Dorothy Gray preparations nestling in a blue-green metal week-end case bring a substantial blessing on your head (for four dollars and a half!) A leather beauty case, moiré lined, is an exciting thing to receive ($16.50) and she may even deserve the handsome Dorothy Gray dressing case which is fitted with Dorothy Gray preparations and has space besides for overnight things ($65).

DOROTHY GRAY

683 FIFTH AVENUE, NEW YORK

These, and many other charming Dorothy Gray preparations, may be obtained at leading shops everywhere, and at the Dorothy Gray salons in

CHICAGO   LOS ANGELES   SAN FRANCISCO   WASHINGTON   ATLANTIC CITY

1927

1
2   3   4
                5

1. Unmarked — Silvertone, Pressed Powder Compact. Cartoon character: "Betty Boop," painted celluloid lid inset with domed face and rolling eyes, framed mirror, 2"dia x ¾". Rare.

Betty Boop was a very popular animated cartoon and comic strip character in the mid 1930's.

2. Mascot/ASB — Goldtone, Loose Powder Compact. "Valise" with rigid handle, cases has padded black lace over ivory and scattered spangles, puff with logo, case signed, framed mirror, 3" x 2½" x ⅞" (tapered). $100.00 – $125.00.

3. Pilcher — Goldtone, Loose Powder Compact. Brushed finish, case with embossed black piano player and keyboard, cased signed, framed mirror, 3⅛"dia x ½". $150.00 – $175.00.

4. Elgin American — Goldtone, Combination Case. Portrait case, engine-turned lid circle scrolling with black enameled border and reverse, lid compartment has matchbook styled lipstick tissues (see below) celluloid topped slip case picture pocket on back of hinged metallic mirror, puff with logo, case signed, 2"sq x ¾". $125.00 – $150.00.

5. Tokalon — Goldtone, Loose Powder Compact. French pantomime character: Pierrot, head and collar lid transfer, case signed, framed mirror, 2"dia x ⅜". Rare.

1   4
2   3   5

1. Unmarked — Goldtone, Loose Powder Compact. Telephone dial lid with black enameled case, embossed goldtone circles with painted numbers and letters, case glued mirror, 3½"dia x ½". $150.00 – $175.00.

2. Coty — Goldtone, Loose Powder Vanity Case. Belt buckle lid with black enameled and embossed buckle, embossed rouge and puffs with logo, case signed, case glued mirror, 3¾" x 2¼" x ½". $125.00 – $150.00.

3. Zephyr — Silvertone, Loose Powder Compact. Roulette wheel lid inset with green enameled case, red and black numerals on workable wheel, folded paper instructions and playing board, reverse decal with Empire State Building & "Souvenir of New York…" (obscured), fleece puff with logo, case signed, framed mirror, 2½"dia x ⅝". Rare.

4. Bollack Et Cie — Silvertone, Loose Powder Compact. Telephone dial lid with black enameled domed case, embossed silvertone circles with painted French numbers and letters, case signed: "Made In France," framed mirror, 3⅜"dia x ½". $175.00 – $200.00.

5. Unmarked — Goldtone, Loose Powder Compact. Telephone dial with green case enamel. See #1.

243

2 4
1 3 5

1. Richard Hudnut — Silvertone, Pressed Powder Pendant Vanity Case. Lid with Art Deco profiled faces in turquoise and ivory enamel, attached lipstick and ring, spring activated lid and interior hinged mirror, domed case signed: "Deauville," framed mirror, case — 2¼"dia x ⅜". $300.00 – $350.00.

2. Richard Hudnut — Silvertone, Pressed Powder Pendant Vanity Case. Presentation box, lid with Art Deco profiled faces in red·and black enamel (same case as #1) red and black enameled case. Box — 6" x 3¼" x ⅞". $350.00 – $400.00. Set: rare.

3. Richard Hudnut — Silvertone, Pressed Powder Vanity Case. See #1 for same case without pendant. $250.00 – $300.00.

4. Richard Hudnut — Silvertone, Pressed Powder Vanity Case. Lid with Art Deco full face in gray and blue enamel, rouge embossed with logo, domed case signed: "Three Flowers," double hinged metallic mirrors, 2¼"dia x ⅜". Very rare.

5. Richard Hudnut — Silvertone, Pressed Powder Vanity Case. Lid with Art Deco profiled faces in blue and ivory enamel, pressed rouge, domed case signed: "Three Flowers," double hinged metallic mirrors, 2¼"dia x ⅜". Rare.

There is no hint as to the designer(s) of these fabulous Art Deco cases. Artistic quality sadly did not follow on the case enameling. It is very poor, so some slight flecks are allowed within these values. A mint case would set its own value between dealer and collector.

1   2

1. Wadsworth — Goldtone, Loose Powder Sling Carryall. "Pandora" with presentation box for carryall.

2. Unmarked — Black Velvet "Sling." Ivory taffeta lining, black silk tassel and goldtone slide ring for goldtone cylinder carryall, double access, lipstick,

clear plastic comb, puff with logo, case signed, hinged framed mirror, sling — 12" x 4", box — 5½"sq x 2½", case — 2"dia x 3½". Ref: 1952 ad. Set: very rare.

It's the total set complete or nothing with this value rating.

WADSWORTH'S

Pandora

THE NEW SLING CARRYALL

Here's a glamour-accessory that makes sense, too! Concealed in the depths of this velvet beauty is a shining cylinder that magically holds all your party needs.

Black velvet bag lined in champagne satin, complete with multiple-use carryall in satin silver or black enamel. $17.50

Other Pandoras, sparkling with jewels— $20 to $35
plus Federal Tax

THREE USEFUL SECTIONS —

- Top section with lipstick case and comb
- Another with powder case— puff—mirror
- Third holds cigarettes (Or keys or money, or what-have-you!)

WADSWORTH
COMPACTS
made in the jewelry manner

Harper's Bazaar, 1952

Chapter Six

FACE POWDER BOXES, TINS & PUFFS

1
2

3
4

5

1. Tetlow's — Gossamer, Face Powder Box. Color: White, 3"dia x ⅞". $35.00 – 50.00.

Henry Tetlow introduced Pussy Willow in 1916 with tints; this powder, however, is white which may predate colors by many years.

2. Allen's — Swan Down, Face Powder Box. Color: Pink, 2⅞"dia x ⅞". $25.00 – $40.00.

3. Bourjois — Java, Face Powder Box. Main box lettering in French, reverse has information in five languages, color: Blanche, 3"dia x 1½". Ref: 1919 ad. $50.00 – $65.00.

Bourjois began making rice face powder in 1832 and was still selling it in the original designed script-lettered box one hundred and ten years later.

4. Tappan's — Swan Down, Wood Face Powder Box. "Trial Size Complexion Powder," color: White, 2"dia x 1". $35.00 – 50.00.

5. La Blache — Face Powder Box. Color: White, Ben Levy Co. signature, 3"dia x ¾". Ref: 1924 ad. $25.00 – $40.00.

"...A FORMER GENERATION WHO THINKS...THAT A PAINTED SURFACE PRODUCES A PAINTED SOUL, AND ONCE YOU HAVE INVESTED IN A BOX OF JAVA RICE [POWDER] AND A RABBIT'S FOOT, YOU ARE HEADED FOR PERDITION. THROW OVERBOARD HERE AND NOW THAT ELEVENTH COMMANDMENT IDEA THAT MAKE-UP IS ONLY PROPER WHEN YOU'RE NOT FOUND OUT."

ANNE ARCHBALD
THE THEATRE, APRIL, 1917

Early in the nineteenth century when cosmetic houses had their beginnings, face powder was born. Made from pounded rice by chemists who had to make a fast shift in clientele when powdered wigs lost their aristocratic owners and the whole idea of powdered hair became passé. The French nouveau riche of the chaotic post-revolution world, not one to let a prosperous industry be interrupted by politics, found that the old wig powder formula worked just fine on the face and voilà! Business as usual.

Powder was almost a necessity in those good old days of appalling complexions and hair loss from such ravages as small pox, typhoid, plague, etc. Theatrical make-up, although not a social anathema, was home-made and primitive. It included mascara of lampblack, glycerin and rose water (a stab at deodorants), a wet red ribbon for rouge and lip coloring, and goose grease to make the powder stick (not too well in a warm room). The French tragic actress, Rachel, who was renown for her high facial blush, had her name enshrined in the cosmetic world eclipsing her artistic fame. This sought-after blush, duplicated in a powder tint, was from tuberculosis, which killed her in 1858 at the age of 37.

Introducing windburn the automotive industry was the next important social step for cosmetics. Moving much faster than any previous conveyance and usually open to the elements, those women who were wealthy enough to use a car were losing their salon pallor at a faster rate than the car travelled. Soaps and cremes began the battle. "Applied before going on an automobile ride, face will not become red and smart, will remain perfect for hours without recourse to powder rags..." The stress was always on the creme ingredient. Milk and milkweed, almonds and arsenic, all came together as "skin food" or tonics for sick skins. This trend towards applied healing rather than vanity has persisted. The two main apostles of this idea were Elizabeth Arden and Helena Rubinstein. Arden's early ads featured a model with a mummy-like head wrap ready to do cosmetic battle with aging, while Madame Rubinstein's uniform was a white lab coat lacking only a dangling stethoscope to give her more than pseudo-medical authority.

Powder rags or powder impregnated papers and rouge bags were early ways of sneaking a wipe or two — usually "mailed in a plain package for 35¢" in 1913. Rouge, conversely, was used to accent the fact that one was rich enough to have or ride in an auto, or to fake the windburn ruddiness. Discreet nature colors of rose bloom and pink violets were acceptable, and powder colors were mainly flesh or white. Pink and cream were additional tints in a La Blache 1909 ad. Rachel and brunette showed up in 1917 and were never cheap. A 1913 ad for French actress Gabys Deslys sponsored products were priced at $1.50 a box.

The two World Wars forever changed women, cosmetics, and life in general. As women drove ambulances in 1917 and ferried B-17 bombers in 1944, advertising switched to planned obsolescence in every field, and cosmetics followed. Never a necessity and later not a health factor, justification of prices and product sometimes became a funny game. Powder went from pressed in the 1900's to loose, back to pressed, and finally to a form of liquid or creme; each time it was touted as new and improved. Over the years, powder boxes came in all sizes, shapes, materials and hype. The adjectives used to explain why one powder process was better than another created a whole new vocabulary. Some advertising adjectives used were bolted, air-spun (by propellers!), silk sifted, sheer-sifted, wind-milled, silk-screened, homogenized, feather-pressed, and velvet-pressed. These processes to make powder airborne, also made the transfer from box to compact a challenge. Tiny shovels were offered, shoe horns proved helpful, but the ultimate tool was the metal fingernail file. Using the broad end for serious powder transfer and the pointed end for a handy small dip, no woman was without her all-purpose boudoir tool.

Fragrances and tints were later added; color coding to eyes and hair or skin was schemed, which required complete adherence to total product line usage or all bets were off on beauty results. The battles began pitting one cosmetic line against another on the merest advertising thread of a different name for the same product or a secret priceless ingredient from Cleopatra's tomb.

But no fault can be found with the deathless legacy of graphic design left behind by unknown and well known artists alike whose art has now surmounted any of the products they were hired to extol. Spanning almost a century, the powder box has survived in all its unique charm. Of sturdy wood, cardboard, celluloid, and metal, the powder box, although begun as a thing of beauty, became a hardworking container for sewing notions, buttons, hairpins, and other household minutia. Sadly their survival time is growing short with current careless handling. They deserve a chance to be cherished again.

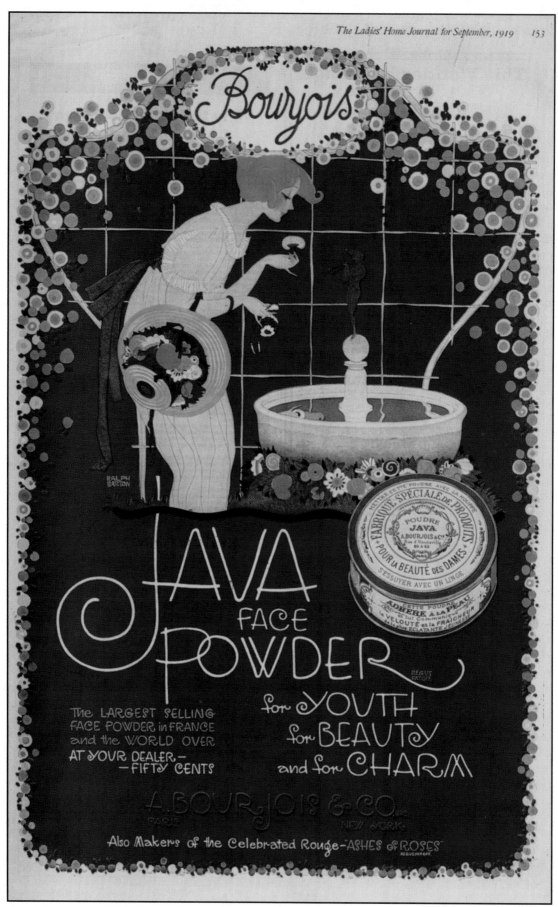

The Ladies' Home Journal, 1919

1 3
2 4
5

1. Madame Berthé — Jordeau Face Powder Box. Color: Blush, French and English information, 3¼" x 2¼" x 1½". $25.00 – $40.00.

2. Franco-American Hygienic Co — Dearest Complexion Powder Box. Color: Neutral, 3"sq x 1¼". $20.00 – $35.00.

3. Freeman's — Face Powder Box. Color: Flesh, reg. 1903, 3"sq x 1¼". $35.00 – $50.00.

4. Marcelle — Face Powder Box. "Cold Cream Poudre," color: Peach Bloom, paper for related products enclosed — shown, 3⅜" x 2½" x 1½". $45.00 – $60.00.

5. Franco-American Hygienic Co — Cutigene Toilet Cream Tin. "Night Cream," 2½"dia x 1". $10.00 – $25.00.

<pre>
1   4
2   5
3
</pre>

1. Melba — Lov'me Face Powder Box. Color: White, 3½" x 3½" x 1¾". Ref: 1928 ad. $50.00 – $65.00.

2. Houbigant — Quelques Fleurs Powder Box Slip Case. Unopened, color: Blanche, 3"sq x 1⅝". Ref: 1925 ad. $45.00 – $60.00.

3. Marriot — Face Powder Box. Color: Rachel, reverse (shown) has cosmetic tax stamps affixed totalling 4¢; Congress passed this tax in the mid-thirties causing a great deal of protest by women — which went unheeded. 3"dia x 1½". Rare.

4. Dame Nature — Face Powder Box. Color: Naturelle, paper for related products enclosed (not shown), reg. 1924, 3"dia x 2". $35.00 – $50.00.

5. Boncilla — Face Powder Box. Color: White, paper for related products enclosed (shown), 3⅛"sq x 1½". Ref: 1923 ad. $60.00 – $75.00.

Beauty's
Alphabet
Keeps You Lovely

You can have the beauty of exquisite color on lips and cheeks, a satin finish to skin — once you learn the A B C of Beauty. This alphabet of make-up really *creates* — and *maintains* — loveliness for its users.

A — *Melba Lov'me Rouge* — achieves a "natural" apple blossom flush for cheeks.

B — *Melba Lov'me Lipstick* — gives a warm radiance to lips.

C — *Melba Lov'me Face Powder* — endows the complexion with a velvety smoothness.

The effect is really captivating!

A — Here's the dainty nickel-silvered case that holds Lov'me Rouge, remarkably smooth and soft, scented with Lov'me, and delicately tinted. Use it for clever accents to the cheeks, ear lobes, and tip of chin! The effect is natural and lovely!

Send 10c for a Sample of the fine Melba Face Powder! Also Booklet: "The Melba Technique — the Way to Charm". Just address:

B — Lov'me Lipstick in an orchid enamelled holder. So pure, you could employ it as a cream for chapped lips! In the new colors for day and evening use. Used by the smartest women.

MELBA *Lov'me*
PARFUMERIE MELBA, INC.
Dept. 20   236 Spring Street, N. Y. C.
Paris   New York   Toronto
Chicago   Los Angeles

C — Lov'me Face Powder is expertly blended to harmonize with every tint of complexion: white, rachel, naturelle. It always is packed in a lavender box of modified triangular shape, such as is pictured above.

Woman's Home Companion, 1928

1   4
2   5
3   6   7

1. Nyal Co — Nylotis Face Powder Box. Color: White, reg. 1919, 3"sq x 1½". $50.00 – $65.00.

2. Palmolive — Face Powder Box. Color: White, four color products booklet (shown) 3"sq x 1½". $45.00 – $60.00.

3. Jonteel — Face Powder Box. Color: White, "Compact Dresser Package," pressed powder with puff (shown), 3⅛"dia x 1¼". Ref: 1919 ad. $65.00 – $80.00.

4. Golden Peacock — Tonic Powder Box. Color: Naturelle, 3⅜" x 2¾" x 1½". $50.00 – $65.00.

5. Jarvaise — Suz Anne Poudre Box. Color: Brunette, reverse has an NRA Blue Eagle stamp which dates it 1933, 3"sq x 1⅜". $35.00 – $50.00.

6. Golden Peacock — Face Powder Box. Color: Flesh, "New Style Package Adopted 1933," 2½"sq x ¾". $20.00 – $35.00.

7. Vida-Ray — Face Powder Box. Color: Dresden (Natural #2), 3½"sq x ⅝". Ref: 1945 ad. $25.00 – $40.00.

This is Peaches & Cream

This is Peaches

Announcing two new popular shades

1. PEACHES-AND-CREAM*—a new tan-and-rose shade of JAVA Face Powder, radiant and soft, with the quality of autumn sunshine in it.

2. PEACHES*—a new delicate shade of tan with the faintest touch of pink in it, catching the glow of wind and sun.

IN honor of JAVA's 50th anniversary, we present to the women of America these two exquisite new shades.

Peaches-and-Cream and *Peaches* already are sweeping the country in their popularity, and it is worthy of note that JAVA* is the only popular-priced face powder having the distinction of offering them.

To the druggists of America we say that never before have they had a better opportunity of giving satisfaction to their face powder customers than through these two new lovely shades of JAVA.

To the women of America we say that wherever they see the window display shown below, they will find a druggist eager and willing to serve them with the finest toilet goods preparations.

BOURJOIS
Famous Parisian JAVA *Face Powder*

The *BOURJOIS COLOR CARD* is an innovation which makes it easy for your druggist to show you at a glance which shade of JAVA Face Powder is best adapted to your complexion. Ask to see it.

ASHES OF ROSES

BOURJOIS
Famous Parisian JAVA *Face Powder*
ASHES OF ROSES or MANDARINE ROUGES

The Powder of Economical Luxury—

The World's Finest Rouges

ROUGE MANDARINE

Bourjois Ashes of Roses Rouge No. 83

Bourjois Rouge Mandarine No. 83

PARIS (France)   A. BOURJOIS & CO., INC., 27 West 34th Street   NEW YORK

The Ladies' Home Journal, 1923

1
2
3
4
5

1. Langlois — Cara Nome Face Powder Box. Color: Rachelle Light, blue satin hinged lid interior, 3¼" x 2¼" x 1⅜". $35.00 – $50.00.

2. Watkins Perfumers — Garda Face Powder Box. Color: Flesh, products brochure enclosed and puff with logo (both shown), 3½" x 2¾" x 1⅞". Ref: 1921 ad. $65.00 – $80.00.

3. Kolynos Co — Nalgiri Face Powder Box. Color: Rachel, lift lid with tab, 3⅛"dia x 2". $50.00 – $65.00.

4. Stearns Perfumer — Day Dream Face Powder Box. Color: Style Tan, "Gives a Natural Sun Effect," 3"sq x 1½". Ref: 1919 ad. $50.00 – $65.00.

5. Andrew Jergens Co — Woodbury Facial Powder Box. Color: Naturelle/Flesh, reverse information shown, 3¼"dia x 1½". $65.00 – $80.00.

1   4
2   5
3

      6

1. Elizabeth Arden — Poudre D'Illusion Box. Color: Special Rachel, gold satin hinged lid interior shown, snap flap box closure, 3½"sq x 1¾". Ref: 1934 ad. $45.00 – $60.00.

2. Coty — L'Aimant Air Spun Face Powder Box. Color: Muted Beige, celluloid sleeved lid with Lalique puff design, this box has red background rather than more common Coty orange, 3½"dia x 1½". Ref: 1928 ad. $30.00 – $45.00.

3. Woodworth — Fiancée Face Powder Box. Color: Naturelle, orange satin hinged lid interior shown,

papered wood frame, 3½" x 2⅞" x 1⅝". Ref: 1928 ad. $65.00 – $80.00.

4. Colgate Co — Florient Face Powder Box. Color: Flesh, "Flowers of the Orient," 3"dia x 2". Ref: 1922 ad. $50.00 – $65.00.

5. Coty — Emeraude Air Spun Face Powder Box. Color: Rachel No. 1, 3½"dia x 1½". Ref: 1954 ad. $20.00 – $35.00.

6. Houbigant — Quelques Fleurs Face Powder Box. Color: Rachel, 2¾"sq x ⅞". $20.00 – $35.00.

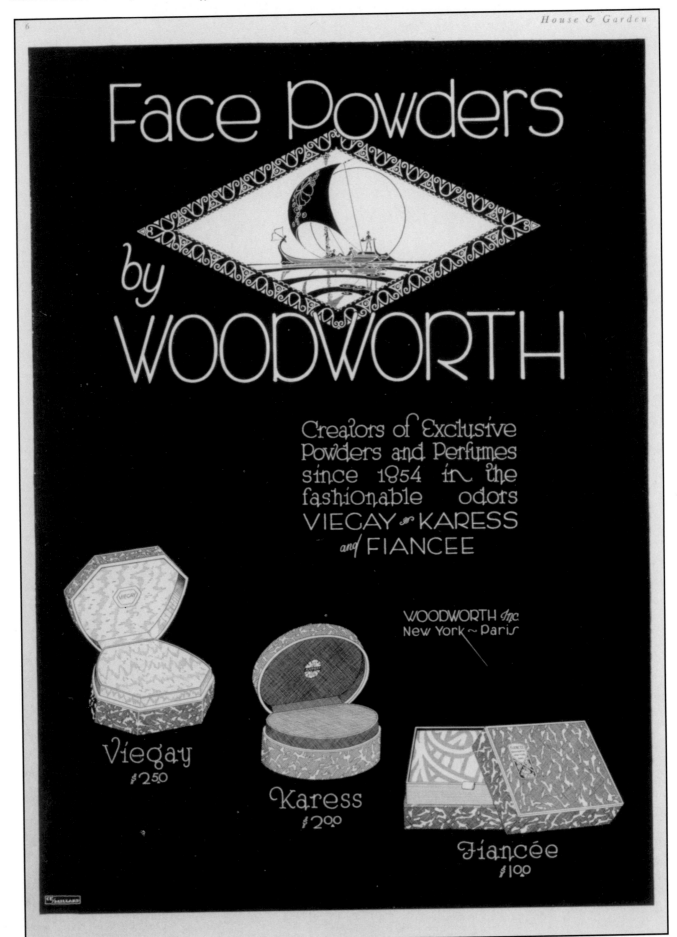

your
Face and
your
Fortune

Before frock, figure, or manner, a woman is judged by her face . . . "a pretty girl", "a distinguished looking woman", "smart", or "beautiful" is said according to the impression given by a face—and its all-important make-up.

And one really can't afford (for fortune's sake) to use powder of a lesser quality than the finest—Houbigant Face Powder. For 150 perfumed years, Houbigant has created the finest powders in all the world, and none is quite so delightfully fragrant, velvety-soft, and lastingly adherent. The exquisite odeurs are Subtilité, Quelques Fleurs, Le Parfum Ideal, Mon Boudoir, and Le Temps des Lilas. Its true tones are naturelle, rachel, rosée, ocre rosée, ocre, and blanche—$1.50.

The same powder, but in compact form, with rouge, is in the new double compact—designed by a Parisian jeweler. The compact is six-sided—unusually good-looking—thin, and light in weight—$2.50.

We would like to send you five sachets perfumed with the five odeurs mentioned above, and the booklet, "Things Perfumes Whisper". Please write for them. Houbigant, Inc., Dept. 153, 539 West 45th Street, New York.

HOUBIGANT
PARIS

Ladies' Home Journal, 1927

```
1    5
2    6
3  4 7
```

1. Co-Ed — Deluxe Face Powder Box. Color: Naturelle, 3¼"sq x 1⅞". $35.00 – $50.00.

2. Plough's — Black & White Face Powder Box. Color: Flesh, "Favorite Bouquet," large products brochure enclosed (shown), 3¼" x 2¼" x 1⅜". $45.00 – $60.00.

3. Keystone/Reliable Co — La Jac Face Powder Box. Color: Nut Brown, 2½"sq x ¾". $25.00 – $40.00.

4. Newbro Mfg Co — Queen Face Powder Box. Color: Gypsy Brown, 2½"sq x ¾". $20.00 – $35.00.

5. Hi-Hat Co — Face Powder Box. Color: Spanish Rose, 3"dia x 1⅝". $35.00 – $50.00.

6. Plough's — Black & White Face Powder Box. Color: Naturelle, reverse information shown, 2¾"dia x 1½". $40.00 – $55.00.

7. Hi-Hat Co — Jockey Club Face Powder Box. Color: High Brown, 2½"sq x ¾". $35.00 – $50.00.

1   3

2   4

1. Richard Hudnut — Gardenia Face Powder Box.
Color: White, blue satin interior envelope closure with
gold foil seal, shown open, 3¼"sq x 1¾". Ref: 1927 ad.
$45.00 – $60.00.

**2. Richard Hudnut — Three Flowers Face Powder
Box.** Reverse information — see #4.

3. Richard Hudnut — Three Flowers Travelette. See
page 262, #4 open.

**4. Richard Hudnut — Three Flowers Face Powder
Box.** Color: Rachel No. 1, products brochure enclosed
(shown) and reverse shown #2, 3⅜"dia x 1¾". $50.00 –
$65.00.

1   4
2   5
3   6

1. Richard Hudnut — Three Flowers Powder Box. Color: Naturelle, "Boudoir Compact or Refiller," pressed powder with fleece puff, paper instructions enclosed, 2⅝"dia x ⅝". $65.00 – $80.00.

2. Richard Hudnut — Three Flowers Soap Cake. Gift wrap with silken cord and gold foil seal, 2½"dia x 1". $25.00.

3. Richard Hudnut — Three Flowers Face Powder Box. Color: Rachel No. 2, "Hypo-Allergenic," 3¼"sq x 1⅝". $45.00 – $60.00.

Note how the Three Flowers Femme has become updated.

4. Richard Hudnut — Three Flowers Travelette. See page 261, #3 closed, contents: tube of vanishing cream in box, tube of cleansing cream in box, glass perfume bottle with cork stopper, face powder box, color: Naturelle. Box — 4⅜" x 3⅛" x 1⅛". Rare.

5. Richard Hudnut — Marvelous Face Powder Box. Color: Rachel No.1, "Continental Type," 2¾"sq x 1½". Ref: 1937. $35.00 – $50.00.

6. Richard Hudnut — Gemey Face Powder Box. Color: Rachel No. 2, "Dark Brunette," 3"dia x 1½". Ref: 1936 ad. $45.00 – $60.00.

ALL THE WORLD
SAYS
"Merry Christmas"
WITH THE

FRAGRANCE *Gemey*

The Frenchman's "Joyeux Noël," the Hawaiian's "Melika Maka," the Italian's "Buon Natale"—they all mean "Merry Christmas!" And in 75 lands the men who know what women want will say "Merry Christmas" this season with ...fragrance Gemey.

For this young, fresh, joyous perfume has charmed its way into the feminine hearts of five continents. And Richard Hudnut now presents America with these gifts of glamor... powders and perfume, compacts and cologne ...all distinguished by this single thread of fragrance...Gemey.

See the gay gift showing at your nearest perfume counter...in packages as lovely as their contents. Find the one that's right for her (prices range from $1 to $10). She'll be thrilled to join the company of the world's loveliest women, the women who know...and wear ...fragrance Gemey!

In crystal clear dressing table flacons ... $2.50, $4.50 and $15. Special Stocking-Gift size ... $1.

by RICHARD HUDNUT
New York   Paris

London . . . Toronto . . . Buenos Aires . . . Mexico City . . . Berlin
Barcelona . . . Budapest . . . Capetown . . . Sydney . . . Shanghai
Rio de Janeiro . . . Havana . . . Bucharest . . . Vienna . . . Amsterdam

To cheer her Christmas day—an *intimate* treasure—Toilet Water Gemey! $1.50

Two gifts—Gemey Perfume, world-beloved—Gemey Powder, filmy-fine. $2.25

A gala giftbox—five "can't-do-withouts," in the world-favored fragrance Gemey. $5

For her dressing-table: Fragrance Gemey —with a luxury De Vilbiss atomizer. $5

Glamor for glamorous girls: Double Compact, $2. Triple Vanity with lipstick, $2.75

"To Mary with love"—a handsome Cigarette Case, Lipstick, Double Vanity, $10

An intimate gift to last all year—eight personal luxuries that breathe Gemey. $10

She's "tops"—and so is your gift—this slim gold-plated Cigarette Vanity, $7.50

Tip to a Man-in-a-quandary—Gemey Perfume, Face Powder, Compact. $3.50

McCall's, 1936

```
1        4
2        5
3        6
```

1. Kaye Martine — Face Powder Box. No color listed, hinged lid with ribbon tab, 5" x 3½" x 2¼". $25.00 – $40.00.

2. Princess Pat — Face Powder Box. Color: Brunette (Rachel), Ivorene ringed drawer for entry, reverse information: "The Only Almond Based Face Powder," 3½" x 2¾" x 1½". Ref: 1932 ad. $65.00 – $80.00.

3. Bourjois — Evening In Paris Face Powder Box. Color: Rose Indian, reverse information: "This is a Temporary Victory Package. The contents are

Unchanged." See #6 for interior, 3¼"sq x 1¾". $50.00 – $65.00.

4. Harriet Hubbard Ayers — Face Powder Box. Color: Peach, 3"sq x 1½". Ref: 1927 ad. $35.00 – $50.00.

5. Sterling Products — Bonnie Day Face Powder Box. Color: Naturelle, 3"sq x 1½". $25.00 – $40.00.

6. Bourjois — Evening In Paris Face Powder Box. See #3 — interior color coordination instructions.

1
2   4
        5

1. Henry Tetlow Co — Pussywillow Face Powder Box. Color: Cream Rachel, 3¼"sq x 1½". Ref: 1920 ad. $65.00 – $80.00.

2. Houbigant — Translucid Face Powder Box. Color: Rachel, Sheer-Sifted, 3⅝"dia x 1½". Ref: 1941. $45.00 – $60.00.

3. Colgate & Co — Piquante Face Powder Box. Color: Flesh, 2⅞"dia x 1⅞". Ref: 1924 ad. $100.00 – $125.00.

4. Truvey — Face Powder Box. Color: Naturelle No. 1, information in French, 2¾"dia x 1½". $45.00 – $60.00.

5. Lady Arlene — Face Powder Box. Color: Hi Brown, moisture proof, 3"sq x 1⅝". $45.00 – $60.00.

Ladies' Home Journal, 1944

Du Barry Beauty in Black

Hat, John-Frederics
Jewels, Marcus & Co.

FOR YOUR FALL LOVELINESS . . . DU BARRY BRINGS YOU A RADIANT NEW COMPLEXION TO LIGHT THE DARK DRAMA OF BACK-IN-TOWN FASHIONS

A fresh start now . . . it's time for a new fall complexion. Every woman enjoys the stimulating change to her first dark frock after the pastel prettiness of summer. Every woman knows that it demands the contrast of a fresh, delicately glowing complexion.

Let Du Barry coax back that soft dewy skin texture with satin-smooth creams and lotions, to help counteract the drying effects of summer wind and sun. Du Barry Cleansing Cream for Dry Skins and . . . under your make-up . . . a light film of Du Barry creamy liquid Foundation Lotion.

Then veil that fading tan with Du Barry warm Rose Beige Powder, and accent it vividly with the new Du Barry lipstick and rouge tint for fall, Rose Cerise. When you enter a room, listen to the whispers . . . "Who is that lovely woman in black?"

Ask the Du Barry beauty advisor, at better cosmetic counters, about the Du Barry "Beauty-Angle" way to complexion loveliness. Du Barry Cleansing Cream, 1.00; Foundation Lotion, 1.25. Complete your lovely new complexion with Du Barry Rose Beige Face Powder, large box, 2.00 . . . Du Barry Rose Cerise Lipstick and Rouge, each 1.00.

Du Barry BEAUTY PREPARATIONS

By Richard Hudnut . . . Featured at better cosmetic counters and in the Hudnut Salon, 693 Fifth Avenue

Vogue, 1941

1   3

2   4

1. Marie Earle — Perfection Face Powder Box. Color: Roseraie, Pour Le Visage, 4"sq x 2¾". Ref: 1933 ad. $125.00 – $150.00.

2. Yardley — Old English Lavender Face Powder Box. Color: Rachel No. 1, product information on reverse, 2⅞"dia x 1½". Ref: 1927 ad. $65.00 – $80.00.

3. California Perfume Co. — Hygiene Face Powder Box. Color: White, 3¼"oct x 2⅝" x 1½". $75.00 – $100.00.

4. Roger & Gallet — Face Powder Aluminum Box. Embossed Birds of Paradise lid with orange tinted ground, lid has Lalique signature (no room for "R"), silver foil identification sticker in reverse cartouche,

Made In France, removable interior cardboard box, 3"dia x 1⅛". Ref: 1924 ad. $250.00 – 300.00.

This is the American version, the rare early French version has "Fleurs d'Amour Paris" — "Poudre Naturelle and R. Lalique, Roger et Gallet" stamped on reverse. No lid signature. Other lid variations: more feathering and missing tiny rim frame.

Unlike the Cheramy aluminum box, also designed by Lalique, (see page 279, #9) these cases are extremely soft. Early uses of aluminum were praised for its silver-like qualities without the tarnish, but its excellent malleability also proved to be its downfall. Finding these boxes in fine to mint condition without dents, and competition from Lalique collectors, makes their value very negotiable.

Marie Earle does in "Gold" *her* <u>New</u>
COMPACT

Symbolic of the season's glamourous fashions, here is a new Marie Earle Compact—*gold-toned*—slim, patrician, resplendent. On its cover a quatre-foil inlay, at its sides carved flanges, in tones of old ivory and *cafe-au-lait*. *Double*—in its powder-and-rouge version, pictured above—$2.50. *Single*—with powder *or* rouge—$1.50. Isn't this the "important" small gift to send your most fastidious friends? A smart *new* box, too, for Marie Earle's superior Face Powder! Its tones are ivory and green, with a rich ivory-tinted motif on the cover! This box introduces Marie Earle's *newest powder tone* —"Soleil"—a warm, luscious, flattering tint midway between "peach" and "sunburn"—$3.

Marie Earle Salon for superb "facials"—714 Fifth Avenue.

Marie Earle dresses Anew her Fine FACE POWDER

AT THE BETTER SHOPS

New Yorker, 1933

```
1      6
2  3       8
4    7  9
5        10
```

1. Max Factor — Hollywood Face Powder Box. Color: Rachelle, Society Make-Up, 2⅜"dia x ½". Ref: 1938 ad. $15.00 – $25.00.

2. Richard Hudnut — Le Debut Powder Box. Color: Naturelle, 2"octagon x 1". Ref: 1929 ad. $50.00 – $65.00.

3. Colgate Co — Eclat Face Powder Box. 2½"dia x ⅝". $15.00 – $25.00.

4. Jardin — De Rose Face Powder Box. Color: Flesh, Trial Size, 1½"sq x ⅝". $25.00 – $35.00.

5. Jonteel — Pressed Powder Box. Color: White, has products paper, (puff shown) may be refill for page 15, #6, 1¾"dia x ¾". Ref: 1921 ad. $50.00 – $65.00.

6. Rawleigh's La Jaynees Face Powder Box. Color: Natural, 3"dia x 1⅜". $45.00 – $60.00.

7. Primrose House — Chiffon Face Powder Box. Color: Brunette, 2½"dia x ½". $10.00 – $20.00.

8. Pompeian Co — Beauty Face Powder Box. Color: Naturelle (nude), travel size, 2½"dia x ¾". $35.00 – $50.00.

9. Kerkoff — Djer-Kiss Face Powder Box. Color: Rachel, 2½"dia x ½". Ref: 1924 ad. $25.00 – $40.00.

10. Elizabeth Arden — Ardena Face Powder Box. Color: Shade 2, Invisible Veil, 1⅝"dia x ⅝". $15.00 – $25.00.

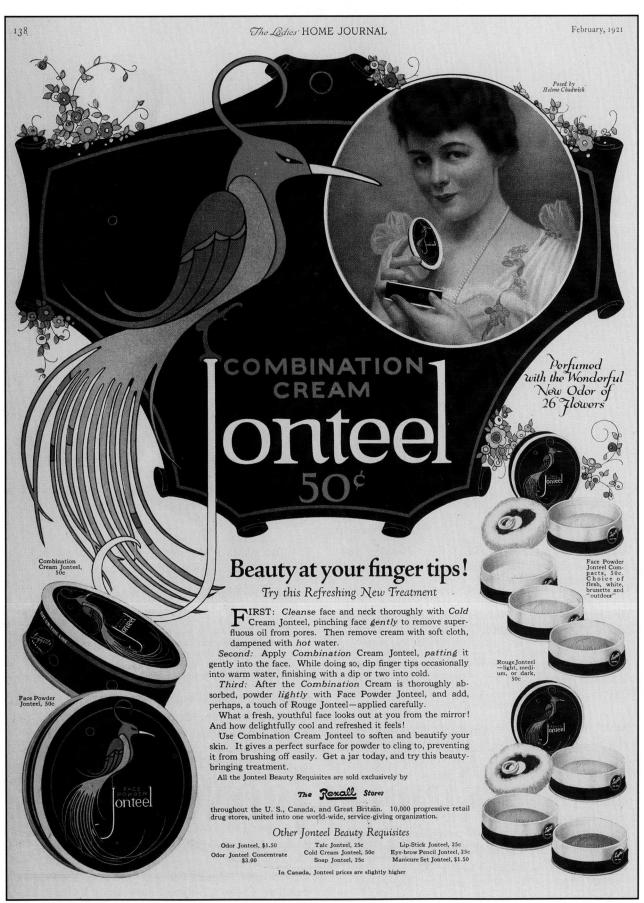

Posed by Helene Chadwick

COMBINATION CREAM
Jonteel
50¢

Perfumed with the Wonderful New Odor of 26 Flowers

Combination Cream Jonteel, 50c

Face Powder Jonteel, 50c

Face Powder Jonteel Compacts, 50c. Choice of flesh, white, brunette and "outdoor"

Rouge Jonteel —light, medium, or dark, 50c

Beauty at your finger tips!

Try this Refreshing New Treatment

FIRST: *Cleanse* face and neck thoroughly with *Cold* Cream Jonteel, pinching face *gently* to remove superfluous oil from pores. Then remove cream with soft cloth, dampened with *hot* water.

Second: Apply *Combination* Cream Jonteel, *patting* it gently into the face. While doing so, dip finger tips occasionally into warm water, finishing with a dip or two into cold.

Third: After the *Combination* Cream is thoroughly absorbed, powder *lightly* with Face Powder Jonteel, and add, perhaps, a touch of Rouge Jonteel—applied carefully.

What a fresh, youthful face looks out at you from the mirror! And how delightfully cool and refreshed it feels!

Use Combination Cream Jonteel to soften and beautify your skin. It gives a perfect surface for powder to cling to, preventing it from brushing off easily. Get a jar today, and try this beauty-bringing treatment.

All the Jonteel Beauty Requisites are sold exclusively by

The *Rexall* Stores

throughout the U. S., Canada, and Great Britain. 10,000 progressive retail drug stores, united into one world-wide, service-giving organization.

Other Jonteel Beauty Requisites

Odor Jonteel, $1.50	Talc Jonteel, 25c	Lip-Stick Jonteel, 25c
Odor Jonteel Concentrate $3.00	Cold Cream Jonteel, 50c	Eye-brow Pencil Jonteel, 25c
	Soap Jonteel, 25c	Manicure Set Jonteel, $1.50

In Canada, Jonteel prices are slightly higher

The Ladies' Home Journal, 1921

Woman's Home Companion, 1919

1. Leroux — Une Brise Parfumee Face Powder Box. Color: Rose Pink, French and English information, 2⅞"dia x 1". $65.00 – $80.00.

2. Richard Hudnut — Du Barry Face Powder Box. Color: Naturelle, oval miniature travel size, 1⅞" x 1⅜" x 1". $25.00 – $40.00.

3. Heather Co — Face Powder Box. Color: Naturelle, 2½"dia x ⅝". $35.00 – $50.00.

4. Andrew Jergens Co — Woodbury Face Powder Box. Color: Fiesta, 3"sq x ¾". Ref: 1952 ad. $20.00 – $35.00.

5. Andrew Jergens Co — Face Powder Box. Color: Peach Bloom, "New! All Shades Styled by ALIX, World Famous Fashion Creator," metallic bottom, 2¾"dia x ¾". Ref 1943 ad. $45.00 – $60.00.

Rivaling Coty's famous Lalique Puff Logo, Jergens hired two names to promote this new powder: ALIX and Alberto Vargas. Vargas — better known for the Esquire Varga Girl Calendars, designed this lid and the Varga Girl ad images, which lasted only a few months because of contractual problems. The signed Varga/Jergens ads are now highly collectable.

6. Stafford-Miller Co — Carmen Complexion Powder Box. Color: Flesh, "Sample Box," 1⅞"dia x ⅝". $25.00 – $40.00.

7. Edna Wallace Hopper — Face Powder Box. Color: Flesh, 2¼"dia x ¾". Ref: 1932 ad. Rare.

Edna Wallace Hopper was a Broadway figure in forgettable roles from 1891 to 1920. She retired at age 56. However, in the twenties she had a face lift filmed and toured movie houses for eight years with a successful lecture series on how to remain beautiful with her beauty products.

8. Andrew Jergens Co — Woodbury Facial Powder Box. See page 256, #5 for larger version, "Trial Size." 1¾"dia x ½". $25.00 – $40.00.

9. Richard Hudnut — Du Barry Face Powder Box. Color: Peach, oval travel size, 2¼" x 1⅞" x 1⅛". Ref: 1940 ad: $40.00 – $55.00.

10. Luxor Ltd. — Complexion Powder Box. Color: Rachel, 2⅜"sq x ⅝". $45.00 – $60.00.

11. Andrew Jergens Co — Woodbury Pressed Powder Box. Color: Golden Dream (Rose Rachel), Dream Stuff, "New! Tinted Foundation and Powder in One." 2¾"dia x ¾". Ref: 1951 ad. $25.00 – $40.00.

1	6	8
2	7	9
3		10
4		11
5		

Hello—Gorgeous!

You're lusciously lovely
... with your
Alix-Styled Shade of

New Jergens Face Powder

FOR LOOK-ALIVE ALLURE

Newest today—that alive, alert look. It's yours—with new Jergens Face Powder! Because Jergens shades were styled by Alix, famous fashion designer and colorist, to *awaken* and enhance your loveliest skin tones—no matter what your type!

FOR VELVETY GLAMOUR

Watch men's eyes stop and adore your new Jergens complexion—so smooth, so lush! You see, the texture of Jergens is *velvetized* by an exclusive process—bringing your skin a finer, younger, more flawless look (helps hide tiny lines and skin faults).

YOUR GLORIFYING SHADE

Naturelle—to give flower delicacy.
Peach Bloom—for young, blossomy loveliness.
Rachel—a glamorous, pearly shade.
Brunette—for alluring, vivid beauty.
Dark Rachel—for that tawny, dramatic look.

BIG BOUDOIR BOX, $1.00 ... TRY-IT SIZES, 25¢ AND 10¢

Modern Screen, 1943

Entirely New Idea in Make-up

Jergens "Twin Make-up"

Two lovely make-up aids—in one box
to give you that young dewy-fresh look

IN A JIFFY, you've the loveliest make-up ever!

First, sponge on Jergens new Velvet Make-up Cake that beauty experts are crazy about. Little skin flaws seem to disappear. Your face looks smoother!

Then, smooth on Jergens Face Powder in the heavenly new shade styled for your type of skin. How young you look! And you needn't repowder for ages longer.

This new Twin Make-up brings you your just-right shade of make-up cake *right in the same box* with *your* shade of face powder.

Only $1.00 for this whole exciting new Twin Make-up! Look naturally-lovelier in an instant! Ask for Jergens Twin Make-up today! (Jergens Face Powder, alone, comes also in regular boxes at 25¢ and 10¢.) Made by the makers of your favorite Jergens Lotion.

$2.00 Value for $1.00

Jergens new Velvet Make-up Cake with matching Face Powder

• Boxed together, for the first time— Both for $1.00—less than many girls pay for a make-up cake alone! Choose the powder shade that lights up your type of skin; your twin harmonizing shade in make-up cake is right in the same box. (5 sets of shades—one specially styled for you!) Get Jergens "Twin Make-up" today!

Photoplay, 1943

1946

```
1   4        8
2        5   9
3        6   10
         7
```

1. Houbigant — Goldtone, Pressed Rouge Compact. Color:?, enameled lid with flower basket logo, case signed, framed metallic mirror, 1⅝" x ⅜". Ref: 1927 ad. $25.00 – $40.00.

2. Richard Hudnut — Goldtone, Pressed Rouge Compact. Color: Stage, embossed Du Barry lid logo, fleece puff with logo, case signed, framed mirror, 1⅝"sq x ⅜". Ref: 1940 ad. $35.00 — $50.00.

3. Richard Hudnut — Goldtone, Creme Rouge Compact. Color: Carmeen No. 8, embossed Du Barry lid logo, case signed, framed mirror, 1½" x 1⅛" x ⅜". Ref: 1940 ad. $25.00 – $40.00.

Both #2 and #3 are from Page 163 — Du Barry Kit. They could be purchased separately as purse items.

4. Lady Esther — Goldtone, Pressed Rouge Tin. Color: No. 3, signed lid with logo, no mirror, 1⅛"dia x ¼". $10.00 – $15.00.

5. Watkins Perfumers — White Metal, Pressed Rouge Compact. Color: Bright, green enameled case, Clary King lid signature, puff with logo, box signed, framed mirror, 1½"dia x ½". $15.00 – $25.00.

6. Coty — Goldtone, Pressed Rouge and Lipstick Duo. Color: Bright, lipstick: Vibrant, Sub-Deb labeled, red plastic tandem carrier, case and presentation box signed, framed mirror, 2¼" x 1¾". Ref: 1947 ad. Set: $25.00 – $40.00.

7. Revlon — Plastic, Pressed Rouge Tin. Color: Ultra Violet, ivory puff with logo, case signed, no mirror, 1⅜"sq x ½". Ref: 1946 ad. $10.00 – $15.00.

8. Bourjois — Bimetal, Pressed Rouge and Lipstick Duo. Color: Cerise, lipstick: Medium, goldtone with pewter winged lid insets, Armand paper for rouge, case signed: Evening In Paris, part of gift set. Ref: 1949, 1½"dia x ½". Set: $20.00 – $35.00.

9. Princess Pat — Goldtone, Pressed Rouge Compact. Color: English Tint, Art Moderne lid with signature, paper label, puff with logo, framed metallic mirror, 1½"dia x ⅜". $25.00 – $40.00.

10. Milrone — White Metal, Pressed Rouge Glove Compact. Color:?, black enameled diagonal lid motif, puff with logo (shown): "Charm," case signed, framed mirror, 1¾" x 1¼" x ⅜". $35.00 – $50.00.

Richard Hudnut, 1936

1. Marinello — Goldtone, Pressed Rouge Compact. Color:?, pink enameled case with Art Deco puff, case signed, framed mirror, 1½" x ⅜". $25.00 – $35.00.

2. Harriet Hubbard Ayers — White Metal, Pressed Rouge Compact. Color:?, lid and puff with logos, case signed, framed mirror, 1½"dia x ⅜". $15.00 – $20.00.

3. Paul D. Newton Co — Goldtone, Pressed Rouge Compact. Color:?, peach enameled case with Peggy Newton lid logo, paper label signed, framed mirror, 1⅝"dia x ¾". Ref: 1950 ad. $10.00 – $15.00.

4. Luxor Ltd. — Goldtone, Pressed Rouge Compact. Color: Encharma, egg shaped signed case, framed mirror, 1¾" x 1½" x ½". $25.00 – $35.00.

5. Deere — Goldtone, Pressed Rouge Compact. Color:?; see page 279, #8 for larger case, signed lid with embossed logo, framed mirror, 1½"dia x ⅝". $35.00 – $50.00.

6. Lorie Inc — Goldtone, Pressed Rouge Compact. Color: Dubonnay, ivory enameled lid, paper label and puff: Adrienne/Lorie, framed mirror, 1½"dia x ⅜". $15.00 – $20.00.

7. Leon Loraine — Goldtone, Pressed Rouge Compact. Color: Yankee Red, metallic brown enameled lid, paper label, puff with logo, signed case, framed mirror, 1¾"dia x ½". Ref: 1936 ad. $15.00 – $20.00.

8. Geo W. Luft Co — Goldtone, Pressed Rouge Compact. Color: Theatrical Red, incised lid with blue plastic dot, case, box and puff signed: Tangee, framed mirror, 1½"dia x ½". Ref: 1947 ad. $15.00 – $20.00.

9. Celina — White Metal, Pressed Rouge Compact. Color:?, incised lid with domed reverse, embossed rouge, no other identification, framed mirror, 2"dia x ⅜". $25.00 – $35.00.

10. Franco-American Hygienic Co — Goldtone, Pressed Rouge Compact. Color: Deep, hammered finish, signed box and case, framed mirror, 1½"dia x ½". $20.00 – $25.00.

11. Elmo — Goldtone, Pressed Rouge Compact. Color: Rose, signed paper and case, framed mirror, 1½"dia x ⅝". $15.00 — $20.00.

12. Richard Hudnut — Goldtone, Pressed Rouge Compact. Color: Nasturium, starred case, paper label, case signed: "Three Flowers," framed mirror, 1½"dia x ½". $25.00 – $35.00.

1	4	8	11
2	5	9	12
3	6	10	
	7		

SAMPLE FACE POWDER AND ROUGE TINS

Although little gems of design, these tins have no mirrors, hinges, or internal parts. They were cheaply made to be given away, and they are not scarce. The values depend on condition, as always, and should range from $10.00 – $15.00.

Armand	Symphonie Face Powder
Armand	Armand Cold Cream Face Powder
Cheramy	Cappi Face Powder
Glebeas Co	Adoration Face Powder
Geo W. Luft Co	Tangee Face Powder (revolving lid)
Geo W. Luft Co	Classic Face Powder
Geo W. Luft Co	Tangee Rouge/sample card
Geo W. Luft Co	Tangee Rouge/sample card
Geo W. Luft Co	Tangee Creme Rouge (aluminum)
Luxor Ltd	Krasny Face Powder
Mello-Glo	Facial Tone Powder
Princess Pat	Rouge (refill)

Meet the girl men want to kiss

SMOOTHLY alluring lips—soft as velvet—with a provocative glow of color like the heart of a rose—no wonder men are fascinated!

Tangee Lipstick is her "magic wand"...yours, too, if you want loveliness. Orange in the stick, Tangee changes to your *very own* shade of blush-rose on your lips. Its special cream base helps keep lips satin-smooth in all weather. It isn't "paint", so it won't rub off.

Get Tangee today...in the 39¢ or the $1.10 size ...equally ravishing for blondes, brunettes or redheads, thanks to its magic color-change principle. Or send 10¢ with the coupon for 4-piece Miracle Make-Up Set containing Tangee Lipstick, Rouge Compact, Creme Rouge, Face Powder.

BEWARE OF SUBSTITUTES! There is only one Tangee —don't let some smart salesperson switch you. Be sure to ask for Tangee *Natural*. If you prefer more vivid color for evening wear, ask for Tangee Theatrical.

World's Most Famous Lipstick

TANGEE
ENDS THAT PAINTED LOOK

Be Popular! Check up on your charm with Tangee Charm Test, sent with Miracle Make-Up Set.

4-PIECE MIRACLE MAKE-UP SET

The George W. Luft Co., 417 Fifth Ave., New York City . . . Please rush "Miracle Make-Up Set" of sample *Tangee Lipstick*, Rouge Compact, Creme Rouge and Face Powder, also Tangee Charm Test. I enclose 10¢ (stamps or coin). (15¢ in Canada.)

Check Shade of   ☐ Flesh   ☐ Rachel   ☐ Light
Powder Desired   ☐ Peach   Rachel

Name_____
         (Please Print)

Street_____

City_____State_____ SG79

Screen Guide, 1939

SAMPLE FACE POWDER AND ROUGE TINS

The only variation from page 284 values is the Kissproof Treasure Chest. These cardboard boxes were usually filled with product samples and could be used for light travel. They also became containers for every imaginable beauty item and suffered early fates. Survivors in excellent condition, with outstanding artwork intact, should be sought. If in fine to mint condition with original products, value should be increased by half. 3⅝" x 2⅝" x ⅞". $40.00 – $60.00.

Armand	Lip and Cheek Creme Rouge
The Belco Co	Radio Girl Face Powder
Colgate & Co	Florient Face Powder
Don Juan Co	Rouge (plastic)
Heather	Rouge
Richard Hudnut	Three Flowers Rouge (plastic)
Jaciel	Face Powder
Kissproof	Rouge
Louis Philippe	Rouge Incarnat/Angelus
Luxor Ltd.	Face Powder
Mai D'Or	Face Powder (brass)
Palmer	Gardenglo (cardboard)
Pompeian	Night Cream
Rawleigh Co	Las Jayness Face Powder

Sweet LITTLE PRINCESS..DEAR LITTLE GIRL

Her Midsummer Night's Dream is sure to come true because she discovered how a Certain Color Tone gave her the Look of Fashionable Innocence...

That 'Little Girl' look has always been completely disarming, and the quickest way to the "steely-est" heart . . . And now, since the Paris Openings, it's necessary for fashion-rightness.

But don't be misled! Clever realness and genuine sincerity must be the keynote if effective "innocence" is to be achieved. And you're going to achieve it with cosmetics! Imagine! Cosmetics for innocence! Which means that unless you take great care, your illusion of naiveté, may not be real enough to work. But you CAN make sure it will be . . .

. . . One certain color-tone makes it easy for anyone, of any complexion type—blonde, brunette or in-between—to create the sweetest imaginable innocence . . . the true 'Little Girl' look.

HERE IS THE SECRET. The very essence of sweet girlishness is the color-tone 'English Tint' by Princess Pat. It definitely has the spirit of flying curls and lacy things. It gives to your lips and cheeks that irresistible something that "grown-ups" always want to touch.

POWDER HAS IT...the 'Little Girl' scheme is complete . . . even to English Tint shade of world famous Princess Pat almond base face powder . . . the only powder with the important virtue of almond base softness. English Tint powder is indispensable for sincere demureness.

ROUGE HAS IT...What a baby blush it gives! English Tint shade of Princess Pat duo-tone rouge is innocence itself. No one would suspect that the sweetness of English Tint complexion came from rouge. It's genuinely moisture-proof, too.

LIPSTICK HAS IT...English Tint comes in the grandest lipstick ever; one that smoothly, softly creates adorable 'Little Girl' lips. It's the English Tint Princess Pat Royalty Lipstick.

English Tint make-up is thoroughly in tune with Summer . . . light . . . gay . . . and sweet as sweetest clover. It's the thing for now. You simply must be little-girlish . . . at once! Obtain your English Tint shades of Princess Pat lipstick, rouge and powder wherever fine toiletries are sold.

SPECIAL—LITTLE GIRL KIT!

So that you can see for yourself how important Princess Pat English Tint make-up really is we will send you a real kit containing powder, rouge and lipstick — together with special instructions. Just fill in the coupon and include a dime to cover part cost of mailing and handling. You'll love this stunning 'Little Girl' make-up. You need it now.

Mail Coupon Today

English Tint **PRINCESS PAT**
'Little Girl' make-up

PRINCESS PAT, DEPT. 489, CHICAGO
Rush me the 'Little Girl' Make-up Kit right away—English Tint powder, rouge and lipstick. I enclose 10c in full payment.

Name..

Street...

City..State.........
IN CANADA, GORDON GORDON LTD., TORONTO

True Romance, 1939

Sheet Music Ad, 1920

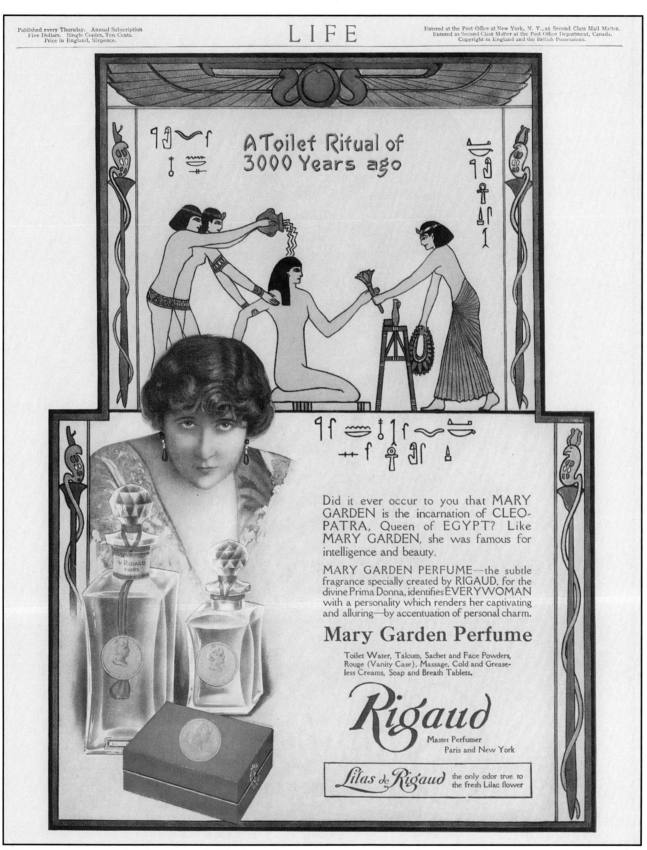

A Toilet Ritual of 3000 Years ago

Did it ever occur to you that MARY GARDEN is the incarnation of CLEOPATRA, Queen of EGYPT? Like MARY GARDEN, she was famous for intelligence and beauty.

MARY GARDEN PERFUME—the subtle fragrance specially created by RIGAUD, for the divine Prima Donna, identifies EVERYWOMAN with a personality which renders her captivating and alluring—by accentuation of personal charm.

Mary Garden Perfume

Toilet Water, Talcum, Sachet and Face Powders, Rouge (Vanity Case), Massage, Cold and Greaseless Creams, Soap and Breath Tablets.

Rigaud

Master Perfumer
Paris and New York

Lilas de Rigaud the only odor true to the fresh Lilac flower

Life, 1916

The Ladies' Home Journal, 1923

Rigaud
16 Rue de la Paix
·PARIS·

First the
ROUGE
and then a touch of the soft, clinging
FACE POWDER
—each fragrant with that bouquet of rare flowers from which emanate the sympathetic vibrations characteristic of

Mary Garden
Perfume

This fragrance enriches the entire series which includes

Breath Pastilles	Lip Rouge
Brilliantine	Liquid Soap
Cold Cream	Nail Polishes
Coffret	Powder
Eau Dentrifrice	(Solid)
Eye Lash	Sachet Powder
Beautifier	Shampoo
Eye Brow Pencil	Smelling Salts
Extract	Soap
Face Powder	Talcum Powder
Greaseless	Tissue Cream
Cream	Toilet Water
Hair Tonic	Tooth Paste
Lip Stick	Vanity Case

1918

December 7, 1940

5¢ A COPY

Collier's
THE NATIONAL WEEKLY

How to Fight in Alaska
By COREY FORD and ALASTAIR MAC BAIN

Collier's, 1940

for August 1940

BEFORE USING MAYBELLINE

What a Difference Maybelline Makes

Stop . . . Look . . . Compare these two pictures of the same girl. Hair, nose, mouth, complexion — exactly alike. Everything the same, *except her eyes*. It's easy to see what Maybelline eye make-up means. The difference between blankness and beauty. Between dullness and sparkle. Between hidden charm and instant attraction!

Don't doubt your own eyes. See what Maybelline Eye Beauty Aids can do for *you*. Lashes always take on this dark sweeping loveliness with Maybelline Mascara — and notice how this makes the eyes appear larger, more brilliant. Depth and color are subtly accented with Maybelline Eye Shadow — and brows are tapered so naturally with Maybelline Smooth-marking Eyebrow Pencil. Bring out the beauty of *your* eyes to your own thrilling satisfaction — today! You can get generous purse sizes of Maybelline Eye Beauty Aids at any 10c store.

Maybelline
EYE BEAUTY AIDS

Maybelline Solid-form Mascara in stunning gold-colored vanity. 75c. Refills 35c. Shades — Black, Brown, Blue.

Maybelline Cream-form Mascara (applied without water) comes in dainty zipper case. Black, Brown, Blue—75c.

Maybelline Smooth-marking Eyebrow Pencil in Black, Brown (and Blue for eyelid liner).

Maybelline Eye Shadow in six flattering shades. Blue, Gray, Blue-gray, Brown, Green, Violet.

Mademoiselle, 1940

Blush Rose

Elizabeth Arden's own flashing
dashing, wonderful pink!
keyed to this blonde blonde spring.

Blush Rose...an out-and-out flatterer—clear...unexpected...authentic as the first robin's trill.
A wondrous make-up shade, dashing on blondes...gentle on the dark-haired beauties.
And vivid, beyond measure, against the pale honeyed tones of this Spring's fashions. Wear it today...the velvet
softness of a rose-petal gathered to your lips and fingertips.

Blush Rose in lipsticks...creamy and of exceptional brilliance on the lips...1.00, 1.50, 1.75, 2.50.
Gold Rush Automatic Lipstick...2.50; Matching Compact...7.50 • Blush Rose in ever-smooth, ever-lasting Nail Lacquer...1.00
Beautiful precision-blended Illusion Powder...1.50, 2.00, 3.25.   all prices plus taxes except compact

Elizabeth Arden

691 FIFTH AVENUE, NEW YORK 22 • PLAZA 3-5846

Presenting you at your loveliest . . .

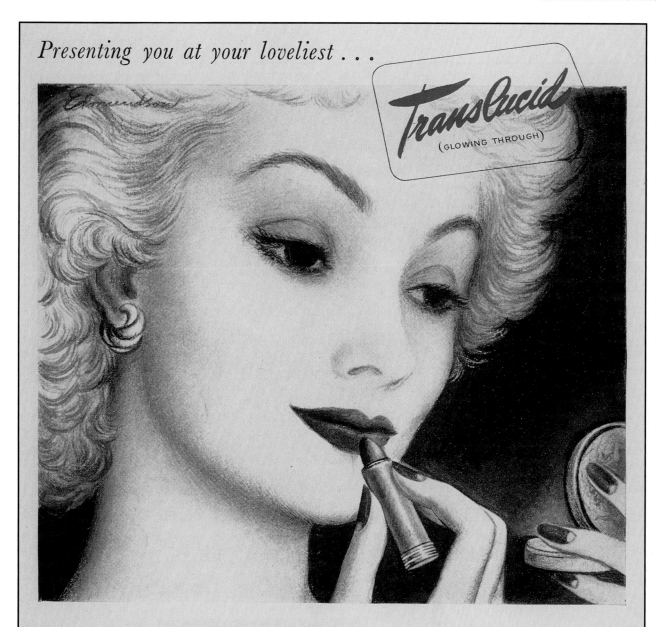

Translucid
(GLOWING THROUGH)

"SHEER MAKE-UP for sheer beauty" by HOUBIGANT

Now, let Houbigant show you new loveliness . . . with Translucid, the silken-sheer make-up that actually seems part of you. Smooth, subtle as mist, Translucid permits your warm, natural skin tone to "glow through". . . giving you new, *sheer* beauty to delight you and your mirror!

TRANSLUCID FOUNDATION LOTION —gives a wonderful sheer, satin-smooth effect . . . keeps make-up fresh for hours. 4 shades $1.50

FACE POWDER—sheer-sifted expressly to wear with the Lotion. Stays on marvelously. 7 beautiful shades . . . $1.50

ROUGE and matching LIPSTICK—7 thrilling shades, perfect with the new fall costume colors . . . . $1.00 each

VANITY—big, capacious, feather-weight! $1.50

EAU DE COLOGNE—introduced at the request of women who delight in the fragrance of Translucid make-up . . $1.50

Vogue, 1941

MEMO
for
MEN
only!

Here's the perfect
gift! Something every
woman wants . . .
and no woman has!
She'll use it every
day . . . think of you
always! Lovingly, too!

YOU'LL TREASURE your new Ultra-Matic Compact for years.
You'll thrill to its luxurious high-fashion "golden look". So will he!

Now Yours—The First Golden Metal Compact With Refills That Click-In, Click-Out...Instantly!

Now—say "goodbye" to unattractive plastic compacts.
At last, enjoy the luxurious feel of Hazel Bishop's breath-taking
new Ultra-Matic Metal Compact that looks exactly like its
solid gold original—that compliments your appearance
and reflects your good taste!

Hazel Bishop Ultra-Matic Make-up Refills are so simple to
change. They click-in and out with push-button ease!
You not only enjoy new beauty—but new economy, too!
For Hazel Bishop Ultra-Matic Make-up Refills are only 79¢.

You'll love Hazel Bishop's new All-in-One Make-up,
for nothing equals its lightness, cling, covering power. And
Hazel Bishop Make-up never streaks, cakes, or turns orangey.

*In your choice
of 3 brilliant
jeweler's designs.*

*The most exciting new
gift to give or get!*

$2.50
plus tax

*INCLUDING EXCLUSIVE
CLICK-IN, CLICK-OUT
MAKE-UP REFILL*

New! HAZEL BISHOP *Ultra-matic*® COMPACT MAKE-UP

PATENT PENDING

Esquire, 1958

Woman's Home Companion, 1954

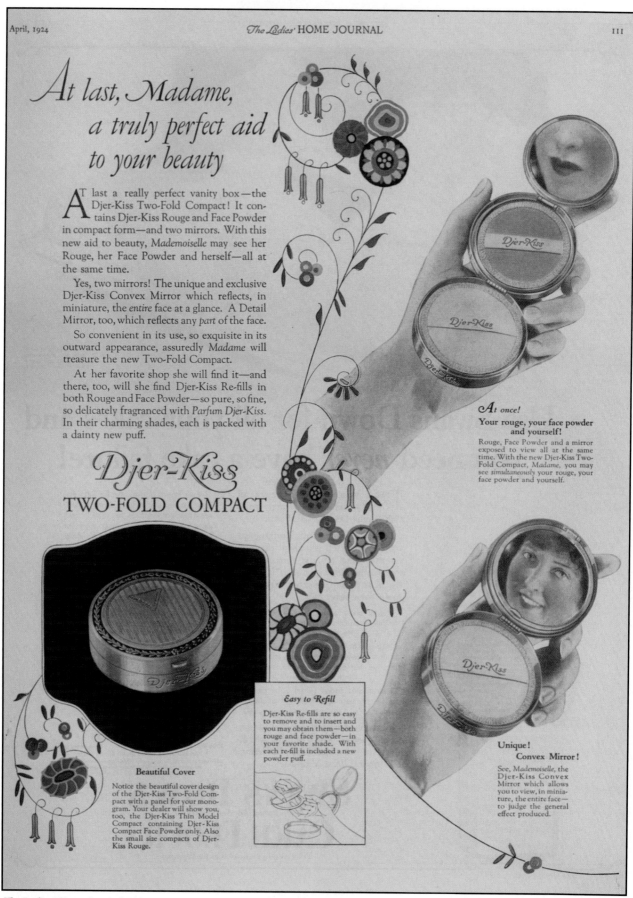

April, 1924   *The Ladies'* HOME JOURNAL   111

At last, Madame, a truly perfect aid to your beauty

At last a really perfect vanity box—the Djer-Kiss Two-Fold Compact! It contains Djer-Kiss Rouge and Face Powder in compact form—and two mirrors. With this new aid to beauty, *Mademoiselle* may see her Rouge, her Face Powder and herself—all at the same time.

Yes, two mirrors! The unique and exclusive Djer-Kiss Convex Mirror which reflects, in miniature, the *entire* face at a glance. A Detail Mirror, too, which reflects any *part* of the face.

So convenient in its use, so exquisite in its outward appearance, assuredly *Madame* will treasure the new Two-Fold Compact.

At her favorite shop she will find it—and there, too, will she find Djer-Kiss Re-fills in both Rouge and Face Powder—so pure, so fine, so delicately fragranced with *Parfum Djer-Kiss*. In their charming shades, each is packed with a dainty new puff.

Djer-Kiss
TWO-FOLD COMPACT

At once!
Your rouge, your face powder and yourself!

Rouge, Face Powder and a mirror exposed to view all at the same time. With the new Djer-Kiss Two-Fold Compact, *Madame*, you may see *simultaneously* your rouge, your face powder and yourself.

Beautiful Cover

Notice the beautiful cover design of the Djer-Kiss Two-Fold Compact with a panel for your monogram. Your dealer will show you, too, the Djer-Kiss Thin Model Compact containing Djer-Kiss Compact Face Powder only. Also the small size compacts of Djer-Kiss Rouge.

Easy to Refill

Djer-Kiss Re-fills are so easy to remove and to insert and you may obtain them—both rouge and face powder—in your favorite shade. With each re-fill is included a new powder puff.

Unique!
Convex Mirror!

See, *Mademoiselle*, the Djer-Kiss Convex Mirror which allows you to view, in miniature, the entire face—to judge the general effect produced.

The Ladies' Home Journal, 1924

Perfume

DJER·KISS

by KERKOFF

KISSES GIVING, KISSES TAKING
. . . that's the impulse of the straight-to-the-heart
DJER-KISS Fragrance, Perfume $3.50, $2. Toilet Water
$1.50. Cologne $1. Dusting Powder $1. Sachet, de luxe
size $1. Talcum, de luxe package 50¢ . . . Make up and
kiss with DJER-KISS Foundation Film, Face Powder,
and Lipstick. Each $1.
DJER-KISS . . . triumph of a great perfumer's art.

Vogue, **1941**

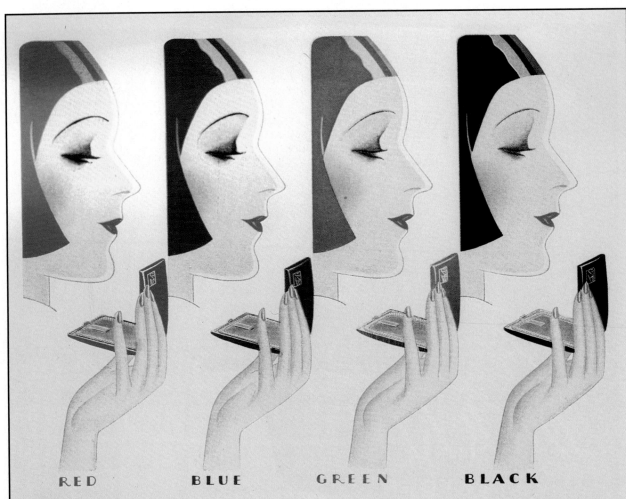

RED BLUE GREEN BLACK

The smartest compact imaginable
....yet only 50¢ and $1

YOU CAN scarcely believe it at first. Such delightful compacts—so gaily colorful, so intriguingly *chic*—for such astoundingly low prices. You'll want one to match each costume—a mode adopted by the very smartest women.

Then, after you have admired the outside of the case—*open!* Inside a generous supply of exquisite powder—soft, clinging, delicately fragrant. And (if you choose the double compact) rouge as well—unbreakable mirror, two puffs. Refills always obtainable. Look for these Tre-Jur compacts in your favorite shop today. Single, 50c; double, $1 —in red, blue, green or black.

TRE  JUR

If your dealer cannot supply you, order direct, enclosing price and stating color of case and shade of powder (flesh or rachel) desired. Address House of Tre-Jur, Inc., Dept. E, 19 West 18th Street, New York City.

Hearst's International–Cosmopolitan for April 1930

Hearst's International-Cosmopolitan, **April 1930**

Pictorial Review, 1929

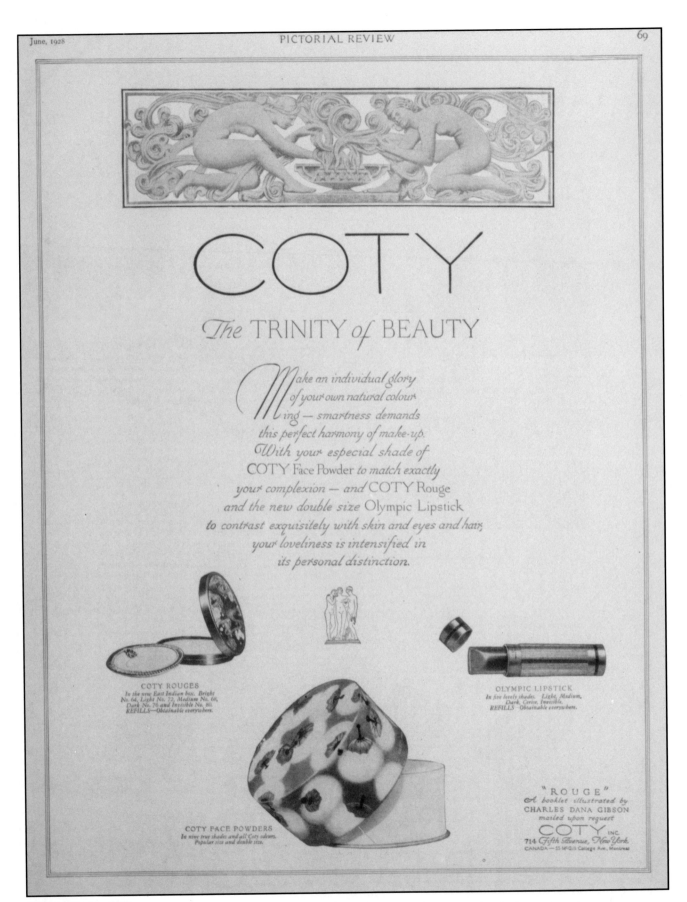

PLATO

TRE-JUR

This Picture is the Tre-Jur
Trademark. It has become the American Symbol for feminine charm. Before it is stamped
on a Tre-Jur product, that product must represent the *utmost* in the world of toiletries.

Tre-Jur Compacts are as ingenious as they are
beautiful. Each is a little inspirational idea,
designed to fill a particular need. Each contains the finest quality of cosmetic and a value
never before achieved. . . . At most toilet goods
counters you will find Tre-Jur in your own
shade of powder or rouge—or by mail from us.

THE HOUSE OF TRE-JUR, 19 W. 18th St., New York

THE "TRIPLE"
*Combines powder, rouge, and lipstick in a delightful case with the
famous sliding drawer—$1.25.*

NEW—TRE-JUR FACE POWDER
*Loose powder of exquisite quality, delicately scented
and silken soft, in a wondrously lovely box—50c.*

"THINEST"
*A shallow masterpiece of handy
circumference. Ample powder
and full-sized puff—$1.*

The Ladies' Home Journal, 1925

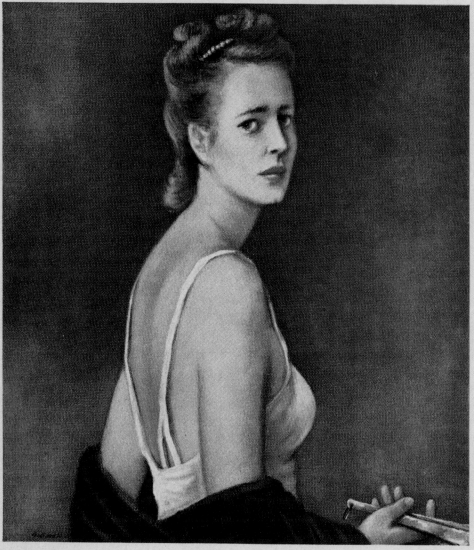

Harper's Bazaar, 1947

Costume, Bergdorf Goodman
Beauty by Du Barry

CALL TO COLORS! NEW Du BARRY SPRING MAKE-UP...

Emblem Red!

THERE'S a new spirit in the air. The styles this spring are crisp, dashing...*military!* Created in the same tempo are the vivacious new Du Barry Lipstick and Rouge—Emblem Red! It's saucy...it's gay...it has that Yankee Doodle spark so grandly "right" for 1941. You'll love it with beige and navy. It does things to the new browns, too. Truly, it's a challenge...a "call to the colors"!

Drop in on the Du Barry Beauty Advisor at any of the better cosmetic counters. Ask to see Emblem Red Lipstick...matching Emblem Red Rouge...complementing Du Barry Face Powder, soft, glowing Special Rachel.

Du Barry

Du Barry Emblem Red Lipstick ... easy-spreading, long-lasting! Du Barry Emblem Red Rouge... cream or cake...young, exciting. Lipstick, Rouge......each **1.00**

B E A U T Y   P R E P A R A T I O N S
by Richard Hudnut ... Featured at better cosmetic counters and in the Hudnut Salon, 693 Fifth Avenue

Du Barry Face Powder ... singularly smooth, clinging, gossamer-light. Subtle shades to enhance your natural skin tones. Large box......**2.00**

Vogue, 1941

Gold-finished Compact Powder case in the Mode "Moderne" $1.00

HOUBIGANT
PARIS

HOUBIGANT, PREMIER CREATOR OF MAKE-UP AND PERFUME REQUISITES FOR THE PURSE, INTERPRETS THE MODE OF PARIS . . . . . FOR THE WORLD

■

HOUBIGANT COMPACTS
. . . retain the fine texture, the smooth spreading and adherent qualities of the loose powder, because they are loose powder, compressed by an exclusive process. The rubbing of the puff will instantly revert them to loose form. Refills are . . . 50c

Gold-finished double Vanity: Lip Stick and Compact Powder. $2.00

Three essentials: Compact Powder, Rouge and Lip Stick in a gold-finished case. $2.50

Engine-turned modernistic design — Platinum-toned Double Vanity — containing Compact Powder and Rouge, the latter in a separate shielded compartment. $1.75

Lip Stick in silver finished holder with green enamelled design. . . . $1.00

Purse size Parfum fitted into a gold-finished case. Choice of odeurs: Fleur Bienaimee, Bois Dormant, Au Matin, Quelques Fleurs, Le Parfum Ideal and others. $1.75

Ladies' Home Journal, 1931

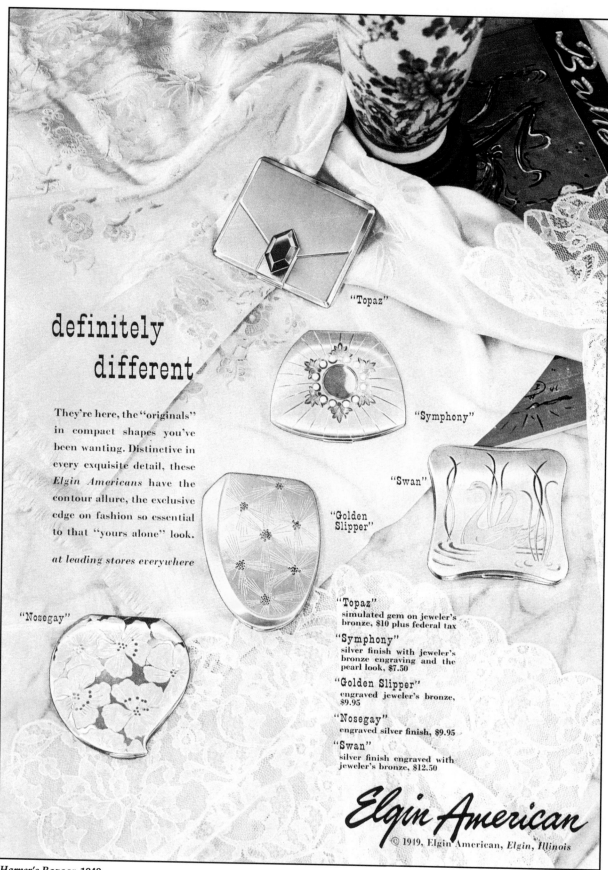

definitely different

They're here, the "originals" in compact shapes you've been wanting. Distinctive in every exquisite detail, these *Elgin Americans* have the contour allure, the exclusive edge on fashion so essential to that "yours alone" look.

at leading stores everywhere

"Topaz"

"Symphony"

"Swan"

"Golden Slipper"

"Nosegay"

"Topaz"
simulated gem on jeweler's bronze, $10 plus federal tax

"Symphony"
silver finish with jeweler's bronze engraving and the pearl look, $7.50

"Golden Slipper"
engraved jeweler's bronze, $9.95

"Nosegay"
engraved silver finish, $9.95

"Swan"
silver finish engraved with jeweler's bronze, $12.50

Elgin American
© 1949, Elgin American, Elgin, Illinois

Harper's Bazaar, 1949

a Wadsworth *Powder Case*

from two
to twenty-five
dollars and up

Vogue, 1945

Vanity Fair, 1928

The Odor Charms

Delightful odors from faraway lands combine to give Pussywillow Powders the fragrance of a lovely flower garden.

The soft smoothness of Pussywillow Face Powder and the soothing coolness of Pussywillow Talc de Luxe are as pleasing as the odor.

Both are unconditionally guaranteed.

Pussywillow Face Powder in white, cream, flesh, pink or brunette is 50 cents a box.

Pussywillow Talc de Luxe, white only, is 35 cents.

Trial Portion of either Free.

Miniature box of face powder sent for a dime. State shade wanted.

Henry Tetlow Company
1200 Henry Tetlow Bldg.   Philadelphia, Pa.

We have been face powder specialists since 1849

"Sifted through silk"

© H. T. Co. 1920

McCall's Magazine, 1920

Courage

A new Bourjois perfume reflecting the gallant spirit of today!

BOURJOIS *New York ~ Distributor*

Vogue, 1942

Glossary

Acanthus — Plant leaf used as an architectural motif such as capitals on Corinthian columns.

Art Deco — Art movement with beginnings in the 1920's featuring linear flora, fauna, and human forms.

Art Moderne — Art movement which broke with Art Nouveau traditions and was concurrent with Art Deco, emphasizing sharp cubistic and geometrical patterns.

Bakelite — Protected trade name for synthetic resin and plastic material — usually opaque.

Baroque — Design with much ornamentation and curved lines.

Bas-relief — Slight pattern projection on a flat surface.

Beauty Box — A vanity case containing cosmetic items other than powder and rouge — such as eye make-up.

Bevel — Sloping angle of a surface.

Bijou — A small and exquisite trinket.

Cabochon — A rounded stone without facets.

Can Compact/Vanity Case — Early twentieth century box-shaped hinged cases containing mirror and puffs, with removable interior fittings for storage of: buttons, pins, shirt studs, snuff, etc., usually with very tight closures.

Carryall — Cosmetic case which serves as a purse substitute:
- *Baton* — Long oval carryall, resembling a staff of office, with or without a carrier, with sliding band closure.
- *Clutch* — All carryalls without carriers.
- *Demi* — Early carryalls holding coins, combs, powder or puff, and a miscellaneous compartment — no cigarettes.
- *Petite* — Name given by Evans for small box carryalls with lighter and cigarette compartments.
- *Portmanteau* — Name given by Volupté for clutch carryalls that open like a briefcase and have no handles.
- *Purse* — Carryalls with detachable cloth carriers.
- *Standard* — Name given by Evans for the classic carryall.
- *Super* — Pseudo Minaudières or oversize carryalls usually carried as a clutch.
- *Vanity* — Smaller carryalls with attached exterior items to handles, such as lipsticks or perfume bottles.

Celluloid — Trademark thermoplastic material used as substitute for ivory, horn or tortoise shell.

Chameleon Finish — Case light reflections created by interacting glossy and brushed case lacquer application.

Champlevé — Enamel fused into design cells which are sunk into the metal baseplate.

Chasing — Ornamental metal work using engraving or embossing techniques.

Chatelaine — Ornamental chain hung from a brooch or belt from which are suspended small objects — keys, note cases, boxes or mirrors.

Chevron — "V" shaped bars or lines.

Chinoiserie — European interpretation of oriental motifs.

Cloisonné — Fused powdered glass placed in separate case cells formed from thin stripes of metal.

Clutch — Woman's purse with no wrist handle.

Cofferet — Small box for holding valuables.

Collet — Non-prong ring mounting for stones.

Compact — Small cosmetic case containing only face powder and a mirror.

Cornucopia — Horn of plenty.

Damascening — Several layers of different metals cut with a tool to expose their color characteristics.

Ebonite — Black variety of vulcanized rubber capable of being cut and polished for combs, buttons, and cases.

Embossing — Carved or hammered design that is raised above a flat surface.

Engine-Turning — Ornamental engraving done by machinery.

Faux — French: fake, false.

Femme — French: female figure.

Filigree — Lace-like ornamental metal work.

Flapjack — Round thin compact resembling a pan-cake.
Cookie — to 2½"diameter.
Baby — 2½" to 3½"diameter.
Standard — 3½" to 5"diameter.
Super — 5" to 6"diameter.

Floret — Any of the individual flowers making up the head of a plant.

Gazelles — Usually "Leaping," small, swift antelope which became a favorite Art Deco leitmotif. Early use by Raymond Loewy as a Neiman Marcus Logo in 1923.

Glove Vanity/Compact — Small rectangular case which fits in the palm of a gloved hand.

Goldtone — Any gold colored metallic finish.

Granulate — Roughen surface by the addition of granules or tiny bulges.

Guilloché — Layers of transparent enamel over a prepared metal surface, generally engine-turned.

High-Relief — Sculptured figures which project by more than half from background.

Incising — Engraving or carving into a flat surface with a sharp tool.

Kamra — Case resembling early collapsible camera cases.

Logo — A word, letter, symbol or character representing an entire phrase or name.

Lucite — Trademark name for acrylic or plastic material, high translucency.

Lunette — Crescent shaped.

Marquetry — Decorative inlay of wood.

Monogram Cartouche — An ornamental outline which offers space for initials or name.

M.O.P. — Mother of Pearl — hard pearly interior layer of certain marine shells.

Nickel Silver — Hard alloy of nickel, copper and zinc.

Niello — Black compound of silver, copper, etc. used to fill engraved portions of metal for highlighting.

Object D'Art — French: art ornament.

Passementerie — Heavy fabric trimming usually of gold or silver gimp, cord or braid.

Pâte de Verre — French: glass substance resembling jade or other carved gemstones.

Pavé — Decorative stones placed close together so that very little case metal shows between the mountings.

Pendant Cases — Compact or vanity case suspended from a chain or ring.

Petit Point — Small needlepoint stitch.

Pewter — Dull silvery-gray alloy of tin and lead.

Plexiglas — Trademark name for thermoplastic synthetic resins.

Portrait Case — Picture frame feature in compacts and vanity cases for snapshot insertion.

Porcelain — Hard white nonporous variety of ceramic ware.

Post Deco — A revival of Art Deco motifs after WWII; namely, the leaping gazelle. The design lines are rounder and the flora is more realistic.

Powder Disk Compact — Case has a small hole/slot in bottom allowing replacement of used pressed powder disk.

Purse Kit — A small fabric or leather case with a snap closure, usually containing compact, lipstick/perfume and comb.

Quatrefoil — Flower or stylized design with four petals or florets.

Repoussé — Decoration achieved by pushing out the metal into relief by reverse tooling.

Reverse — The exterior back of an object

Rhinestone — Artificial gem made of glass.

Rococo — Ornamental design of swirls, imitating shellwork and foliage.

Shagreen (Faux) — Rough granular surface resembling sharkskin.

Silvertone — Any silver colored metallic finish.

Sterling — Standard pure silver with minute variable alloys.

Tambourine — Small drum-like instrument with loose brass jingles in the side rim.

Trifids — Three lobes or parts.

Vanity Case — Portable case with mirror, powder and rouge, sometimes called a double compact.
> *Carrying Case* — fitted miniature travel case with mirror and make-up accessories attached to lidded bottom compartment. Case has lock and key for jewelry storage.
> *Combination Case* — Contains additional features other than powder and rouge: coin holders, combs, etc.

Kit — A small slipcase for a compact with a lipstick mounted in an exterior sleeve.
Kit Bag — Cloth pouch with drawstring closure, mirror and puff accessories — no compartment for powder.
Pouch — Fabric or metal mesh bag with a vanity case serving as a lid.
Triple Case — Vanity case with lipstick.

Velour — Fabric or finish with a soft velvet-like nap.

Vermeil — Gilded silver or white metal.

Votary — A worshipping figure.

Wedgwood — Fine pottery with a white cameo-like relief on a tinted background.

White Metal — Generic term for any unidentified silver looking metal composition.

Bibliography

◆◄▬▬▬►◆

BOOKS:

Arwas, Victor. *Art Deco*. London: St. Martin's Press, 1976 (PB).

Arwas, Victor. *Art Deco*. New York: Henry N. Abrams, Inc., 1980.

Battersby, Martin. *The Decorative Twenties*. New York: Walker & Co, 1969.

Battersby, Martin. *The Decorative Thirties*. New York: Walker & Co, 1971.

Becker, Stephen. *Comic Art In America*. New York: Simon & Schuster, 1959.

Contini, Mila. *Fashion*. New York: The Odyssey Press, 1965.

Corbett, Ruth. *Daddy Danced The Charleston*. New Jersey: A. S. Barnes & Co, 1970.

Culme, John. *The Jewels Of The Duchess Of Windsor*. London: Thames & Hudson, 1987.

Dorner, Jane. *Fashion In The Twenties & Thirties*. London: Ian Allan Ltd., 1973.

Drake, Nicholas. *The Fifties In Vogue*. New York: Henry Holt, 1987.

Gerson, Roselyn. *Ladies' Compacts*. Radnor, PA: Wallace-Homestead Book Co, 1989.

Hillier, Bevis. *Art Deco*. London: Studio Vista/Dutton, 1972 (PB).

Keen, Brigid. *The Women We Wanted To Look Like*. New York: St. Martin's Press, 1977.

Klein, Dan. *All Color Book Of Art Deco*. London: Octopus Books Ltd., 1974.

Le Gallienne, Richard. *The Romance Of Perfume*. Paris: Richard Hudnut, 1928.

Lesieutre, Alain. *The Spirit & Splendor Of Art Deco*. London: Paddington Press, 1974.

Lewis, Alfred Allan. *Miss Elizabeth Arden*. New York: Coward, McCann & Geoghegan, 1972.

Loewy, Raymond. *Industrial Design*. Woodstock, New York: Overlook Press, 1979.

McClinton, Katherine Morrison. *Art Deco*. New York: Clarkson, N. Potter, 1972.

Maryon, Herbert. *Metalwork & Enamelling*. New York: Dover Publ., 1971 (PB).

Maxtone, John. *The Only Way to Cross*. New York: The Macmillan Co, 1972.

Mendes, Suzy. *The Windsor Style*. London: Grafton Books, 1987.

Nadelhoffer, Hans. *Cartier*. London: Thames & Hudson, 1984.

Neret, Gilles. *Boucheron*. New York: Rizzoli, 1988.

O'Higgins, Patrick. *Madame (Helena Rubinstein)*. New York: The Viking Press, 1971.

Proddow, Penny. *Hollywood Jewels*. New York: Henry N. Abrams, 1992.

Rainwater, Dorothy T. *American Silver Manufacturers*. Hanover, PA: Everybodys Press, 1966.

Raulet, Sylvie. *Art Deco Jewelry*. New York: Rizzoli, 1989.

Raulet, Sylvie. *Van Cleef & Arpels*. New York: Rizzoli, 1987.

Schiaparelli, Elsa. *Shocking Life*. New York: E. P. Dutton & Co, 1954.

Snowman, A. Kenneth. *The Art of Carl Fabergé*. Boston, MA, 1952.

Vargas, Alberto. *Vargas*. New York: Bell Publ. Co., 1984.

Weber, Eva. *American Art Deco*. Greenwich, CT: Dorset Press, 1985.

PERIODICALS:

The American Perfumer, May 1931.

The American Perfumer, February 1935.

The American Perfumer, August 1935.

Drug Topics, June 1930.

Harper's Bazaar, 1931 to 1963.

Junior Bazaar, 1946.

St. Louis Dispatch, November 30, 1941.

St. Louis Globe, December 2, 1928.

Theatre, 1909 to 1925.

Vanity Fair, 1917.

Vogue, 1938 to 1963.

BROCHURES:

Richard Hudnut. "Beauty Is Yours." New York: Du Barry Beauty Salon, 1941.

Richard Hudnut. "Marvelous." New York: Du Barry Beauty Salon, 1936.

Armour & Co. "Luxor." Chicago: Beauty Making At Home, 1917.

Helena Rubinstein. "Beauty In The Making." 1932, 1933.

CATALOGUES:

Bennett Bros Inc., Chicago, 1955.
Chicago Mail Order Co., Chicago, 1931–32.
Christie's, Jewelry, 1987 to 1992.
Ft. Deabrborn Mercantile Co., Chicago, 1938.
Plymouth Jewelry Co., New York, 1942.
Sotheby's, Jewelry, April 2–3, 1987.
Wallenstein/Mayer Co., Cincinnati, 1932.

EXHIBITIONS & THEATRICAL PLAYBILLS:

Deco. Rothman's Gallery, Stratford, Ontario: 1925 to 1935, June - Sept., 1975.

Playbills. Hartman Theatre, Columbus, OH: 1911 to 1954.

World Of Art Deco. Minneapolis Institute Of Art: July - Sept. 1971.

ARTICLES:

Ladies' Home Journal. "All In A Day's Shopping." December, 1930.

McCall's Magazine. "Give Gifts For Beauty," Nov. 1928.

Woman's Home Companion. "New Winkles," March, 1932.

Woman's Home Companion. "New Winkles," May, 1932.

Woman's Home Companion. "Powder In The Hand," Jan. 1936.

Index

Schroeder's
ANTIQUES
Price Guide

. . . is the #1 best-selling antiques & collectibles value guide on the market today, and here's why . . .

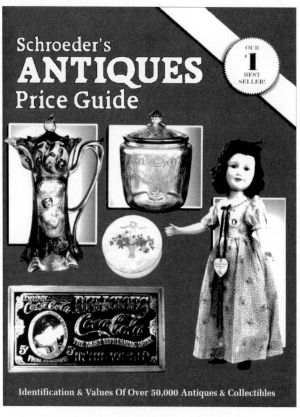

Schroeder's ANTIQUES Price Guide

OUR 1 BEST SELLER!

Identification & Values Of Over 50,000 Antiques & Collectibles

8½ x 11, 608 Pages, $12.95

- *More than 300 advisors, well-known dealers, and top-notch collectors work together with our editors to bring you accurate information regarding pricing and identification.*

- *More than 45,000 items in almost 500 categories are listed along with hundreds of sharp original photos that illustrate not only the rare and unusual, but the common, popular collectibles as well.*

- *Each large close-up shot shows important details clearly. Every subject is represented with histories and background information, a feature not found in any of our competitors' publications.*

- *Our editors keep abreast of newly-developing trends, often adding several new categories a year as the need arises.*

If it merits the interest of today's collector, you'll find it in *Schroeder's*. And you can feel confident that the information we publish is up to date and accurate. Our advisors thoroughly check each category to spot inconsistencies, listings that may not be entirely reflective of market dealings, and lines too vague to be of merit. Only the best of the lot remains for publication.

Without doubt, you'll find
SCHROEDER'S ANTIQUES PRICE GUIDE
the only one to buy for
reliable information and values.

COLLECTOR BOOKS
A Division of Schroeder Publishing Co., Inc.